Alchemy of the Extraordinary

A Journey into the Heart
of the Meridian Matrix

Entrance to Temple in Qingkeping on Hua Shan(Mount Hua) in China

by *Peter Shea*, L.Ac.

with Illustrations by Alex Gama

Disclaimer and note: the majority of information in this book comes from the vast existing public and non-proprietary information related to the subjects of "Traditional Chinese Medicine" and "Classical Chinese Medicine." The author and publisher do not endorse self-diagnosis or treatment by non-medical professionals. Chinese Medicine is a regulated and licensed profession and guidance should be sought for any medical issues. Though acupuncture points and trajectories are described, they should never be needled by an unlicensed, untrained and unsupervised individual. Their inclusion in this book is to assist in meditation and movement and in both cases it is recommended to work with a trained and experienced practitioner of these arts.

The majority of the roots of these teachings come from the oral tradition through the generosity of Taoist Master, Jeffrey Yuen. I take responsibility for where the fruits have fallen far from the tree. P.S.

Soul Pivot Press

Address inquiries to soulpivotpress@gmail.com

For more information, go to www.soulpivot.com

Cover & Book Design: Jean Hardesty-Prater

Glass art by Vaughan Anderson, www.glassworkonline.com.

ISBN: 978-0-692-47364-1

*"The shamans say that the Universe makes you right –
so that whatever you choose to believe
(your working hypothesis),
you will continue to find evidence to support it.
So, why not make your working
hypothesis extraordinary?"*

Alberto Villoldo

Contents

Part 1

Alchemy of the Extraordinary

A Journey into the Heart of the Meridian Matrix

∝⳾∽

Part 2

Background & Preparation for the Alchemical Journey

⚜

Part 3

The Terrain of Our Journey:

The Meridian Matrix and the Curious Organs

∽ಲ∽

࿚

Part 4

Story of the 8 Extraordinary Vessels:

Pathways of Our Destiny

Acknowledgments

I would first like to acknowledge, show gratitude, and give credit to the millennia of creators and contributors, past and present, to the system of Chinese Medicine. This medical system is one of the crowning achievements not only of China but of human civilization. As much as I have incorporated my own writing style, personal spin, and modern parallel concepts to extrapolate and translate ideas, this book is written in the language, concepts, and spirits of Classical Chinese Medicine. It is a living tradition that comes alive in the moment through the creative re-interpretation of its practitioners and participants.

I would also like to acknowledge the authors and creative minds that have helped spread the understanding of human evolution and its relationship to consciousness through their ground-breaking works. Their ideas are interwoven in this book with my own and with Chinese Medicine. I have cited their works in the bibliography and have tried to give them credit along the way. As with Chinese Medicine, their ideas have so deeply merged with my own that it is difficult to cite them specifically.

I want to extend a huge thank you to Jean Hardesty for offering her formatting talents to this book. Your contribution has dramatically increased the quality of this project since the first edition. Thank you for contributing your time and experience to the formatting of the book and guiding me through the editing process. You have taught me a lot about what it takes to complete a book. From "widows and orphans" to proof-reading to numbering the points on the illustrations, your professional touch is greatly appreciated!

Thank you Alex Gama for your inspired illustrations! Your flowing artwork is a quantum leap from the drawings that I did myself for the first edition. Thank you for offering your natural talent to this project. I appreciate the creative touch that your drawings bring to the book. Thank you Vaughan Anderson for your alchemical inspiration. Your glass art is perfect for the cover.

Thank you to my mother and my family for being so kind, generous and supportive throughout my life and during my time in Asheville, where this book needed to be written. Thank you to my wife, Joanne, for her love and companionship over the many years on this journey with me and for co-creating the language used in this book. I thank my children for tolerating having a pre-occupied dad during many hours over this past year.

Thank you to the Daoist Traditions community of students, faculty, and administration for allowing me the opportunity and support to be immersed in this medicine at such a high level and to Dr. Mary Cissy Majebe for being a driving force of the renaissance of Classical Chinese Medicine. Thanks to Josephine Spilka for sharing so many ways of using the 5 Channel System for practical medical applications.

I would like to thank my friend, Kevin Kelley, specifically for being the first person to show interest, print out a copy, and provide me with feedback and positive encouragement to continue working on this book. I would like to thank Caroline Proctor for providing the incentive for having a clear finish date for the 1st edition.

I would like to thank my Chinese Medicine patients for trusting me and allowing me to develop my understanding of this medicine. Thank you to my many Chinese Medicine, Tui Na, Qigong, and Tai Chi teachers along the way for sharing so much embodied wisdom. Thank you to Michael Winn for getting me and my wife to China against all logic and odds. Thank you to Uwe, Cathy, Matt, Sara and our journey circle for holding a loving space to experience the potential of medicine.

And finally, thank you to Jeffrey Yuen, whose on-going spiritual transmission of Chinese Medicine has allowed me to experience and integrate more aspects of this medicine than I ever thought possible. Without these translations and transmissions the majority of these ideas I may never have encountered in the way that I needed to.

Preface

❧

This book is intended to be used as a guidebook for illuminating our journey. It is a map of the unfolding of the spiritual and evolutionary coding of the acupuncture meridian system from the perspective of the Taoist oral traditions. While learning and integrating this system as a student of the Classical Chinese Medicine transmission of Jeffrey Yuen, I always felt that the heart of this complex information from the disciplines of Acupuncture and Chinese Medicine wanted to be accessed by people outside the profession and outside of the treatment room. I have attempted to make this book accessible to any dedicated reader from inside or outside the profession. The book is meant to be read in small sections at a time to inspire a reflective state of mind. The intention of this book is to support the experiential awareness of ourselves as spirit embodied in form.

The Inner Traditions of Chinese Medicine offer one of the most beautiful and sophisticated maps for guiding us safely on this journey. Through doing this work we are cleaning up generations and millennia of baggage in our DNA, our ancestry. We are learning to literally unwind the coil of our genetic code to dilate the amount of multi-dimensional energy coming in through our conduit between Heaven and Earth from the Tao. We unwind our DNA through the process of healing. The separation consciousness of material form becomes reinforced through shock and trauma, through wounds. Our spirit is "wound" into our genetics through wounds. Through healing on a personal and collective level, we are "un-wounding" our species and re-discovering our gifts. Not so that we can fly away, but so that we can have more space for our spirit to be present in our body, in our form, and share our gifts of the spirit with each other and our community. We all have a purpose, a destiny that is unique to us and contains our potential for the greatest good for Humanity.

It is our inner journey that allows us to create the deep space for our spirit to reside in our form. We are at a time when science and technology, what we call external achievements, are hitting a quantum leap. What is needed to ground these achievements is comparable growth on the internal level. The internal level is where our spiritual work takes place in order to reflect out into the world. As we begin to take responsibility for our own healing process, we begin to work through our individual stories. By working through our story we can connect beyond our personal consciousness and recognize that we are a part of the planetary mind of the Earth and that we are simultaneously awakening into the multi-dimensional consciousness of the Universe. This is the experiential reality of the inner journey, of listening with our Heart.

This book uses the timeless wisdom of Chinese Medicine, especially the Taoist perspective, to map this archetypal journey of the soul. Chinese Medicine is an endless wellspring of wisdom. Its roots are deep and its path becomes richer and wider through drinking of its well. Its wisdom is embedded and enfolded into the Chinese characters, its spirit residing in the names of the acupuncture points themselves, in the legends and history of its practitioners and in the living representatives of its traditions and lineages. It is a system that is learned through meditative reflection and application. Its principles emerge from its Inner Traditions, from the spirit residing in each of our Hearts and the Heart of Humanity.

There is a saying in Chinese Medicine, "Learn the form, forget the form." We could also translate this in a more Taoist way and say, "Know the Form, but stick to the Formless." We could further elaborate this to mean, "Know the body, but operate from the Spirit." This is an interesting paradox in Chinese Medicine for there is more information and knowledge available in its many lineages and long history than any one person can know. This means that we can go a long way down the rabbit hole of Chinese Medicine without achieving mastery and can get stuck in the details of infinite complexity. If we do this we often start to limit our experience of life by being stuck in a methodology that is meant to enrich our lives. Spirit is not limited by methodology. However, we do not want to strip Chinese Medicine of its roots and pass it off as just another New Age modality. Chinese Medicine has mapped the functional relationships in the body in a way that is every bit as empirical as modern science and is far beyond being a relative study. These maps describe patterns of truth that are inherent in nature and in having a physical body. This system is a living legacy of the potential of Medicine. But there is always the danger of becoming externally attached to the trappings of methodology, just as there are inherent risks associated with seeking answers outside of our self.

Chinese Medicine stays alive through the constant reinterpretations of those practicing it and living it. It changes over generations and its practice may get streamlined or westernized, etc. but its roots are too deep and vast to be watered down for very long. Chinese Medicine went through this streamlining process very strongly during the Communist Revolution in China and in its transmission to the West. But teachers have come forth to alter the level of closely guarded secrecy of oral lineage transmission to insure that Chinese Medicine has access to its roots during this exciting phase of global transmission and expansion. Many classics of Chinese Medicine were lost over time and many masters of Chinese Medicine died without being able to pass on the entirety of their lineage, but volumes and volumes of classics still exist and the world still has many living masters of Medicine. Furthermore, through the teachings of these living ambassadors, we see and feel the living transmission of information from the collective archives pointing us to the reality that these teachings are never permanently lost. Chinese Medicine has a long history of teachings coming through the ancestors in dreams, visions and channeling. This is the Inner Tradition of Chinese Medicine.

The spirit of Medicine comes alive when we are honoring the guiding universal principles of its wisdom while remaining open to the creativity and spontaneity of the moment. It is these moments of creative inspiration when I feel that I am honoring the medicine and its ancestry the most. Equally as important as having these roots in the tradition is having roots within our own experience. In order to experience the conduit between Heaven and Earth we have to become as authentically our self as possible. This is the challenge of developing our own central channel. Chinese Medicine is always a balance between honoring the past and staying present in the moment, of having a vast body of knowledge but not being blinded by conditioning and pre-conceived notions.

In this book there are many ideas that are traditional and have been generously gifted to me by many teachers and for this I give credit entirely to them and their traditions. For the ideas and embellishments that are my own, I take full responsibility for where I have erred and where I have succeeded in translating and extrapolating on the concepts. The ideas in this book are meant to be inspirational, to catalyze and illuminate the spiritual realities of our lives. These maps can be used in conjunction with movement, touch, acupuncture, meditation, and plant spirituality, to help us integrate and navigate on our way. This is a guidebook for personal and planetary awakening written in the words of Chinese Medicine and Taoism. Listen with your Heart and enjoy the journey!

To Joanne Shea.
Thank you for your loving
companionship on this
extraordinary journey...

Part 1

Alchemy of the Extraordinary
A Journey into the Heart of the Meridian Matrix

A Hero's Journey through the Meridian Matrix

శ్రీక్రిస్తి

Humanity stands at a mythical transition point. We have developed technology that has allowed us to manipulate our external landscape, the material world, to an incredibly high degree. But we have yet to fully accept the challenge of understanding our internal landscape, the spiritual world and the power of the mind, with any degree of sophistication and maturity. It's pretty clear in mythological terms what happens with this approach. It is called a "wasteland"[1] scenario. Humanity becomes alienated from nature and from itself. Our instincts become duller and we can no longer recognize our beating heart as the beating Heart of Humanity and the beating heart of our Mother Earth. Nature does not speak to us and we do not speak to it. At this point of development, the existence of the human soul might even be questioned as a fairy tale. This is a state of materialism that has gotten profoundly out of balance. It is the mark of materialism to believe that the immaterial or insubstantial either does not exist and/or is inherently useless.

This is where a Hero's Journey comes into play. A Hero's Journey is the mythic journey through the ocean of archetypes in the collective unconscious. It is a quest for meaning and purpose, for redemption. It is a search for liberation of the soul, both our own and that of humanity's. It is seeking the expression of the highest potential of the human spirit. We are all living this journey, this quest in our own way. But often times we do whatever we can to keep from embarking on this adventure into the unknown and all the strange forces we may encounter there. There is a fear of unlocking Pandora's Box and entering into the chaos of life without being prepared. Oftentimes we only find the courage to walk this path once we realize that the only way out is through and that there is really only one thing that can get the Hero through such a quest. Maps are useful, but you can only trust your compass, your Heart.

Most of the mythologies we think of in the West look at a Hero's Journey from the perspective of the Warrior archetype. The Warrior is going out into the world to find a solution, to affect change, to win a battle. The only problem is that the Warrior is always fighting on some level, fighting for a better future, maybe fighting for justice or a righteous cause. The Warrior can become the embodiment of resistance, a very tiring and tiresome role, especially on the inward journey where all the things we are fighting against or for exist within our self on some level.

There is also the archetype of the Saint. The Saint is the embodiment of acceptance in the moment. The Saint takes care of things the way they are. The Saint takes care of the dying and the sick while the Warrior may be off seeking the cure for sickness. Some of us are more resonant with one

---

1. *Joseph Campbell - 1972.*

archetype than the other. In truth, we are all composite beings and there is an ocean of archetypal forces guiding the roles we play in our lives. An example of a composite archetype which is less polarized than the Saint or the Warrior is the Warrior-Buddha,[2] patiently observing with active awareness for the right moment for action. This is the application of right timing, an essential component of the alchemical process.

A Quest to Know Our Self

In this book we are going on a quest to get to know our self. And we shall see that there is no other way to awaken humanity to its own potential than to awaken one's self. We will be journeying deep into the Tao, deep into the Meridian Matrix that weaves together the substantial and the insubstantial, the soul and the spirit, the body and the mind, the material and the immaterial. We will be journeying directly to the essence of our being where our ancestry, our DNA, and our instinctual drives connect us to the Tao Field, the morphogenetic[3] record of our personal and collective story. This is where personal and collective evolution takes place and we will be looking specifically at the evolutionary circuitry of the 8 Extraordinary Meridians, or the 8 Extraordinary Vessels, in order to shine light on the unfolding of the evolutionary process.

Practices that work at this level are known as "alchemy" or "alchemical," in the Chinese wisdom traditions. We are at a time when the understanding of these processes can begun being understood medically, scientifically, experientially, anthropologically, etc. These types of practices may very well hold the key to dealing with the types of disease that confound modern medicine. We are at a time when we can participate in cross-cultural alchemical practices and cross-reference them with the models and technologies of modern science. This is the best way to truly understand things like the genetic code and multidimensional energy: through direct experience.

During a Hero's Journey the Hero may encounter what is known in Jungian terms as "the Dark Night of the Soul." This can be experienced in many different ways and can be of varying timeframes. It represents the period in which we are seeking the "light within," "the spirit within matter." We have lost sight of the surface and have been plunged into our depths. Heaven and the light are still there, but we can no longer see them. This often takes place as sickness, loss, or being stuck in an adverse fate from which there appears to be no way out. This can cause a deep crisis of faith as we no longer feel supported by Heaven or Earth. This level of practice was often done in the light-deprivation of caves. Over time we begin to liberate the light within. We begin to be able to see better in the dark, to navigate better through the unknown. The darkness becomes familiar and though we may not embrace it, we are no longer running from it. We begin to metabolize the darkness of the dense layers of form dimensions of consciousness.

---

2. *The Human Design System for archetypal composites based on the crosses of the Weel of the I Ching. 2011*

3. *See the work of Rupert Sheldrake for more information on the Morphogenetic Field.*

The Journey into our depths will also bring us face to face with the many layers of our projection fields and those that are projected onto us by others. We are in the Hall of Mirrors. We exist deep in this web of projection and any insight into the nature of these projections can begin to change our reality on a very physical level. We exist within these projection fields. It is the way it is. We may be able to get a partial break from them on a mountain top, in a cave, deep within meditation, but we return. There is no escape. The only solution is to get to know yourself. You will still be immersed in the projection fields, but you will be able to differentiate self from other and projection from reality. This allows us to refine our receptivity, to tune in our station, and to have more choice in the wavelengths we attune to. We are learning to tune our instrument. The music we play will be unique to us. We all have our own unique vibration that is innate and authentic to us, our energy signature.

Mythology and Spirituality of the Acupuncture Meridian System

The web of the Chinese Medicine Meridian Matrix is better known for illustrating the relationships of our metabolism, of our metabolic functions. This is generally what we call "medicine" in our modern culture. This is what is known as an external approach to reality. This approach is built upon some major assumptions about the material world and physicality. This is the realm of the substantial. It is real, and it is practical but one should be aware of how their presuppositions, pre-conceived notions, alas their beliefs, affect their experience of the material world. The world of the Tao, the world of spirituality, of creator and creation, is a web of manifestation and mystery. The manifestation is created out of the mystery and will return to the mystery. The *Dao De Jing* by Lao-Tze, is a book of reminders that the deeper aspect of the world, the well from which it comes and returns, is the constant reality. The map of the Chinese Medicine Meridian Matrix is known for illuminating the metabolic functions, the manifestations, but it also simultaneously tells the story of the metaphoric functions, the story of the spirit, of the mystery. And it does so through the same template of relationships for both metabolism and metaphor.

The acupuncture meridians and points tell the story of the evolution of the spirit as it experiences incarnation. This is known as the inner tradition, the internal arts. This is the spiritual wisdom gained from reflection and awareness that reveals how the mystery, the spirit, the Tao, the quantum entanglement and the empty space drives the manifest reality of the material world. Every metabolic function is related to many metaphoric corollaries and vice-versa. Metaphor is entwined and entangled with metabolism. They are two aspects of the same thing, somato-psychic and psycho-somatic, the body-mind. This is the reality of Medicine. It is the somatic spirituality of embodiment, of deep, grounded presence within the physical form. Any breakthroughs regarding either the understanding of spirit or the science of microscopic metabolic processes can further the individual and our collective definition and practice of Medicine. Chinese Medicine functions as a bridge, as a rosetta stone, as a naturally fluid container for Medicine, equally comfortable and compatible with western medicine as it is with shamanic practices the world over.

In this book we will be exploring the background and foreground of the mythical, metaphorical and spiritual aspects of Chinese Medicine. This is the world of the Shen, the spirit. The beautiful thing is that the spiritual aspects of the Meridian Matrix are in direct relation to the metabolic functions of the body and both can be worked with in the same way. Activating an acupuncture point or taking an herb will affect the physical and the spiritual and the same medical and philosophical relationships underlying both levels. What we have here is a map that functions well from left brain dominance and right brain dominance and ultimately leads to transcendence of hemispheric dominance and polarized consciousness. This is the journey to the awakening of our Central Channel, our axis between Heaven and Earth and it's unfolding throughout our body and soul via the Meridian Matrix.

The chakras, the vortices that connect our body to the spectrum of consciousness, lie along the Central Channel as do our sphincters, the core of our Ancestral Sinew network. The involuntary aspects of the sphincter system regulate the pressurization of our system in relation to our breath, reflecting how expansive we feel or how pressed upon we feel. The sphincters function through negative pressure, the same term used for sucking, smoking or sipping through a straw. This negative pressure exerted by the physical body aligns the sphincter system with the various levels of the chakra vortices of consciousness. From here this experience of breath and consciousness expands through the distribution of acupuncture points all over the body. Learning how to participate in this process can provide us with agency at the dimensional border of our external energy fields, with the spiritual awareness of expanded consciousness while maintaining a grounded and relaxed awareness of the needs, responsibilities and surroundings of our physical body.

The Meridian Matrix is formed by the interference pattern created by Heaven and Earth. We are essentially a hologram of sorts within this field of the Tao. The acupuncture points are nodes of gravitational flux, the distribution of gravitational pressure throughout the fluid and connective tissue matrix of a living being. They are like a unique constellation, a pattern, signature or encryption, of nodes that are active and nodes that are latent. They are programmed as a mixture of the influence of Heaven, what is known as Astrology and the influence of Earth, what is known as Morphology. We are each a unique configuration of these influences. In holographic terms, this is our standing wave pattern. Astrology consists of vibrational influences, what are becoming scientifically recognized as the affect of the stars and planets through the quantum information that they bombard us with via quantum particle/waves like neutrinos and such. Morphology is becoming understood as genetics.

Our acupuncture points are a guide to our lives, their lessons and their stories. This is called our curriculum. The distribution patterns of active and latent acupuncture points function as strange attractors in our body and energy field that guide our growth and experience. The opportunities to transcend these configurations are the destinations that we are strongly attracted to, the record of our karma. We transcend the polarity between Heaven and Earth by awakening the "empty space," the cultivated balance within each point and within our self that dilates to accept the influx of spirit, of multi-dimensional energy. We can explore our curriculum proactively through the Acupuncture Meridian Matrix. We can do this through reflection, exercise, therapies, plant medicine, minerals, etc. It is a process of awareness and authenticity. This is called cultivation. This is the path of Destiny.

Taking Responsibility for Our Belief Systems

There is a maturity required in taking this journey. It requires taking responsibility for your beliefs, for the mythology of your place in the larger story of the Great Work[4] of ongoing creation known as evolution, or the ongoing evolution known as creation. This is a very tricky thing about mythology. It functions most powerfully when believed. This is the area of religion. We take magical, often seemingly illogical, stories of forces greater than our self and believe in them literally. This takes away some of the uncertainty and doubt associated with being incarnate and gives us access to the power of consciousness, the spiritual force, associated with that myth. The problem with this approach is that it is very often exclusive and in its basest form comes with the dogmatic notion that "my belief is right and therefore yours is wrong." One possible translation of the roots of the word "religion" comes from the Latin for "to connect together." To the degree that any religion separates us from the rest of Humanity it is not serving its higher purpose. In order to soften this potential dogmatic separation many of us have developed a relative sense of understanding of spiritual energies. This sense of relativity is a more intelligent, honest and inclusive approach in my opinion, but it often fails to connect to the visceral power of strong belief and deep faith.

Faith is an active relationship with the universe, with the unknown. Faith takes place in the present moment. Faith is the projection of our beliefs. It has been said that we cannot have an ounce of faith if we have a speck of doubt.[5] Belief is a more passive relationship based on pre-conceived notions and experience and filters out potential information. It is built on the past. Belief is our working hypothesis and the universe provides evidence for it. Often we are unaware of our beliefs and how they got there. Our core beliefs are the foundation of our faith and our faith is our dynamic relationship with the unknown. Our beliefs are at the level of the marrow in Chinese Medicine, the level of the self. Beliefs affect our experience of reality profoundly but they do not change easily. We can begin to take responsibility for our beliefs, but it requires awareness. There is a saying in the martial arts that

---

4. *A term used by Western Mystery Schools to describe the cultivation and evolution of spirituality in the embodied form.*

5. *From introduction to Carol Anthony's* A Guide to the I Ching. *2007*

"the things that we are unaware of control us." An opponent who sees what we are ignorant of can use that against us, until we figure it out, until we gain awareness of it. Life is like this. It is the big awareness exercise. The beauty of awareness is that it provides choice. Without awareness of something we cannot make choices regarding our relationship to it. Once we are no longer ignorant of something we have a choice regarding our actions in relationship to it. But we also now have a responsibility and have to forsake some of the limited protection that ignorance of our actions can provide.

Cosmic Adulthood and a Hero's Return

In order to engage the raw spiritual power of the many faces of the life force requires coming to terms with the way that belief shapes reality. Are we willing to take responsibility for our own beliefs, for our own morality, for our own meaning in life? It is similar to what we learn from body-oriented practices like Tai Chi. We have to commit, whether it is our weight, our hip, our shoulder, or our heart. We have to grow up and learn to take on the commitment to decide for our self what our beliefs are and where our faith lies and to take on the responsibility for what that means to us.

A Hero's Journey is the initiation into the responsibility of adulthood, but it is an adulthood defined by reality. It is a cosmic adulthood. It is independent of social conditioning, although often the most authentically adult choice we can make is to adopt many of the masks and roles of the culture we live in, because they are often defined by reality. If we can learn to play these roles and wear these masks from a place of authenticity we transform these roles through our presence and minimize the amount of suppression it takes to participate in society. Our social roles are infused by aspects of the divine. We see and feel spirituality within the mundane.

Transforming society is part of a Hero's Return. The Hero is destined to return from this Journey into the Meridian Matrix with newfound insight and understanding that can be shared with the community, with the collective. We help bring the tribe back into resonance with the collective unconscious. From this exploration of our circuitry, our web, so deeply entangled with the Universal Web, we bring back some light. We learn to pack light, so to speak. We can learn our purpose, our Destiny. We can learn to use our gifts in a way that can most benefit others. We can learn to let spirit move through us and participate in its divine unseen plan. We can become the miracle we want to see in the world. We can begin co-creating the kind of society that can place spiritual self-awareness, conscious evolution and the pursuit of destiny among its guiding principles and stand by these principles from a place of knowing.

Once again, we are entering the time of a New Mandate,[6] a time of major species-level change that I call the New Mandala of Humanity. We are leaving the time of hierarchical organization and centralized power and entering a

---

6. *Term used in Stephen Karcher's* Total I Ching: Myths for Change 2003

time of decentralizing power from institutions and returning power to the individual. This process is a mirror of the internal process where we are leaving the time of over-identification with our ego as our authority and learning to navigate from a place of connection to the whole. Our personality exists as part of our original nature, however our ego mechanisms are merely for protection and territorial power and must be recognized as such. Our egos exist on a spectrum somewhere between frozen in fear and willful manipulation. It's said that the ego is interested in 3 things: judgment, control, and approval. We can navigate from a better operating system than that as individuals and as a species. We all have our own Central Channel between Heaven and Earth and if we can embody our self authentically, we transmit information to each other directly from the collective intelligence. This synergistic transmission between individuals living their authenticity accelerates the mechanism of human evolution. We are all complements to the whole and have our part to play in the self-organizing Mandala of Humanity. We do this through taking a journey to the center of our self.

The Heart of the Meridian Matrix:
Exploring the 8 Extraordinary Vessels

≪♡≫

The 8 Extraordinary Vessels are part of the larger circuitry of the Meridian Matrix(the terms Meridian, Channel and Vessel will all be used interchangeably). The Meridian Matrix is the circulatory system for the life force, what is known as qi. Qi can be defined as the life force, as energy, as the energy of information, the energy of relationship, the energy of communication, the energy of connection. It is Q.I.: the Quantum Interface. Everything is either kinetic energy or potential energy, but qi is more about the relationship between things. Everything is qi because everything exists in relationship to everything else. In Chinese Medicine there are many specific ways in which we differentiate between types of qi . From the perspective of holistic experience of the Universe, qi is self-evident. Every ancient culture knew of qi because it's everywhere. But it is only available in the present moment.

The inability to sense qi is a clear indication of having the majority of our awareness outside of the moment, resourced in the past or future as a pre-conceived notion or a projection. If we can no longer sense qi in all its manifestations, it is a sign that we have lost touch with one of the most basic instincts, the ability to sense the presence of the life force. It can be felt throughout our body. It can be witnessed and sensed in the patterns of the wind and water, in the growing plants, in the movements of animals. It is a knowing that our blood and the water in the rivers are one and the same. It is, again, the knowing that our heart is the beating heart of Humanity and of Mother Earth. We are stating this very directly because it is a primal concern.

Humanity appears to be too ashamed of its loss of connection to Nature to be able to heal this disconnection. Yes, we have become poor stewards of the planet. Yes, our global leaders have lost all sense of respect and participation in the eco-systems of the planet. Yes, we have made some poor decisions that may require a great deal more work to correct than having made better decisions in the first place. Yes, modern cultures have lost touch with the reality that we are a living part of a living planet. As a species we have become like an auto-immune disorder to the planet. Awakening the evolutionary energy within us holds the key to rectifying this situation of attacking our own planetary self. Re-learning to sense the life force that flows through us and through everything is a good place to start healing this connection.

The Cauldron of Our Alchemical Process

The 8 Extraordinary Vessels lie at the Heart of the Meridian Matrix, at the deepest level of our being where Spirit-Shen and Essence-Jing come together and create life. They are the cauldron for this alchemical process. They are called "extraordinary" for good reason. This is where we can access the spiritual energies that are at the root of life. This is where we can access the quantum consciousness of the sub-atomic level within the nucleus of our cells, within the empty space.

Certainly any culture that can harness nuclear power should be spiritually mature enough to understand the process from an internal perspective. This is where the exploration of the 8x Vessels becomes highly relevant to our times. The 8x Vessels are the part of our being that is associated with the survival and perpetuation of the species, what we now know as DNA and its relationship to what we are coming to understand as the morphogenetic field. As such, the 8x Vessels are associated with adaptation, mutation and evolution. This level of our being is traditionally difficult to access, but it becomes easier and easier to access when it is a matter of survival of the species. We are living in just such times and it is through our personal evolution that we participate in the evolution of our species.

Implications of Accessing the 8 Extraordinary Vessels

The ethics of tapping into this level, similar to ethics issues regarding genetics, have been debated by the ancient Chinese. It is the old debate that "God made us this way and he must have known what he was doing. Let's not tamper with things." This is the sacred ground of ancestry, karma and spiritual curriculum, our blueprint. This issue has new global implications in modern times. This deep level of being that is related to our spiritual evolution is also associated with the survival of the species and is responsible for evolving to adapt to environmental threats. In ancient times, essentially only epidemic febrile diseases, such as measles and small pox, tapped into this level. Now we have xenobiotics(plastics), radiation, hormone therapies, vaccines, genetic engineering, and widespread use of powerful psychoactive drugs, to name a few things that penetrate to this level.

This level of our being adapts according to Disease-Nemesis Theory.[7] An example of this is the development of Polio and Sickle-Cell Anemia to provide immunity to Malaria. They are less of a threat to the continuity of the species than Malaria. This is the default setting of the Source Qi-the Yuan Qi. Interestingly enough we concurrently have greater access to this level personally from the widespread availability of powerful spiritual technologies such as Yoga, Qi Gong, Shamanism, etc. The 8 Extraordinary Vessels are becoming easier and easier to access because it is a matter of survival of the species. If we can shine our awareness into this level of our being maybe we can find ways of adaptation that are more promising than those offered by the default setting of Disease-Nemesis Theory. The health of our species is threatened by our technological achievements and we are finding ways

---

7.   *Cecil-Sterman, p. xxvii. 2012*

to adapt and to evolve. The 8x Vessels govern evolution and the evolution required may very well be one of spiritual evolution.

No exploration of Chinese Medicine would be complete without exploring this level, especially in this era of genetics, information theory, quantum physics, neuro-theology, etc. The theories of the 8 Extraordinary Vessels, in the context of the 5 Channel Systems of Acupuncture, offer a parallel and predictive framework for the discoveries of modern science and medicine. The cross-referencing between these extremely detailed and sophisticated systems is fertile ground and can provide the missing component of in-terrelationship and systems-theory so lacking in modern medical theory. Relationships between the brain, genetics, stem cells, hormones, synaptical arrangement and inhibition, fascial properties, piezo-electric conduction, gravity, temporal perception, aging, magnetic fields, plasma and transpersonal communication are all present in this model.

The reason that this system resonates so consistently with modern developments is a combination of experience and philosophy. Chinese Medicine is a system of applied philosophy. It is a system of philosophy based on empirical observation and put to the test through meditative, medical and martial application. It was an extremely scientific endeavor given the tools of the times. These were results-driven inquiries into the nature of subtle energies, with practitioners of spiritual technology as practical as practitioners of the martial or medical arts. In this fashion and in the context of subtle energy, the channel flows and relationships have been mapped in extreme detail.

We are now able to combine these maps with language and models drawn from science enhanced by technological breakthroughs and it is clear: the ancient Chinese were experiential and theoretical masters of both Newtonian and Quantum Physics. Exploring reality at this level is a trip down the rabbit hole and requires us to come to terms with our dynamic place in the Universe, but the potential discoveries we can make experientially parallel the leading edge of scientific breakthroughs in every field. We are far from the first culture to understand these things in some way and our ability to experience these phenomena personally and directly, in my opinion, is the key to applying them most effectively and responsibly. Culturally, we have just barely begun to participate in the phenomena of the mind/body/spirit.

Spirituality is Just the Way Things Are

As we explore esoteric spirituality there is a sense of mysticism, magic, awe, wonder, and power as well as the pitfalls of superstition, delusions of grandeur, and narcissism to name a few. These are dangers of over-identification with archetypal processes and are part of the challenges of this type of spiritual training. The world is indeed a transcendent place but, in the end, things are the way they are. Always have been and always will be. This quote from Bruce Lee illustrates the concept well:

*"Before I learned the art, a punch was just a punch, and a kick, just a kick.
After I learned the art, a punch was no longer a punch, a kick, no longer a kick.
Now that I understand the art, a punch is just a punch and a kick is just a kick."*

-- Bruce Lee

Spirituality is the same. At first Life is just Life. Then with spiritual discovery, Life is no longer just Life. Then with training, grounding, time and wisdom, Life is just Life again. It is subtly transformed through awareness, but it has become natural again. It is just the way things are. However, we cannot skip the work and exploration it takes to transform this spiritual understanding into something natural. The ancients experienced it and documented it. Science is validating it. It's sacred, but it's no big deal. However, in the process we may be able to discover wonderful things about our self and others and our place in the universe. We may be able to love more and fear less, and we may be able to cure our self of disease processes for which we were told there was no cure.

Alchemy: the Shamanic Journey into the Divine

ورجی

Traditionally the 8x Vessels have been most explored by the spiritual traditions associated with Taoism and it is these Taoists that have left behind the most information regarding their use. The spiritual use of the 8x Vessels is known as Alchemy and the practitioners are known as Alchemists. Alchemy is the process of transformation through discovering the essence, the nature, of something, be it plant, mineral or ourself . The analogy is that of turning lead into gold, what is known as "the Philosopher's Stone" in the West and "the Elixir of Immortality" in the East. Apparently Alchemists are also Poets.

In spiritual traditions, Alchemy can be seen as the process of refining darker and denser states of consciousness into lighter states of consciousness. As we begin to embody our essence, our Jing, we begin to have more presence of our spirit, our Shen. Ultimately this leads to the rebirth of our Pre-natal self, what Taoists refer to as "the Immortal Fetus." In more modern terms this could be called our Light Body, our Auric Egg. We are evolving towards conscious participation in our Light Body which can be experienced as a Cell, or a Self, in the larger, multi-dimensional organism of Humanity. This is the redemption of spirit from matter. This is the story of how spirit came into form and its awakening after a long time gone. This is the return home.

Historically and even currently, there are traditions in Chinese Medicine that divide Alchemy into two camps, "internal alchemy" and "external alchemy." External Alchemy is associated with the use of elixirs, such as minerals and herbs, to facilitate their practices. This is done in the spirit of reducing something to its essence, generally a plant, animal, or mineral product and ingesting its essence to further our practice. This is the beginning of modern science. Just as it is today, the scientific approach of constant reductionism and separation is extremely volatile. Alchemists would use the extracts of the essence of minerals for their spiritual practice. This was the advent of pharmaceutical medicine.

For a time this was in vogue in China and emperors wanted Taoist adepts to teach them their techniques because the emperors were seeking power and longevity. Obviously, something was lost or left out from these practices and heavy metal poisoning from mineral ingestion became commonplace with these practices. Some practitioners survived having gotten poisoned and began to advocate the meditative approach of Internal Alchemy as a better way and began developing techniques solely based on meditation. On a bio-chemical level, internal alchemy is about unlocking our endogenous pharmacy, whereas external alchemy is more about ingesting exogenous substances. The beautiful thing is that the chemicals of all of the most potent plant medicines and entheogens already exist within us. Internal and external are on a continuum.

In the External Alchemy, the exercise is about transforming a substance and or letting it transform you. In Internal Alchemy, it is about transforming negative emotions or thought forms both personal and collective, and/or letting them transform you. In order to do this we need to be able to recognize, to differentiate our self from our conditioned influences and from outside influences. This is our essence, our original nature. In either case, Alchemy is a process of allowing the universe- in the form of substances, events, emotions, energy and thoughts- to flow through us without resistance and being able to transform our experiences into fuel for more expanded states of aware-ness. Through recognition of the essence of our Self we can participate in the expanded transpersonal presence of spirit. This is called Awakening.

Alchemy and Pre-Natal Qi

Alchemy is a process that takes us into the realm of the spirit. This is the domain of pre-natal qi in Chinese Medicine. This is the area of spiritual exploration and also of exploration into our transpersonal nature regarding DNA, Humanity as a species, and the Planetary Mind. The medical tradi-tions of Chinese Medicine have often had little interest in the exploration of pre-natal qi. It is merely regarded as a finite commodity whose development was fixed in utero and which declines throughout our life until we die. This is life as measured by the breaths you take, life as the aging process, life as the entropy of decay. This is the emphasis on the material, the substantial, the body.

In Alchemy there is the understanding that our pre-natal nature is our connection to the cosmos and that how we experience our life affects every-thing. This is life as measured by the moments that take your breath away, life seen as the experiences that feed and shape our soul and the recognition that the purpose and meaning of our spiritual life can transform our life and quite possibly our body in the process. This is the emphasis on the imma-terial, the insubstantial, the soul. This is the reversal of the entropy process, known as negentropy.[8] Or to state it more simply, we can potentially reverse the decay caused by life by allowing more Flow into our life. In the case of Alchemy, more precisely through allowing more Flow through the pre-natal energy system.

Post-natally speaking, we are an open system to air and food. It is the flow of these resources through our system that sustains us. In much of Chinese Medicine as practiced by physicians, the pre-natal system is seen as a closed system. It was once an open system where we were open to the flow of resources through the umbilicus up until birth when the pre-natal system becomes a closed system with no flow moving through it. No flow means death essentially and that is how we are designed. We are pre-programmed for death by having these fixed parameters that do not allow for any flow of resources. This is where Alchemy and the practice of Medicine can be seen as taking a strong turn away from each other. They have radically different

8. *Dechar.*

views regarding the nature of pre-natal qi. As we have already seen, the beliefs of physicians regarding pre-natal qi can often be summed up in one sentence.

Here is the big difference in perspective: we are actually a potentially open system on the level of pre-natal qi. We have a whole energy body of pre-natal qi that is connected directly to the Universe. We are an open system through our ability to tap directly into the Tao Field and accommodate multi-dimensional energy flow through our system. This is the purpose of our pre-natal energy system. We are programmed by design to have a controlled setting on this energy. Physically, we experience our pre-natal energy as our sex drive and libido. However, we rarely experience the consciousness of this energy outside of Peak Experiences such as falling in love or having a child, and the consciousness of the pre-natal remains generally imperceptible. Our accumulated resistance due to social conditioning and habituation is the impedance to this energy from the morphogenetic field of the Tao. The 8 Extraordinary Vessels are a map to our connection to this field and provide a framework for the awakening of our pre-natal energy body, where we attach our etheric umbilicus to the mainframe of the Universe.

Reversing Entropy = Increasing Flow

The Alchemists are known for being seekers of longevity and immortality. Taoism strongly points to the belief of immortality being possible in the body and not simply a metaphor for enlightenment or awakening. The ability to extend the lifespan can be seen as the ability to reverse entropy and get into the settings of the genetic code. However, the mere desire to extend a lifespan in and of itself seems spiritually immature. Life is already immortal. Individual longevity is more the by-product of a way of approaching life, of working with the soul, rather than being an end goal unto itself. But, regardless of how it happens, anything that involves the reversal of the aging process can teach us a great deal about health and disease, so let us take a look at the principles of entropy to see how such a reversal could take place.

Alchemy can be seen as the process of reversing entropy in a system. Entropy is the principle that things, if left to their own devices, will naturally go from a state of more order to a state of less order. This is the principle behind decay, rotting, rusting, aging. It is a process of degeneration, a process of breaking things down. Psychologically, entropy can be defined as the amount of uncertainty in a person's mindset. This uncertainty will create more and more disorder which will cause the organism to use extra energy to maintain focus under the anxiety-inducing state of uncertainty. Stress creates a state of psychological entropy. This psychological entropy of stress is the prime force behind the aging and disease process. It is the inability to optimally deal with constant change and uncertainty in the Universe.

The term "flow consciousness" is a state of psychological negentropy, which is to say it is a positive psychological state. In this state we are able to harness all the power of our mind to focus effortlessly on the task at hand, not using any energy to quell the distraction of uncertainty, doubt, fear, and stress. States of flow consciousness drive the personal and collective evolutionary process. Life is designed to create higher levels of order and self-organization and will do this naturally, unless we put up higher than necessary amounts of resistance. In this sense, Alchemy is the process of learning to flow with life, of putting up less resistance in order to reduce the amount of entropy and decay in a system.

The alchemical process is one of being able to digest, integrate, and eliminate whatever life throws your way. It is the path of least resistance to life. It is the process of acceptance, lack of attachment(lack of grasping and holding through excess tension), transforming what we can into useful energy and letting go of what no longer serves us. Ultimately, the alchemical approach teaches us to allow more life force to flow through us. This activates our gifts that can be shared for the greater good that were stifled by early wounds and social repression. In order to do this we need to be able to accept and love our self and find our purpose, that which allows us to enter into a flow state

Horizontal and Vertical Approaches to Alchemy

Learning to relate to and metabolize the events of our lives and the relationships in our lives is known as a horizontal approach to alchemy. Learning to navigate this level of our inter-relationships is the first step in healing. It allows us to ground and start taking responsibility for our emotions and actions and how they affect others and taking responsibility for how the emotions and actions of others affect us. This teaches us how to heal on a personality level and a social level. In a sense it teaches us how to heal the subtle energies of our post-natal relationships. We are learning to transform and navigate the negative and positive energies of the post-natal, but we have yet to participate in the evolutionary potential of the pre-natal energy system. This level of alchemy is about working with the amount of energy that is already in play. This sort of emotional healing takes place at a much lower charge of energy and is therefore much safer. This work is mainly about becoming grounded. Once we are grounded in the post-natal we can begin to bring in energy that was not available. This is the energy of creation that drives evolution.

This type of healing work prepares us for metabolizing the higher energies of the cosmos directly, which is a vertical approach to alchemy. In order to take in multi-dimensional energies directly, we must learn to be detached enough from our material perspective to hold a non-judgmental, non-polarized space within our self. If we are constantly being pushed and pulled by every unprocessed charge of our story and our emotional bias, we will not be able to hold this neutral space. Holding this neutral space is called being empty. Being empty creates the alchemical process of bringing in multi-dimensional energy or spiritual energy into this plane. This energy flows through our spine, through our energy centers, through our brain and through our DNA. This is Flow.

We create the ability to dilate our axis to take in more energy, which resonates at the genetic level as an opening, an unwinding, of the intercalated double helixes which take in sub-atomic energy through the nucleus. This is experienced as time dilation, which just so happens to be the gateway to immortality. We enter eternity through living more and more in the ever-expanding moment.

Shamanic Roots of Alchemy

Alchemy is a type of divination. It is a matter of interacting with the divine, with the higher patterns of life, with multi-dimensional, spiritual energies. Alchemy is finding ways to enter into connection with the spirits, deep within the eternity found at the heart of every moment. We enter into the Divine, into a connection with the spirits and we come with a quest, with a question. The question is generally about the past or future, about our purpose or direction. After we have had our experience with the divine, we have the opportunity to integrate the experience into our life. We have the opportunity to integrate the higher patterns of light into the material plane for the benefit of our self and our communities. Here is where we see the ancient roots of the alchemical practices.

The alchemical practices of Chinese Medicine are rooted in the pre-historic practices of the ancient Wu, the shamans, essentially back to the dawn of Humanity. The ancient psyche was deep in connection with the spirits. Stories were communicated around the fire, stories of the primordial forces that influenced life and death. At some point this connection to the spirits began to be facilitated or mediated by the ancient Wu, or shamans. Through their own gifts, trials and journeys into the spirit world, the shaman's role is to facilitate the connection of the people with the spirits and with their ancestors. These are energies of consciousness that are still present in the morphogenetic record, the ancestor field. The shaman facilitates the ability of the culture to resonate with the primordial realities of the collective consciousness. Alchemy and shamanism are the facilitation of this connection to the Divine, to the spirits, to the consciousness of the morphogenetic field.

The Pre-Natal Era and the Divine Feminine

The majority of the ancient Wu were women. The Wu were in direct contact with the spirits, often through plant spirituality, trance and ecstatic states. The pre-historic times represent the pre-natal times of Human consciousness. Whole tribes would enter into the shared experience of the Numinous, the shared experience of the pre-natal energy body as the medium of transpersonal connection. These are the universal roots of religion, medicine and culture, gifted and evolved over time from the collective consciousness, from the planet herself. Much of the prejudice against shamanism and plant spirituality seems to stem from subtle and not-so-subtle prejudice against the feminine, the divine feminine and the feminine principle, the Yin. This prejudice is largely responsible for our poor stewardship of the planet culminating over the past 5,000 years.

Even within many of these shamanic traditions around the planet the approach to plant spirituality and spirituality in general became dominated by males. These warrior approaches to healing often tend toward more rigid traditions and aggressive approaches to healing. They can be effective, but, in my opinion, many of these traditions need healing as well. The healing of this rift between male and female, of yin and yang is the core rift in our collective psyche and takes place within us as well as outside us. It is represented by our ability to harmonize these polarities within our self, to create pathways through the corpus callosum connecting the left and right hemispheres of our brain that allow the flow through the vertical axis.

We can return to the spirit of the ancients and the pre-natal era of Humanity for it is always available in the ever-expanding moment. Whenever we experience creative guidance and inspiration in the moment we have returned to the sacred ground of the ancestors, the origins of this medicine. When our experience of time dilates into a continuous experience of the Now and we enter into the pre-natal, we have entered the realm of the Wu.

Part 1 Chapter 4

Putting Our Self in Perspective: Original Nature and the Acquired Mind

Each of us has a direct connection to the Divine. This part of our self is known as our Original Nature. It is who we are beyond the influence of any social influences. We can learn who we are through the process of differentiation, the process of individuation. This is the process of becoming grounded enough in our essence, in our own body that our own consciousness can be recognized within the larger ocean of consciousness, but not merely through the resistance of separation consciousness. As we differentiate our self we begin to recognize the part we play in the larger picture. We begin to see that we are all complementary parts in the Mandala of Humanity. We begin to take responsibility for our vertical axis, our connection between Heaven and Earth. When we can allow this energy to flow through our vessel with minimal resistance, we can begin to move through our life without resistance and begin to move towards our Destiny. We become the conductor of our Destiny.

In order to reduce the amount of resistance that we put up towards the flow of the universal energy, we need to come to a certain level of acceptance, of allowance. As this acceptance grows to become gratitude and devotion, we dilate the flow of energy. We are allowing the life force to move through us, and to move us towards our purpose. Resistance exists in the body/mind as tension. This is the tension of striving, of competing, of self-protection, of hiding our inadequacy or incompetence. This is the world of the ego, constantly trying to protect us and our identity. Our personality is deeper than our ego and we have little to fear in letting go of our ego. Our ego comes back.

Our ego is merely a lens, a screen, a filter, an incomplete perspective. It provides a boundary for us to experience being an individual, to experience being separate from the whole. It is how we organize the world based on our experiences and conditioning. It is not so much a matter of getting rid of the ego as it is a matter of having a large enough perspective to put the ego in perspective, instead of the ego being the perspective. The ego is the post-natal consciousness of having form. It is the conditioned self or the acquired mind. The conditioned self identifies with the perception of being separate from the whole.

Separation Consciousness of the Acquired Mind

"Tension is who we think we should be. Relaxation is who we truly are."

- Chinese Proverb

We use tension to hold on to our ego, to maintain our separation consciousness. This tension is rooted in the trauma and shock of separation from the whole. It is a natural process of coming into form. These deep imprints allow us to contract our energy body enough to experience a life with the freedom of perceived separation. There is a certain amount of residual tension required to be in relation to gravity. Any extra tension is entirely for self-protection. It is a form of armor. Healthy muscle tone and chronically tense muscle tonus are not the same thing.

When we desire to understand and feel a deeper connection to each other and to life, it is the early traumatic imprints of separation, these boundaries that keep us from being able to do so. Healing is the process of learning to be connected to the whole again, learning to navigate our boundaries. We are part of the whole, but we can differentiate ourselves from the whole. We can never truly know our self until we have experienced being part of the whole. Differentiation comes from experiencing unity. This is where practices that allow us to be immersed in an experience of the Divine are so important.

Striving, Resistance and the Conditioned Self

The more we strive to identify with our Conditioned Self, the more resistance we are putting up to our Original Self. This resistance keeps the energy of the vertical axis between Heaven and Earth un-accessible. This limits us to being defined by our horizontal relationships, our social relationships. Not that they are not important, they may be the most important aspects of our life, but we will never be in charge of our own Destiny in this way. The Universe lets us work out our issues on the horizontal axis because this is a safer plane for the ego to participate in. The potential energies are much less powerful and mainly post-natal in nature.

Our resistance meets with social resistance unless we learn to play the games required by our society. This is the inertia of structure. Social structures become habituated into the morphogenetic field to maintain stability, to avoid changing, to avoid mutation, to avoid evolution. This is the self-perpetuating nature of post-natal consciousness and the conditioned self. They are based in form and so define themselves through structure. The movement and function available within these structures is a closed system. The only way to bring in the energy of evolution is through the vertical axis. This brings the flow of new energy, multi-dimensional energy into circulation and this creative energy causes evolution. This flow occurs through the pre-natal energy system. Our conditioned self will put up resistance to this vertical flow. Our original nature will recognize this flow as home. Once we learn to accept these energies without resistance we can express them horizontally through cooperation in community. We will only be cooperated with to the point that we are not in resistance to our own conduction of this energy.

The higher bandwidths from Heaven are intended to conduct charge through us through the power of acceptance. Resistance along the vertical axis creates impedance to this conduction of energy which can cause distress to the organism and can create social resistance to the intentions of the person working with this energy. The only way to conduct this charge is through accepting yourself, through loving yourself. This charge will ground and flow through the authentic aspects of our energy body and will spin off the noise and static of our resistances. This energy brings the power of creativity into play, the power of creation, the power to create. This is how evolution takes place. Your ability to access the energies of the vertical axis come with a responsibility: the willingness to be yourself. Through the creative power of this authenticity you will be able to share your gifts with others. Destiny.

Part 1 Chapter 5

Quest for Quantum Consciousness

✍✎

The Holy Grail at our journey's end and new beginning can very appropriately be termed Quantum Consciousness. We are developing powerful models of consciousness that can be described aptly using scientific terms taken from breakthroughs in every field. Because everything is some form of energy, physics provides some of the most applicable insights and makes a good skeleton key. Quantum physics sets the bar pretty high as far as weirdness goes and weirdness could indeed be translated into Chinese as the same word as extraordinary. The experiences of my life are in accord with the latest theories of science. The experiences of my life and the latest theories of science are all in accord with the spiritual wisdom of the ancients. The modern arenas of politics, religion, energy, economy, and medicine are mostly in active forms of resistance to the application of the latest theories of science, the wisdom of the ancients, and yes, also to the insights provided by the most extraordinary experiences of my life.

Wave Consciousness and Particle Consciousness

Let us start with one of the core insights of Quantum Physics: matter can be either a wave or a particle based on the perspective of the observer. This is sheer genius. Matter can be a particle, which is fixed in time and space. This is the material, the substantial, solid aspect of reality, of form, what we term the post-natal perspective of consciousness. This is the obvious, explicate order of the world. Newtonian principles and practical experience work well with this. This is separation consciousness. Our world has gotten good at this, obsessively separating things into details to the point that we have developed the means to destroy the planet. We have managed to deeply explore the obvious, the explicate order.

Thankfully at the extremely large, small or subtle, the weirdness of the implicate order or the hidden order starts to reveal itself. This is where we see that matter can also be a wave. When matter is behaving like a wave, it has no fixed position and is insubstantial. It begins playing by radically different principles than those of a particle. A wave has a larger relationship to the unknown, to the mystery, that is implied by its unfixed coordinates. It could be anywhere, until we fix it with our observations and expectations. This is how our energy body functions. All matter is energy. Our inability to perceive the subtle flow of energy that is the material world is based on the limitations of our own perception. We tend to see the world through the lens of pre-conceived notions and projections conditioned into us and reinforced by our experiences, which of course tend to validate our pre-conceived notions and projections. This is the explicate order. We tend to calibrate our perception, our senses to the explicate order, eventually tuning out all other potentials and possibilities that are available in the moment, in the empty space in-between. This material consciousness known as "particle consciousness" could also be termed "post-natal consciousness."

Wave consciousness views the world as an ocean if vibration. Wave consciousness tunes into the world through resonance. It is a receptive form of consciousness. We allow our self to be open enough to tune into the frequencies, the vibrations of our self and the world. This level of sensitivity comes with a degree of added vulnerability. It can be difficult and even life-threatening to begin to reconfigure our survival energy, our Wei Qi. This is a spiritual and martial yoga. We learn efficiency, economy of movement and self-defense in order to allow our self to be more open, more receptive. Consciousness itself can be transmitted through waves, through vibrations.

Waves participate in the non-local field of vibration that ancients called "the Tao." Waves are not limited by time and space. They are multidimensional, functioning from the same principles as galaxies, sub-atomic energy, dark matter, etc. We are multidimensional, functioning from the same principles as galaxies, sub-atomic energy, dark matter, etc. This formless, spiritual consciousness called "wave consciousness" can be called "pre-natal consciousness." This type of vibration-based consciousness was essentially all we knew in utero, when we were in an aquatic environment. We can physically generate waves through accessing the torsional movements of the ancestral hydrostatic skeleton. In this way, our form is already programmed to participate in this level of consciousness, but it requires healing our relationship to all the traumas and imprinting since birth and really since the hardening of the bones that lock us out of the marrow level and the flow of hydrostatically generated movements, both individually and evolutionarily. The 8x Vessels provide a template for this journey.

Observer Consciousness

Whether matter behaves more like a particle or a wave depends on the perspective, even the expectations, of the observer.[9] If the observer goes to measure the results of the experiment as a particle, that is what they find. If the observer goes to measure the results of the experiment as a wave, that is what they find. In this way, the universe validates our working hypothesis. Until the observer goes to measure his experiment, matter is essentially a wave or a particle, or both. In this way the design, the expectations, the choice of what to look at, completely affect the results of any experiment. Understanding that we affect everything through our observation comes with a large amount of responsibility. It is the responsibility of co-creation. We can choose to view everything as a particle and accept the material world at face value. This is a soul-less viewpoint but it might possibly simplify things. Or we can learn to be more centered amidst a vast amount of uncertainty.

9. *Quantum Physics truth.*

We learn to navigate quantum consciousness through becoming comfortable with relativity, with relational understanding. In quantum physics nothing even exists until it is in relation to something which is similar to our definition of qi. Life requires entanglement. Relativity is like learning to swim. Relativity is a property of motion and the whole universe is moving. Relativity is the doorway to quantum consciousness. However, relativity is not an end state. It is like never opening the box to see if there is a particle or a wave. It is like never conducting the experiment at all. We have to place our attention, our intention somewhere. We have a perspective on the whole which we can share. Choosing where to place our attention is where we begin to move from the more non-committal aspects of relativity into the responsibility of quantum adulthood.

Getting Centered: Navigating Relativity

Herein lies some of the dangers of the inner path, we wander into a forest of relativity and uncertainty, a forest of the unknown and find that relativity is only a perspective, it is not a solution. It is almost like the opposite of belief in that it provides no direction home and offers only the random feedback of random chance from external reality. Random chance is a certain pathway to the default setting of our Fate. With relativity, we begin swimming in a loss of certainty. There is really only one constant that we can know and that is our self. Everything else is relative to our position.

In the Martial Arts we train this understanding spatially through knowing our center and being aware of all the dynamic angles and vectors as they relate to our center. When we interact with the *I Ching*, the Book of Change, we train this understanding temporally. We learn to find our center through the flow of events over time. There are situations and decisions that come and go and we just need to be aware of how to remain centered in our actions and non-actions. It is this centering that allows us to begin orienting our self within uncertainty and within the pure potential of the unknown. We are learning all the angles, all the perspectives and they require that we know our self, our position, our presence.

Emotions Ground the Channel

We begin developing the awareness of being aware, the awareness of consciousness. We can keep expanding the angle of perception, the depth of our perspective as we grow into more spiritual or transpersonal modes of consciousness. In order to ground and sustain this expanded awareness into the material world, we have at least one more thing besides time and space to address: our emotions. We cannot be present by thinking our way through our life. We have to feel our way through. Our emotions provide us feedback as to how we are doing personally and socially. Emotions let us know how we are treating each other and how we are treating our self. Emotions allow us to expand and contract in relation to perceived positive and negative stimuli. They connect Humanity as an organism. They show us how we interact with the Field through vibration.

Emotions are a frequency of vibration, a quality of vibration. As we see in Chinese Medicine 5 Element theory, emotions are mediated via the organs and acupuncture channels, which are the "channels" that modulate the frequency that connects inner and outer through resonance. Emotions exist on a spectrum. When we develop clarity in relation to these emotional channels, we develop and embody the virtues of these emotions, the broader bandwidth of these signals. It is not merely about embodying higher vibrations. These higher vibrations/emotions are anchored through the work we have done with the denser vibrations/emotions. In this way we are like a radio or an instrument and we are learning to "tune" our self to receive and transmit signals. The broader bandwidth of frequency we can embody allows us to be more constant and stable in our presence, in our truth.

In Information Theory, signals represent truth and the rest of the information is noise. Once we can embody our truth, we can transmit and receive useful signals. We have clarity. Unprocessed, suppressed, and repressed emotions exist as noise in our system and keep us from going "on-line" into the world of direct transmission of signal. The unresolved charges of emotion distort the clarity of reality and dampen the signal. These undigested emotions provide the homework, the unfinished business of our spirituality. These unprocessed emotions relate to our stories.

In Chinese Medicine we say that the emotional record of our lives is stored in the blood as well as in the marrow. Unprocessed emotions will keep us from being fully grounded in transpersonal states of awareness and will generally keep us from ever experiencing these states. Our emotional energy is how we connect with spiritual energy. It is our "analog-to-digital" converter and can be "tuned" into receiving the digital messages of spirit. This is the beginning of the development of quantum consciousness, of spiritual consciousness. This book will explore these models in the language of Chinese Medicine in order to help us tune into the spiritual levels of consciousness.

In order to develop a perspective on our emotions and our experiences we need to learn to observe them. We are learning to be a neutral observer working with the first lesson of the emerging quantum consciousness: "the observer always affects the outcome of the experiment." This leads to the interesting potential that maybe the most powerful way to affect an experiment is to become the observer. Be the observer in your own experiment. The experiment is our life and spatial, temporal, and emotional relativity all teach us how to observe, how to pay attention. Through where we choose to put our awareness, we can begin to live our experiment through our presence. This is the nature of multi-dimensional consciousness.

In order to experience a more expanded perspective, keep resonating with the part of you that is observing. Who is observing you observe? Who is aware of you trying to be more aware? But again we are not simply trying to dissolve into an ocean of relativistic consciousness. The experience of unity is just the beginning of developing a higher level of ability to differentiate the essence and spirit of things, especially the ability to differentiate the self. Each more expanded level of consciousness comes with an expanded set of responsibility. Personal evolution allows us to participate to a higher degree in co-creating reality. Creation is creating more of our self in the world.

Flowing at the Speed of Life

Through cultivating awareness we develop a sense of the universe as a process. We can learn to flow with that process and to let it flow through us. We have done some homework on the nature of our resistances. This is an important pre-requisite because once we begin allowing the full force of spiritual energy, of multi-dimensional energy to flow through us we have to allow it to flow. It is similar to high velocity activities. If we are not going fast enough, not allowing enough energy, then we do not gain the essential support of the centripetal effect of gravity. Without this added support we can never take the turns smoothly enough, with enough grace. It is the same in Tai Chi standing postures. We have to surrender to gravity a little beyond our comfort zone to engage the buoyant support of gravity. We have to allow a little more flow than we at first are comfortable with.

As we approach higher velocities, there is a tendency to want to overuse our brakes to remain at lower velocities. This will make us clumsy when navigating the twists and turns in the road. Sure we are safer when we crash at lower speeds, but we are also less stable and have not engaged the force that elevates an activity into a skill, a talent, or an art. We have not engaged the flow. At higher energy levels we need to develop similar understanding to that required for moving at higher velocities. We have to learn to look where we want to go and not to look where we do not want to go, because we will go where our eyes go and we will go there quickly. We will gravitate towards where we place our focus. We navigate through our intentionality and directionality, through the choices we make. These are the responsibilities of quantum consciousness. As we engage higher and higher states of flow, we begin to move towards choicelessness, because at these velocities it is clear when we are leaving the flow and we naturally move in the direction that centripetally holds us to our path.

We start by learning to make choices we can live by. We are learning to navigate from pure awareness. Our intentionality and directionality will affect every outcome and these will be reflections of our underlying beliefs about the universe. Part of our developing awareness is to take responsibility for these core settings, regardless of how they got there. To some degree, spiritual awareness is giving up your "right" to go on auto-pilot. We are learning to allow the multi-dimensional energy, the spirit, to flow through us in an accelerated manner. Like gravity and velocity we have to let go enough to engage the flow to enough of a degree to be able to feel its support. This is the flow of the Tao, the flow of creation. Through this flow, evolution occurs with joy and surprise at its own creativity.

This force flows through our pre-natal circuitry, through the 8x Vessels, through our marrow. This includes our brain and our DNA. As such its flow is largely dependent on our settings, otherwise known as our beliefs. In order to engage this flow and apply it to our life we have to understand the nature of beliefs. There are aspects of our beliefs that we will never understand without cultivating our awareness at the level of the marrow. Many of our beliefs originate in what is known as the collective unconscious, the morphogenetic field and our ancestry. Our beliefs shape our reality on every level. Rigid belief systems will not allow multi-dimensional flow through our DNA. This is why some of the alchemical practices have names like "Brain Washing" and "Marrow Washing." We need to do some housecleaning to be able to expand our perspective, to observe our own beliefs influencing our perception and behavior.

The Strange Attractors of Our Destiny

The flow of spirit is likened to chaos in Chinese Medicine. In Chaos Theory, chaos has an "order" all its own and some of the principle aspects of this order are known as "attractors," or "strange attractors." If this were being translated from Chinese, these could just as easily be known as "extraordinary attractors." Our beliefs function like strange attractors that manifest the experiences that provide us the opportunity to learn our lessons. The strange attractors are programmed into our curriculum. They are the equation of the relationship between our lessons and the destinations of our story.

Alchemy is the process of shining awareness into the nature of these attractors. The more we get to know our self, the more we begin to understand our beliefs and can change our beliefs. We improve upon the configuration of the attractors through arranging our marrow, our neuro-genetic patterns, more and more coherently. We do this by working with the master control of our brain's neural patterning, the Heart. Through entrainment with the Heart's magnetic field, the brain orchestrates its patterns. Through creating patterns of higher and higher levels of coherence, patterns of peace, love and understanding, we begin to see through our belief systems. We begin to unlock the principles underlying our beliefs. Extracting the essence of our beliefs, the core principles, allows us to let go of our resistance to the flow.

When we learn our lessons we engage more of the flow of the universe. This is the energy of our Destiny. Our Destiny is a working hypothesis, a purpose, an intention. Our life is the experiment, the canvas, the clay, the story. This is our creation story, our mythology. It is time for our story to be told. Every one of us is unique and stands at the crest of the wave of evolutionary momentum going back to the Big Bang, the first creation story. We can stand for something. We can make a stand. We can stand up to our self and to the world. Trust that you have gifts and are a gift to humanity. Cultivate that faith. Be the hero of your own story.

"If you're not the hero of your own novel, then what kind of novel is it?
You need to do some heavy editing."   – Terence McKenna

Applications of the 8 Extraordinary Vessels

Chinese Medicine is applied philosophy. In Chinese Medicine there is always an application for a concept. In the realm of the 8 Extraordinary Vessels there are many applications. These applications are related to the practice of medicine, martial arts, and the meditative arts. The main ways that these meridians have been applied is through acupuncture, herbology, movement and meditation. The 8 Extraordinary Vessels were traditionally used by the spiritual traditions to create higher levels of spiritual awareness and in the martial traditions to gain access to deeper levels of power. This could result in longevity, increased vitality, healing ability, a deeper appreciation of being alive, and perhaps even some miraculous gifts and abilities.

The 8x Vessels have been used by acupuncturists for millennia to address diseases of the constitution or of a spiritual/karmic nature. The 8x Vessels have been seen as a reservoir and canal system. The goal is to maintain appropriate levels in the reservoir and be able to deliver these reserves efficiently wherever and whenever they are needed. As such any progress in the efficiency of these reservoirs will carry over into every aspect of your life. This Yuan Qi-Source Qi can support a medical process, a growth process, the expansion of consciousness, movement on the path of destiny or the force behind a kick. These applications are all related to coming to acceptance of yourself, liberating energy from your memory/story, and letting that energy of the authentic self become available for application in the present moment. This is called the dissemination of the pre-natal into the post-natal.

Medical Aspects of the 8 Extraordinary Vessels

In working with the 8x Vessels medically, we can help people work on any symptoms or processes that are related to the Essence/Yuan Qi Level. This includes genetic disorders, auto-immune disorders, structural disorders, cancers, problems related to reproduction, pregnancy, birth, early childhood imprints and trauma, complications from vaccines, developmental disorders, brain function, geriatrics, PTSD and more. We may not always be able to "cure" but we can allow for optimal unfolding of the process and help shine the light of awareness into the nature of the problem on many levels. We may be able to alleviate some degree of the symptoms and suffering that come with someone's karma and someone's genetic make-up, even if we can't "change" their medical condition. We can help people feel more natural within their body and their life, to be more comfortable with their self, to be more comfortable in their skin. We can help catalyze the processes of healing that come from awareness and acceptance and guide the person into the areas of themselves that may require change in order to transcend a disease process. Often the disease process is intimately tied into who we are and who we have become.

With awareness comes choice. With awareness we can take more responsibility for who we are and how this shapes our lives. In the words of Chinese Medicine, "there are no incurable diseases, only incurable people." This saying is not coming from a place of judgment. It is stating that our ability to heal and transcend disease is often directly related to our ability to grow, to change, and to adapt on whatever level, perhaps even every level if that's what it takes. Often it is the sheer repetition and habits of the mind and personality that create decay. We stop growing and crystallize into our form and experience the inherent entropy of form. It is like being addicted to our beliefs. What may be required is the change of perspective that comes from a change of heart. Grace. Miracles. Possibilities. These are not things that someone else can do for you or can come in a pill. They come from our connection to the source, to all things, to the Field, to the Tao, to God. Like all healing, the 8x Vessels guide us to being able to open up this door.

According to Chinese Medicine if qi is moving we will not experience pain and disease, but if qi is stagnant we will experience pain and disease. All of Chinese Medicine is designed to restore flow. The 8x Vessels are the valve on the miraculous potential of the multi-dimensional energy of the Universe. The 8 Extraordinary Vessels circulate at the Yuan Qi/Source Energy level and are where we can restore the flow to the deepest, densest fluids in our body, the Jing-Essence, the hormones, the cellular metabolism, the cerebro-spinal fluid, and the bone marrow. The 8x Vessels can be used as restorative medicine to build up the resources in the body or to improve the body's efficiency in the usage of these resources.

Just by allowing contact to be made with one's original nature is a huge opportunity for growth and healing. This is enough for many people to find improvement in their lives. But the potential of this level of our being is that of transformation, the transformation of our experience of our self and our connection and perspective on the world. Chinese Medicine says, "change the belief, change the illness." Beliefs belong to the brain marrow, a component of the Jing-Essence and Yuan Qi level. A change of belief manifesting as lasting brain change and genetic change is an attribute of the 8 Extraordinary Vessels. This is the miraculous potential of there being no incurable diseases. It all depends on our ability to have a change of heart, a change of perspective.

Destiny and the Spiritual Aspects of the 8 Extraordinary Vessels

Spiritually speaking, medical cure is not necessarily the goal. The goal would be more along the lines of being at peace with yourself and your place in the universe, which may or may not improve one's medical condition. However, accessing this deep level of being, of the spirit moving through our essence is another story. We can often restore hope quickly, as it is a matter of the Shen/Spirit. This is the first step. Then generally to change our marrow is an act of directed focus of will over a period of time, traditionally said to be 90-100 days, or a season. Or we can participate in a transformative peak experience and integrate it over the course of a season. But bear in mind that grace can do this instantly. In Chinese Medicine this is "vaporizing the phlegm that mists the heart-mind." In working at this level we are holding space for grace. In one model we could use the 70% rule of Tai Chi which says to leave 30% of an activity open for the qi to come in. Another one I like is "it takes a 100% of our efforts to meet God half way."[10] Though the math is quite different they are saying the same thing: there is an outside force that can work in your favor and it is worth learning how to connect with it. In working at this level, we need to keep in mind that although a person may need to change in order to transcend a disease process, this does not mean that there is anything wrong with who they are. Often acceptance is the biggest change possible.

Perhaps the two most explored ways of accessing the 8x Vessels are acupuncture and qigong. The former has been used in the medical traditions and the latter more in the alchemical traditions. They are both effective means of accessing these energies. Herbal Medicine can access the Yuan Qi and, as importantly, can access the Shen and enhance its ability to connect with the Yuan Qi. The shamanic use of plant medicines can provide profound direct experience with our Yuan Qi that can be invaluable in guiding our process. Working with spiritually powerful people can activate these channels. The 8x Vessels are resonant in nature to the channels involved in all yogic traditions. Just reading about the wisdom contained in the philosophy of the 8x Vessels is transformational in and of itself.

---

10. *Anthony, several times throughout book 2007.*

Part 2

Background & Preparation for the Alchemical Journey

Wu Ji and Tai Chi- Creation of Separation

❧

"The Dao that can be told is not the eternal Dao"- beginning of Dao De Jing

Wu Ji- The Primordial Mystery of Empty Space

To begin we will explore the beginning, or the before the beginning. This is the concept of Wu Ji. This is the great void, the primordial emptiness from which all things come. This is the energy of zero. It is inseparably related to the energy of one. It is difficult to speak of the nothing. Math is a better language for describing the indescribable. However, in Taoism we like to say something cannot be described and then go on to describe it in great detail. Essentially, Wu Ji is the empty space. As nature has issues with vacuums, emptiness creates a vacuum suction which then fills with energy. This has been called "zero-point energy" or "ground state energy." This is the background "resting state" of the universe. From Wu Ji comes Tai Yi. Or from the Zero comes the One. Together they are creation, the seed of pre-natal qi, before the birth into the world.

Figure 2.1: Wu Ji to Tai Yi to Tai Chi to Trinity with Wu Ji in the Center

---

Tai Yi- Undifferentiated Unity of Pre-Natal Qi

Tai Yi means the "great one." Tai Yi is the undifferentiated unity before the creation of the universe, before things start moving. This is the stillness that exists before the movement of duality. It is the unity or neutrality before the creation of the polarity that comes with manifest or material existence. Tai Yi and Wu Ji are a somewhat inseparable "unity/emptiness." This is the Mystery. Wu Ji is instantly filled by Tai Yi through the vacuum energy of empty space. This is the spiraling energy of creation. This is the spiritual energy of universal self-awareness. This is the limitless and liminal world of consciousness from which all form arises. This is the unity before the differentiation process of self-awareness creates the "half-illusion" of separation in the material world. Thus the One begets the Two. Tai Yi becomes Tai Chi. The universe enters "detail-oriented" consciousness, creating endless divisions in order to get to know itself better. We repeat, or recapitulate, this process of pre-natal qi becoming post-natal qi through our birth into the world and within every moment of our life. The 8x Channels are a window into the moment-by-moment awareness of our own creation, unfolding at the sub-atomic level and through the transcription of DNA creating RNA to create proteins to keep us materializing.

Tai Chi: Walking through the World of Yin and Yang
Manifestations of Duality and Separation

From Wu Ji comes Tai Chi, or from the one comes the two. Tai Chi means "the Supreme Ultimate" and its symbol is the Yin/Yang symbol where life is experienced as polarity, as the interplay of opposites, and our consciousness and perception exist in duality. This is the world of post-natal qi, of yin and yang, where everything is perceived as separate. This is the world of sensory perception. It is an opportunity to get to know our self and others as differentiated beings. With the material world comes the constant division and sub-division of differentiation. We are designed to compulsively discern things from each other. This serves several purposes. One purpose is that the ability for individual survival requires knowing self from other and knowing safe from harmful. The other purpose is that we have an opportunity to explore what it means to be alive and conscious of our self as an individual, to individuate, to get to know our own nature.

The manifest world is a world of constant movement and change. It is the world that exists over time and has been set into perpetual motion since the beginning of time, perhaps the Big Bang. It is the post-natal world that is created from the mystery. It is not a world of harmony-by-design, it is a world of movement. Polarity drives constant motion. Lack of awareness of the differentiation of polarities creates endless overcompensation. It is the nature of our survival energy to over-react. This creates great tension and the difficulty in this is compounded by the "either/or" nature of the decision-making process.

Discerning between polarity requires a certain amount of judgment. This is natural, however the highest spiritual aspects of our consciousness cannot exist within judgment. So our perception becomes "trapped" in the inertia of time and the highly compelling illusion of separation. There is a creative "solution" to this paradox and we can temper this separation anxiety through awareness. Our awareness of the nature of motion and polarity can allow us to stay more towards the center. We can begin to use the energy of polarity to create a dynamic "neutral space," a gap, a space in-between. We can create stillness within the motion. We can enter into the empty space and participate in the mystery of creation. We can create a trinity of yin, yang, and the neutral or empty space in-between.

Yin	Yang
Feminine	Masculine
Earth	Heaven
Dark	Light
–	+
Parasympathetic	Sympathetic
Stillness	Motion
Receptive	Active
Blood	Qi
Nurturing	Protecting

Figure 2.2: Examples of Yin & Yang

Yin/Yang is the fundamental theory of all life, Earth, post-natal qi. All cultures had this deep innate understanding of polarity. It is the foundation of any living philosophy based on nature. All things can be divided into relative categories of yin or yang. Yin and yang can relate to each other and turn into each other in several ways. Yin and yang are clearly demonstrated at the level of Newtonian Physics and the principles of Force, Attraction, Resistance and Repulsion. Deeper knowledge of Yin/Yang brings us to the level of Relativity and begins to allow for the understanding of the subtler aspects of energy, motion and time. It is the cultivation that leads us to trinity consciousness of Yin/Yang and Wu Ji which allows for the level of Quantum Physics and beyond. It is here that we return to the world of pre-natal qi.

The word Tai Chi is often translated as "Supreme Ultimate." Tai Chi is another word for the Yin/Yang symbol. Tai Chi Chuan can be translated as "Supreme Ultimate Fist," indicating its martial heritage. Tai Chi Chuan as an official martial art form is not more than a few hundred years old. It is a marriage between Kung Fu and the ancient principles of Daoist philosophy and Daoist Qigong . The Principles of Tai Chi are timeless and take us into the Wu Ji. These arts have their roots in the 1,000's of years of ecstatic trance states of the ancient shamans, the Wu. Tai Chi has been called "spirit boxing," or "swimming in air"- the activation of the evolutionarily embedded hydrostatic skeleton. Tai Chi is about using polarity to transcend polarity. Harmony.

Figure 2.3: Tai Chi

The Trinity- Simultaneous Awareness of Unity and Duality

"The new formula in physics describes humans as paradoxical beings who have two complementary aspects: They can show properties of Newtonian objects and also infinite fields of consciousness."   Stanislav Grof

Figure 2.4: Wu Ji in Center, Dilated Wu Ji, Wu Ji Column

One of the spiritual applications of Tai Chi and Qi Gong is to use polarity to transcend polarity. In doing this we do not simply return to Wu Ji, we create a third thing, a combination of unity and duality, a trinity that is at the heart of spiritual alchemy. This transcendence occurs through using polarity to create a container where the dynamic magnetism of yin and yang creates a neutral space. This concept is both relatively simple and sheer genius. It is like holding two magnets together and letting the tension create a space where they cancel each other out. This strategy is based on the principle that our Shen, or spirit or unity consciousness, cannot exist within polarity, within the judgment that creates separation. With this line of thinking, our spirit cannot reside in the material plane, i.e. cannot reside in our body.

However, if we create an empty space, spiritual energy comes in through vacuum suction. This energy is not easy to maintain for we are highly con-ditioned to the polarized consciousness required by our physical body and its material plane existence. But we have now been scientifically shown to be 99% nothing at the sub-atomic level, so emptiness is the vast majority of our nature. Experiencing this alchemical process of creating empty space begins in our heart. As we learn to extend this empty space energy, we begin to awaken our pre-natal circuitry as modeled by the 8x Vessels. As this grows to fill our auric egg we activate the spiritual connection system of our solar plexus where humanity is experienced as one organism.

The challenge at this period of evolution is operating from this spiritual navigational system with our full survival awareness intact. As this mode of awareness demonstrates itself to be more efficient at survival than the mere over-compensation of unconscious animal instincts of predator/prey and dominance/submission, these evolutionary traits will be awakened in more and more people. The arts of Tai Chi offer a unique solution to conflict resolution one in which cultivated cooperation with the forces of pressure and compression creates a tensegrity bubble that is stronger than the mere application of tension and resistance while also being able to neutralize it. This is done through developing relaxed structural integrity which allows us to enter into the pre-natal body, the ability to articulate our fluid body, our hydrostatic skeleton around the pivots of our bones, our endoskeleton. In the process of neutralizing our connective tissue resistance, a stillness of the mind is created, an embodied neutral space for the spirit.

Qi Gong translates as an activity involving Qi, the life force that requires Gong, time and discipline to develop. It is a relatively modern term used mainly since the 20th Century. Previously it was known as Dao Yin, which means "guiding qi." Qi Gong= Breath + Intention + Movement. Intention can convey focus, feeling or imagination, like an artist or actor. Movement can mean alignment, posture, or internal movement of qi. Qi Gong has a strong emphasis on the breath and creating equilibrium in our osmotic pressure. All Tai Chi is Qi Gong(albeit an extremely sophisticated Qi Gong), but not all Qi Gong is Tai Chi.

Figure 2.5: Qi Gong: Breath + Movement + Intention

Part 2 Chapter 2

The Three Treasures:
Building Blocks of Our Experience

❧

The Three Treasures- The Candle of Our Life

The process of life according to Chinese Medicine is often illustrated with the concept of the Three Treasures. These are Jing(Essence), Qi(Energy) and Shen(Spirit). These are often explained with the metaphor of our life being like a candle. The Jing(Essence) is like the raw materials such as the wax and wick. There is a certain finite quality to them. The Qi(Energy) is the metabolic process that generates the flame and also consumes the candle. The Shen(Spirit) is the light given off by the candle, the radiance that is the essential purpose of the candle in the first place. From one perspective, we are the raw material trying to refine ourselves into a light-giving source. From another perspective, we are the light that is consuming the physical materials in order to sustain itself.

One of the fundamental principles of the spirituality of the 8x Vessels is that life is the process of Shen consuming Jing, of spirit consuming essence. This is akin to the idea that we are spiritual beings having a material experience. We could also call it consciousness exploring form, but in this case the consciousness is metabolizing the form it is using to get to know itself, to gain self-awareness. This is the premise that life wants to get to know itself and it does so through us. Life learns and self-replicates in order to evolve more creative and efficient ways of experiencing itself.

One could also say that spirit metabolizes form and generates experience and learns from these experiences. One could say that spirit metabolizes essence and we experience this metabolic rate as time. In any case, it is the individual's self-exploration that creates the experiences that are recorded by the Yuan qi, the Source qi, for the purpose of evolution to benefit the survival of the species. In this sense, we are always truly at the crown of creation perched on the evolutionary wave with a state-of-the-art vehicle capable of self-awareness with the potential to consciously participate in the process of evolution.

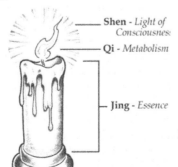

Shen - *Light of Consciousnes*

Qi - *Metabolism*

Jing - *Essence*

Figure 2.6: Three Treasures- Jing, Qi, Shen

Jing: Raw Material of Our Self

The Jing is housed by the Kidneys in Chinese Medicine. The Kidneys are the Water Element in Chinese Medicine. The Kidneys relate to our DNA, our Yuan Qi/Source Qi, our reproductive energy, our bones, our marrow, our Will and ultimately, our Wisdom. They are our batteries and empower us with the ambition and drive to go out and explore the world, to use our Will to shape the world. This is our Earthly energy, the primal drives that insure that life will go on and allow us the opportunity to create enough experience in our lifetime to learn our lessons, to grow into Wisdom, to download the essence of our experiences into the collective mainframe for others to learn from.

The Kidneys represent our self. This is our original nature, unconcerned with the social order and social models of morality, it is more concerned with our survival and the perpetuation of our creativity into the future. The Jing is a pre-natal resource associated directly with our Yuan Qi, our Source Qi. In general, Jing is seen is a non-renewable resource, with a certain inheritance given from the parents at birth. In some ways we are more or less unchangeable, such as blood type, certain bodily features, ethnicity and gender. The ability to change gender through surgery and hormonal supplementation is an example of the Yuan Qi exploring its limits. Alchemy and the 8x Vessels are seen as affecting the Jing level, with the potential of affecting the settings of our DNA. The reverse-aging practices of longevity are another example of the Yuan Qi exploring its limits. DNA is being shown to be an open-ended system without a cap on its ability to reconfigure even within one generation.

Shen: the Spirit of Consciousness

The Shen or Spirit is related to the Mind in Chinese Medicine, which is housed in the Heart. This is our piece of consciousness, our piece of Mind. The Big Shen is consciousness itself, or spirit. It is impersonal and omnipresent. The Little Shen is our individual consciousness running through our program, consuming the form and generating experience. This is the energy of Heaven, or our Purpose and represents the more transpersonal aspect of ourselves as members of the Circle of Humanity, the human species. This is where we experience the altruism and empathy of being connected to everything.

The Shen manifests as light which can be seen in the eyes and also in the glow of the aura. The cultivation of Shen can consume the Jing rapidly due to its accelerated conversion of essence into consciousness which can cause things like premature aging and graying of the hair common in certain types of spiritual practices. In the alchemical approach to spirituality there is the potential to cultivate a relatively sustainable conversion of Jing-Essence into Shen-Spirit. It becomes a matter of getting to know your Self. Life is not a contest of who can live the longest or defy the disease process or even who can accomplish the most spiritual growth or amass the most material goods. The purpose is up to you. Knowing one's purpose is one of the effects of shining the light of the Shen into the dark potential of the Jing. This is the Fire element illuminating the Water.

Qi: Metabolism and Relationship

Qi is the energy of relationship. When two or more things have enough resonance with each other a connection is made. This quantum connection now becomes greater than the sum of its parts and activates the life force. This is the energy of communication, connection and relationship. This is information and as such, it is faster than light, or more correctly, exists outside the time-space continuum. These connections can be illuminated through the power of our intention and focus, what is known as the Yi. When our intention is aligned with the principles of gravity and force, this Qi can harness great power. If our intention is solely to manipulate this energy, we will consume our Jing faster. If our intention is to participate with this force, we can become a conduit and a battery that can sustain and support us. This is one of the many aspects of Tai Chi and Internal Alchemy.

It is our Qi that we use to manage the relationship between the Jing and the Shen. It is the relationship between the two and our management of Qi is the rate of metabolism of our Jing-Essence. If we burn our candle too hard, we will burn out eventually. How this manifests depends on our constitution and our Destiny. Never learning or choosing to allow any substantial combustion at all can also fail to nourish the spirit with less than desirable consequences. Living life as conservation of qi merely for the sake of conserving qi also has its own pitfalls, as in and of itself it serves no purpose. It can be like watching a team with a one or two point advantage that stops playing well as it tries to preserve its lead instead of moving forward. The use of our Qi, of our energy, is the art of living life and it requires being nourished by our choices, our connections and our relationships and perhaps even being guided by our purpose.

Part 2 Chapter 3

Pre-Natal and Post-Natal Energetics

அஇ௧

The concepts of "pre-natal" and "post-natal" are fundamental to the message of this book. The 8x circuitry is pre-natal by nature and life proceeds by the unfolding or conversion of pre-natal energy to post-natal energy. Our post-natal energies are also replenished through air and food. Where this is insufficient, we begin to draw from our pre-natal resources. When we have nourished ourselves sufficiently, we can bank some of the extra. The traditional image is that of the 8x as reservoirs that support the waterways of the Primary(post-natal) Meridians. This can also be seen as the pre-natal Jing-Essence being like a savings account, endowment, or inheritance and the post-natal qi is like a checking account. If we invest wisely, we may be able to live off the dividends or interest. When we overdraft or cannot live within our means we drain the resources. As the resources dry up, we age, when the resources are gone we die. This book is not about looking at this pre-natal process as a closed system. Using that model as a default setting of life creates a "survival of the fittest" mentality and a scarcity of resources for those that can't or won't compete(interestingly enough, Darwin co-opted his phrase from economic theory). This book asks the question, "what is the untapped potential of the pre-natal energy body and how can it transform our post-natal experience?"

Post-Natal Qi- the Material World and the Acquired Mind

The above waterways and banking system models of qi represent a very material-based perspective, which is the perspective of the post-natal. The post-natal is the material world. If you believe that that is all there is, the above model is for you. If you believe that embodying the light of consciousness into and through the depths of the physical body holds the potential to transform the experience of the material world, then you may find the pre-natal models very helpful. Wu Ji and Tai Yi are pre-natal aspects of energy and yin and yang are post-natal aspects of energy. The material world is subject to the experience of physical separation and the inherent trauma that it brings. The material world is subject to the world of survival and all the over-reactions of predator and prey consciousness. The material world is subject to all the social contracts and behavioral conditioning of culture. In short, it is the ego, the acquired mind. It is not a bad thing. It is necessary for individuation, but it creates the perfect challenges to its own transcendence. That is part of our curriculum, our karma. This transcendence is the re-awakening of the awareness of the pre-natal energy body within the post-natal material body.

The post-natal is extremely important. It is how you live your life. There is no conflict with the material world. It's just that that is not all there is. In Chinese Medicine we talk about substantial and insubstantial. Matter and Vibration. Body and Spirit. Blood and Qi. Jing and Shen. Particle and Wave. Newtonian and Quantum. By becoming increasingly aware of the insubstantial in life we begin to be able to participate with the energy of the relationship between the two. We begin to be able to cultivate the empty space that brings in spiritual energy and the miraculous potential therein. As we do this with our 8x Vessels we also do this microcosmically at the cellular level and macrocosmically in our external energy body.

The post-natal model is more the medical model than the alchemical model and is only a portion of the story. This model, like most post-natal models of anything, is entirely materialistic and therefore self-limiting by nature, similar to Darwinism and Newtonian science. It is practical and applies common sense but it does not take into account the transformational power of the Shen-the Spirit. This may be valid in many approaches to medicine but at the 8x level, life is seen as Shen experiencing Jing. Spirituality, mind, or consciousness is fundamental to the 8x circuitry. I would go so far as to say that without this understanding we have no business accessing the 8x vessels. It is through the cultivation of the Shen-Spirit that we can access multi-dimensional energies. These energies operate through the pre-natal qi network.

Pre-Natal Qi- Spiritual Awareness and Original Nature

Traditionally, it has often been the understanding that the pre-natal cannot be affected much, especially for the better. It's the model of the candle. As it burns we age, and when the candle's gone, it's over. This is a very materialistic viewpoint, representative of a great plague of materialistic thinking that is threatening our planet. As with all materialistic thinking, it's a half-truth. It's the limited attitude of life being about how many breaths you take or heartbeats you have and then you die. The Spirit understands that life is about the moments that take your breath away or make your heart flutter with joy. Obviously, you inherit your parent's DNA and ancestry and the changes you can make to your body may be limited to a certain degree. The far more interesting aspect is to what degree we *can* participate in the pre-natal unfolding into the post-natal and what does that look like?

When we work at the pre-natal level we are working with someone's spiritual curriculum and their Original Nature. It is an exploration into the self and the meaning of life. As we shed light on our self we can take care of unfinished business, look at incomplete lessons, and maybe suffer less, fear less, love more, and have more energy available for the present moment. We also might find that we are capable of optimizing our gene expression in ways never before thought possible and using our energy on a quantum level.

Let us take a look at the things that impact our pre-natal, our Jing-Essence. We have mentioned radiation, xenobiotics, epidemic febrile diseases, vaccinations and the like that can penetrate to the Jing level. Here we will look at the ways our Jing gets consumed in life. We have the obvious ways of burning the candle such as overwork, over indulgence in sex, drugs, alcohol, long-term illness, malnutrition, childbirth, etc. There are also less obvious ways that the Jing gets affected over time. It is the natural process of imprinting our essence. This happens over and over again. Birth, bonding, walking, talking are some of the very core imprints that become lifetime settings in the pre-natal qi.

After these core imprints, essentially anything that impacts us enough to be recorded in our long-term memory and emotional memory taxes our Jing. This is the process of life, a process of learning. According to Chinese Medicine we have rhythms of when the windows into our Jing are more available. These are called the cycles of 7 & 8, or 10 or 12 in some traditions. These are life changes where we will be more greatly impacted at the pre-natal level. These are opportunities to change for the better at a deep level or to further crystallize the patterns we have set in place.

The Imprinting of the Jing to Create the Consciousness of Separation

A powerful method of the imprinting of Jing is through shock or trauma. It is a natural imprinting method for individuation. When we are born we still have our fontanelle open and our Shen-Spirit is connected to all that is. In order to view our self as separate we need to deeply contract our energy body to create a boundary between us and the unity of being. This is generally done through experiencing trauma or perceived trauma. It is said that at these junctures of imprinting separation that we develop limited perspectives on the world that are represented by the 5 Element types. So everyone is a product of some degree of traumatic separation and the deeper the degree of trauma and repetition of trauma, the deeper the "scarring" of the Jing. Shock separates the "Heart-Kidney Axis," our connection between Heaven and Earth. This shock allows the pre-natal qi to become accessed.

The point of this understanding is to help recognize that although we are born a certain way and suffer the shocks of being alive, we can learn to heal these impacts on the deepest levels. While this may not create more pre-natal qi per se, the degree that we can learn to optimize our pre-natal expression and connection between Heaven and Earth is wide open. Separation creates a valve on the expression of our self, of our pre-natal expression into the world, our creativity. Often it is not a case of a lack of resources as it is the settings on the valve. Working with the 8x and the pre-natal is working directly on these settings. What the alchemical practices bring to the 8x, which is the perfect complement to the acupuncture medical models, is the inclusion of our energy body as it extends from our body, our auric egg.

We will be exploring how auric egg awareness is related to our pre-natal awareness and the 8x vessels.

Multi-Dimensional Energy = No Shortage of Energy

The concept of the multi-dimensional energy of the pre-natal is similar to the modern scientific understanding of Dark Matter and Dark Energy. The 1st Law of Thermodynamics which states that matter and energy cannot be created or destroyed is true, but it is thinking in the material terms of 3 dimensions. It is making the assumption that the only energy available in the system is the energy and mass within 3 dimensions and there can never be any more or less. This "Law" may be true but thankfully we now know that we have been playing with only a fraction of the energy in the system. The 1st Law did not account for the potential energy of the invisible Dark Energy, which may be 90% of the energy of the universe. In humans, this multi-dimensional energy manifests through the awareness of the Shen, through the expansion of consciousness.

Through participating in the awareness of pre-natal energetics, we have the opportunity to interact with the untapped potential of this multi-dimensional energy. Through the re-discovery of the evolutionary processes embedded in the hydrostatic skeleton of the Jing Qi, the pre-natal water element of the Kidneys, we empower our self to be a receptacle for the spirit. This is how we begin to see where these ancient understandings developed from. Anthropologically speaking, the pre-historic periods from whence these traditions arose represent the pre-natal aspects of human social development. The goal of this book is to use the classical teachings of Chinese Medicine along with modern scientific insights to shed light on the direct experience of the numinous, the shamanic experience of the ancient Wu, as available as it ever was for those able to experience beyond the limitations of 4 dimensions.

Pre-Natal	Post-Natal
Jing-Essence	Ying Qi- Nutritive Qi
Yuan Qi- Source Qi	Wei Qi- Protective Qi
In Utero	In Vivo
8x Vessels	Primary Channels
Original Nature	Acquired Mind
Evolutionary Energy	Inertia of Conditioning
Curious Organs	Zang-Fu Organs
Reproductive Energy	Digestive Energy
Hormones	Blood
Brain	Choice
Marrow	Body Fluids
Bones	Muscles
Temperament	Emotions
Ethnicity	Society
DNA	Proteins/ATP
Destiny	Life Path
Ancestry	Ego

Figure 2.7: Pre-Natal and Post-Natal Comparisons

The Mothership Connection-
Simultaneity of Pre-Natal and Post-Natal Awareness

As we have seen, pre-natal qi on one level is just that, the energy and dynamics that occur in utero. From post-natal consciousness, it is fixed and finite and cannot be changed, because it already happened. However, all spiritual traditions are working from the premise that some aspects may be fixed, but others can be changed, can be healed. The liberation of this pre-natal energy can fundamentally change the reality constructs that have consensually limited humankind. According to the *Dao De Jing*, once wonder and awe is lost, we enter into the realm of morality and social convention, "the husk of true faith." All spirituality points to a time, deep in the past and also deep in the Now, when we experience the direct wonder of life.

The potential offered to humanity by being able to consciously enter the wonder, the yang, the external, is untapped as a global collective. The price of sustainable entry however is being able to enter the mystery, the yin, the internal. Modern culture has been extremely patriarchal and lost connection to the yin, the internal, the feminine, the mystery. Once we lose this awe and this sense of mystery we enter post-natal levels of being that are real but offer no solution to suffering, personal crisis or global crisis. The pre-natal dynamics are a reconnection to the dynamics of being inside our mother. We all came here in a mother, a womb, indeed a Mothership.

Pre-natal awareness allows us to begin recreating some of those buoyant, aquatic, safe, nurtured and contained aspects of the womb. While in the womb our spirit is still connected to unity consciousness. Through working with the pre-natal qi we can reconnect our umbilicus directly to the source and claim our space between Heaven and Earth. The 8x vessels are templates to the structure and function of our auric egg, that most transpersonal aspect of our self. Our auric egg allows us spiritual space/boundaries, a womb with a view, where we can consciously hold space for spirit. Our aura is a seed, an egg, our epigenetic bubble, a cellular membrane in the collective of humanity and we are awakening to it. It is the coherence, the peace in our heart that allows the aura to come into definition, that allows the signal, the truth, to emerge from the noise, the information. The level of definition and integrity in our auric egg, representative of our character, is the flowering of our pre-natal body and is our vehicle, for participation in multi-dimensional space.

The Human Battery: Heaven/Earth/Humanity

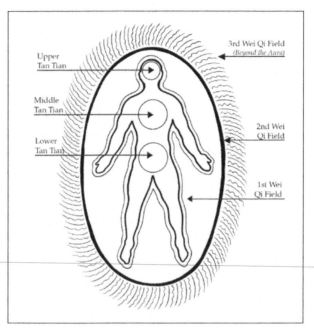

Figure 2.8: 3 Dan Tians with 3 External Wai Qi Fields

Humanity- the Pivot of the Heaven/Earth Axis

This is the foremost trinity in the Chinese cosmology and the one that all others relate to in some degree. In this trinity, Humanity occupies a central position in relation to the forces of Heaven and Earth. This trinity can be condensed to be the Three External Qi Fields, the Three Dan Tians, and the Triple Heater mechanism. Such is the elegance of the relational way of perceiving of what are called "systems of correspondence." The 5 Elements, the Bagua(the 8 Directions) and the *I Ching*(the 64 Situations) are other examples. The universe acts as a fractal and the microcosm and macrocosm will reflect similar proportion, ratio, and relationships whether dialed in to the very small, the very large, the very subtle, or the size we physically interact at. Changes made at one part of this fractal spectrum will reflect and resonate in others.

We are the pivot of this Heaven and Earth axis. We can participate in the quality and quantity of this connection between Heaven and Earth if we are willing to do some deeper self-exploration. The forces of Heaven and Earth are powerful but they are designed to remain unconscious from the post-natal perspective. They are transpersonal, multi-dimensional forces that require a willingness to expand our awareness beyond the physical. We are already in relationship to this axis, it is a matter of if we choose, or are chosen to gain awareness of our self in relation to this axis. Heaven and Earth create a standing wave pattern through the interference waveform they generate. This is the material hologram of life. This intersecting grid creates the acupuncture points, intersection points on this cross between Heaven and Earth. These are the gravitational lines of flux, the distribution of gravitational pressure over a form, a mass. We are essentially fluid and connective tissue and the acupuncture grid is formed by the spherical distribution of the vertical pressure of gravity. These points of distribution lie partially activated and partially dormant as the strange attractors of our spiritual blueprint. If we choose to activate them to their potential, we can create the pathways of our spiritual evolution, the birthright potential of our Destiny. This is the realm of the 8x Vessels. They are the conduit, the mediators of this divine connection.

Heaven is considered the Creative Force and represents the yang polarity. Earth is the Receptive Force where the seed of Heaven can manifest in the material plane and represents the yin polarity. Humans are in the middle existing in polarized consciousness until they can evolve to sustain conscious neutrality and bring in larger bandwidths of energy from the cosmos. This bringing in of larger bandwidths is called involution. It brings multi-dimensional energies into the material plane and drives the process of evolution. This happens through the Yuan Qi, the pre-natal qi. Humanity evolves to the point where it can consciously participate in this process. When we bring in wider bandwidths the energy is intended for Humanity. It is creative energy that may come through one individual but its goal is for the betterment of all. This is the energy of purpose. One who has achieved this self-realization is called a Zhen Ren, or True Person. One simply becomes real and plays their part. They become their natural self. This is the flowering of the pre-natal energy body in the post-natal world.

Heaven represents the yang polarity. It is light, it is fire, it is expansive, it is the sun, the stars, the neutrinos and other sub-atomic particle-waves that emanate the consciousness of stars. It is the higher consciousness. When it enters our body through the Crown, it becomes yin. It becomes descending and calming, creating stillness and peace. It becomes the energy of our parasympathetic response, our relaxation response. It is represented by the Heart.

Earth represents the yin polarity. It is the darkness of the water element, it is the substance of life, it is dense, it is the animals, the plants and the minerals. It is the manifest world. When it enters our bodies it becomes yang. It is activating and generates movement through the legs. This is the energy of our sympathetic nervous system, our survival response. It is represented by the Kidneys.

Microcosm of the Heaven/Earth/Humanity
Axis- the Three Dan Tians

In order to better understand how to operate our battery, let us look at the microcosm of this trinity, the three Dan Tians, or Alchemical Elixir Fields. The Upper Dan Tian is at the level of our head/cranial cavity and is related to Heaven and the Shen. The Middle Dan Tian is at the level of our Heart/ thoracic cavity and is related to Humanity and Qi. The Lower Dan Tian is at the level of the naval/lumbar spine/pelvic cavity and is related to the Earth and to Jing. These are our access points within our body to participate in the Heaven/Earth conduit. These centers are located along our spine/our axis/ our tai chi pole.

Learning to participate in this conduit is a form of spiritual evolution. The body is extremely self-regulating and has many safeguard mechanisms, but if we overload the circuitry before it has developed the pathways and connections, it can result in spiritual, psychological, social, moral, behavioral, emotional, and physical symptoms. The best advice I can offer is to balance Yin approaches and Yang approaches. Spiritual technologies that are powerful at one or the other can be highly useful however you may have to fill in the gap. You are responsible for your own evolutionary process, not your teacher, their teachings, or some system.

Each Dan Tian is related to one of the 3 bony cavities, the cranium, thoracic cavity and the pelvis. The Chinese spiritual systems put a huge emphasis on grounding to the Earth before exploring the realms of the Shen. Here we learn to sense qi at more telluric frequencies in the denser, slower part of the spectrum. The focus is on the Lower Dan Tian, below the navel, which is the only center that can function as an energy storage center. This is the Sea of Qi. The Lower Dan Tian is related to the power of the Kidneys, our Root connection to the Earth, our bones and our Jing. Our Lower Dan Tian connects us to the Earth through our legs and their survival energy of power and movement.

In order to work with this Heaven-Earth connection we need to develop the energy of our Root. We do this through the structure, by aligning our bones with gravity and through working through the lessons recorded in our bones. This is represented by the martial arts and the energy of the warrior. The Lower Dan Tian is directly related to the function of the coelum, a peritoneal organ in animals with a hydrostatic skeleton that allows them to move by pivoting off of this incompressible fluid sac in the same way that we pivot off of our bones. It is the lower body pivot that can withstand compression and allow the pre-natal movement system to be articulated.

The Middle Dan Tian is the Heart Center located at the center of the chest in the thoracic cavity. It is the Sea of Blood. This area rules the blood and also houses the Lungs. This area represents the level of Humanity. It is the knowing/feeling of our connection to the Circle of Humanity, of our being part of one organism, a cell in a larger network. This is where we experience altruism, cooperation, compassion and the peace of being part of a community.

This connects us outward through our arms and our ability to shape the world from the Heart and to make contact with others. This is represented by the Healing Arts and the energy of the Healer.

The Upper Dan Tian is the head, the mental and spiritual center located in the cranium. This is the energy of Heaven. It is the Sea of Marrow. This is the power of the brain and how our mostly unconscious beliefs and those of the ancestors who came before us shape the world we live in. It offers the potential of transformation and liberation from the stagnation of habit and sheer repetition recorded in our relationship to the morphogenetic field. Here we connect with the impersonal forces of spirit and can awaken our senses to see the clarity of our connection to the Universe. This is represented by the Spiritual Arts and the energy of Priest or Priestess.

Gravitational and Multi-dimensional Aspects of the Dan Tians

These energies between Heaven and Earth also have a gravitational component. Aligning with gravity allows relaxation and creates a buoyant reflex if we can surrender to gravity while maintaining our full integrity, structurally and otherwise. This ability to be grounded allows us to handle wider bandwidths without getting knocked off our axis, or getting spun from our integrity. We all have an individual axis between Heaven and Earth and as we align with it, we begin to feel it's force and spin, centripetally and centrifugally, its ability to attract and repulse. It is the development of character, in this case at the level of the bones which generate piezoelectric charges through their liquid crystal collagen matrix in response to the pressure of gravity, movement, and breath. This in turn can be allowed to consciously circulate evenly through our body.

The key to this is the maintenance of integrity without the engagement of resistance, the recruitment of unnecessary tension. This happens on all levels from force, structure, emotion, mental and spiritual. We can achieve and sustain this level of pressurized relaxation through allowing the even distribution of the force of pressure throughout our whole being. This follows the principles of tensegrity[11], the distribution of compression through whole-system integrity, or even distribution through tensile integrity of an organism. When the pressure of life, of gravity, of the atmosphere is distributed this way it becomes absorbed by the Earth and we are truly grounded. This is the physical potential, the capacity of the human battery, achieved through the yoga of tai chi principles.

This charge then circulates and generates a magnetic field at the perimeter of our external qi field, our auric egg, bringing awareness into the previously dormant blueprint of these auric settings. This perimeter creates a container for the 4th element, plasma, which can be contained by a magnetic field. The charge, the polarities of this plasma, balance each other out, essentially creating

---

11.   *See the work of Buckminster Fuller.*

a neutral space. This neutral space allows the Shen to dwell in a non-polarized space on the material plane. The Shen is then able to be connected to higher transpersonal consciousness, which in turn can hook up to a higher power source. The above sounds fantastical and it is. But life is fantastical and we now have the external scientific models to understand the process and the internal experiential models to participate consciously in the process.

The effect of how the dilation of polarity can vacuum suction the energy from other dimensions is similar to how dark energy tendrils create a galaxy, which can now be photographed or how collagenous fibrils form a geodesic structure in the connective tissue to distribute pressure along the principles of tensegrity. Remember, before you learn the art, it is just life. When you study the art, it is no longer just life. When you understand the art, it is just life again. The above is merely a highly technical way of explaining the most natural phenomena, that of the flowering of human consciousness.

The Microcosmic Orbit, the Central Channel and the Chakra Centers

In our body these energy centers are represented by various acupuncture points. Together they form a loop around the front and back mid-line of the body often referred to as the Microcosmic Orbit. We will look at the points most associated with the Three Dan Tians to give us some more strategies for embodying these relationships. The main adherence point to Heaven is Du-Governing Vessel 20 at the top of the head in the Upper Dan Tian. The main adherence point to Earth is Kidney 1 at the sole of our feet if we are standing, and Ren 1 at our perineum, if we are sitting. The main connection point to Humanity is Ren/Conception Vessel 17 and extends outward to others through Pericardium 8, Laogong, at the center of our palms. These are some of the main alignments for the Human Battery exercises known as Qigong. There are many, many more alignments for this gravitational axis, with perhaps the most important other one being focusing on the Lower Dan Tian at the navel or around Ren/Conception Vessel 6. The ability to feel the relationships in our body at these points allows us to engage and monitor our relationship to this axis, and the gyroscopic spinning orbs along this axis which comprise our Dan Tians.

The Microcosmic Orbit is comprised of the Ren Channel along the midline of the front of our body and the Du channel along the midline of the back. They meet and interpenetrate at the tongue/palate and the perineum/tail-bone. Working with the Microcosmic Orbit up the front and down the back is called the water cycle(yin) and up the back and down the front is known as the fire cycle(yang). Points along the Du and Ren meridians also represent the chakra connection points. Including these points creates a triangle around the Lower Dan Tian, a diamond around the Middle Dan Tian, and a triangle around the Upper Dan Tian. The relationship between these points helps us to experience the Dan Tians as spinning orbs, pivoting off the reference points of the microcosmic orbit. These points also create a sort of "serpentine belt" around the Dan Tians.

The 8x Vessels take us deep into our pre-natal body. The wheels/vortices of consciousness known as the chakras lie along the central channel. They are thought to lie along the Primordial Chong Vessel beyond the acupuncture points. Their locations are represented along the Du and Ren Vessels. In the alchemical meditations, these distinctions are not extremely important as the goal is to open up all three vessels into one superhighway and expand it through the other 8x Vessels into one bigger superhighway as large as our external qi field, a fiber-optic connection to multi-dimensional energy.

External Projection/Perception Fields- Feedback Loops of the Dan Tians

Each Dan Tian has an External Energy Field associated with it known as the Wai Qi Field[12], or External Qi Field. The 1st Wai Qi Field corresponds with the Lower Dan Tian, Earth, and is within a few inches of the body. It is directly associated with the physical plane. This Wai Qi Field connects directly with the Wei Qi/Protective Qi of the body that circulates at the level of the skin. This 1st Wai Qi Field represents what is either already, or just about to be, manifest. This level operates from a very Newtonian level of cause and effect. Manifestation moves through the outer Wai Qi Fields towards the field closest to the body and by the time things are at this level they are pretty much bound to manifest. This is how illness and events can be sensed in the auric configuration before they actually occur. The vitality of this level is resonant with the vitality of our Kidneys, our Jing.

The next Wai Qi Field is related to the Middle Dan Tian, Humanity, the Heart, and is located near our wingspan, delineating our auric egg. This is the energy of the Heart, Pericardium and Lungs and our personal psycho-social boundaries, our bubble. Issues of trauma, trust, vulnerability and intimacy obscure our awareness of this Wai Qi Field. This area is associated with the Zong Qi, the Pectoral Qi that is related to our breath and is called Ancestral Qi. Our ancestors are alive in the atmosphere of Mother Earth, on the spirit wind, in our Heart.

We breathe of the same unbroken chain of the ancestors, of the same O2 and CO2 cycle, since the dawn of Humanity. As we clear and integrate our emotions, we learn to relax into our self, to breathe deeply into our self, or moreover, to be breathed deeply by the self. This fills our body with life and fills our External Qi Field with presence. This is where we communicate with spirit. At this level of the aura the impersonal forces of spirit begin to resonate with us personally. There is enough resonance in our heart with the movement and purpose of spirit that we begin to experience emotion towards this energy and internalize it. In short, at this level spirituality becomes personal and we can work with these forces to follow our destiny.

12.   *Jeffrey Yuen. Also see Medical Qigong works such as Jerry Alan Johnson.*

The 3rd Wai Qi Field is related to the Upper Dan Tian, Heaven, the brain marrow and is infinite. Essentially this field is non-local and is anywhere that we put our attention. This is the quantum level of consciousness. This is the impersonal energy of spirit, the chaotic movement of the winds of change, the fertile emptiness from which all things are created. In the brain, the ability to be conscious of any of these levels of the External Qi Field will be in relationship to synaptical patterns, symphonies of synchronized, self-organized neural firing. These are phenomena of the whole brain, reflecting the state of the whole system.

This is a non-linear process, like music and very much like the harmonic overtones generated by music. Transcendent music and voices achieve rich activation of harmonic patterns in the higher overtone sequences, connecting us with the octaves, the levels of spirit. It is difficult to achieve whole-brain patterning through linear learning. This is analogous to "learn the form, forget the form." The form can be a bridge to the next level of patterning, but a bridge is not the new pattern. This is similar to the Buddhist saying of how people often mistake the raft for the shore. Systems are rafts. Language is a raft. Experience is the shore.

The External Qi Fields have a relationship with the 7 layers of the auric body which are in relation to the chakras. The 1st Wai Qi Field would relate to the Physical, Astral, and Mental. The 2nd Wai Qi Field would relate more to the Causal Body, and the Upper Dan Tian relates more to the Buddhic, Atmic, and Monadic Bodies. We will look at the properties of these fields again when we discuss the Hun and the 3 Spirits.

We see this circuitry not only as representing the macrocosm of Heaven and Earth, but also as representing the microcosm of the cellular level. We will discuss these analogies more in the book, but for now I would like to suggest that the Axis is the nucleus(a common idea shown in the relationship between the medical staff of Cadduceus and the serpentine kundalini up the spine) and the auric egg of the 2nd Wai Qi Field relates to the cellular membrane. We are a cell/self in a larger cellular network, the organism of Humanity, and the expression of our health is deeply based in the connection to community and environment experienced at this membrane. This is analogous to the cellular behavior being scientifically demonstrated through epigenetics.

It appears that the cell membrane, based on the quality of its environment and cellular network, may be the actual master control of gene expression, of the unfolding of the self. This line of thinking leads naturally to the idea that our adherence points to Heaven and Earth parallel the telomeres at both ends of the cell. The health of the telomeres affects the health of the cell and as these connection points begin to lose integrity, transcription begins to get interfered with causing aging and many disease processes. Perhaps the best way to navigate the health of our cellular level and the integrity of our genetic transcription is through learning to be aware of and monitoring the quality of one's auric egg. We will elaborate on this model as we begin to explore the relationships of the 8x Vessels and the Curious Organs.

Part 2 Chapter 5

The 3 Levels of Qi

ॐॐॐ

In order to prepare ourselves to dive into the deepest aspects of our being with some semblance of organization, we will be using one of the classical ways of organizing the body. The ancient Chinese looked at many things as trinities. This trinity divides the body into a more superficial level known as Wei Qi- Protective Qi, a middle level known as Ying Qi-Nutritive Qi, and the deepest level known as Yuan Qi- Source Qi. The channel systems connect, communicate between, and distribute resources between the 3 levels.

Wei Qi	Ying Qi	Yuan Qi
Superficial	Middle	Deep
Survival	Interaction	Differentiation
Mood	Emotion	Temperament
Defensive Qi	Nutritive Qi	Source Qi
Skin and Fascia	Blood, Flesh and Organs	Bone and Marrow
Immunity	Digestion	Reproduction
Self-Protection	Conscious Self	Survival of the Species

Figure 2.9: Three Levels of Qi- Wei, Ying, and Yuan

Wei Qi- Survival

The superficial level, or Wei Qi, is translated as Defensive Qi or Protective Qi. This energy is circulated between the skin and muscle and structurally relates to the connective tissue, or fascia. As the most surface level of Qi it is related to contact, the communication systems of the senses, such as touch and vision. As our survival energy it is responsible for movement, from "fight or flight" to all subtler aspects of navigating our vehicle, our body. Internally this movement is the peristalsis that takes place in every system and at every level of the body, from digestion, to blood and lymph circulation. The Wei Qi, being the defensive qi, is related to our Immune System function. This is the elegance of the fractal and metaphoric nature of Chinese Medicine.

The Wei Qi is autonomic. It is automatic and unconscious by design. It has to be or we could not keep up with our survival needs. It is the energy of the autonomic nervous system, but it is much older and deeper than that. It is the instinctual reflex, the mechanical vibration that is picked up by the fascia causing contraction or expansion. This mechanism exists in all levels of life forms right down to the single-celled amoeba. Some version of this exists in plants, though they can't move. In vertebrates the Wei Qi has evolved to become intertwined with the nervous system.

Ideally, this Wei Qi flows freely through the body, insuring peristalsis, movement and survival on every level and also providing us with a semi-permeable force field at the barrier of the skin. This defensive qi protects us in many ways. It is the instinctual energy of our reflexes, it is the metabolic energy that modulates our temperature, it takes care of the autonomic nervous system processes such as breath and heart rate, and it is our immunity taking care of foreign invaders such as viruses and bacteria or external pathogenic factors(EPF's). When flowing freely the fabric of our Wei Qi has coherence and integrity and we have strong immunity and instincts. In many ways this Wei Qi can become "stuck." It becomes busy protecting us from old External Pathogenic Factors(EPF's) such as viruses, bacterias, and fungi that are still in the body in a state of latency.

The Wei Qi protects us from old emotional and physical traumas that are too much to feel, creating body armoring, to protect us from emotion. It does this in conjunction with the blood level and Ying Qi. The Wei Qi can become hyper-vigilant, always monitoring the environment for potential or perceived threat. It can become hyperactive and cause allergies and environmental sensitivities. It can become confused or deranged for various reasons and begin fighting itself causing auto-immune disorders. It does this in conjunction with the Jing-Essence and Yuan-Source Qi pointing to the genetic component of such disorders. The Wei Qi is related to expression, whether it is a movement or gesture or a skin rash. When we suppress our natural expressions, we compromise some of the function of our Wei Qi. This is a major aspect of how disease and aging processes take place.

The Wei Qi is unconscious to us so that it can operate faster than our consciousness and bypass the brain, so that we don't interfere with our own survival and can react to danger with animal instinct. A good example is removing our hand from a hot stove or dodging a speeding object. We can learn to bring awareness to our autonomic response which is what many yogis do when they learn to control their heart rate or body temperature. Martial artists learn to train their defensive reflexes and to ultimately awaken the deep primal defenses that humans have suppressed and repressed. In a sense all "muscle-memory" such as athletic training, musical instruments, or any physical skill for that matter trains the Wei Qi or aligns with the Wei Qi. When this level has been transcended one is said to have good kung fu or be in tai chi, whether a chef, carpenter, musician, athlete or dancer.

Ying Qi- Interaction

The middle level is called the Ying Qi, the nutritive qi and blood. This is the source of our post-natal qi. This energy comes from food and air. This is the metabolic energy from digestion, from the ability to transform and transport nutrients and to separate the useful from the useless, letting go of and eliminating what no longer serves a purpose for us. This energy is related to the blood, the body fluids and the internal organs, known as the Zang Fu Organs in Chinese Medicine. The blood houses our emotions according to

84

Chinese Medicine and each emotion is related to the viscera, the organs. As humans, we have to process our emotions and our experiences in the same way that we process food.

The circulation of emotions is related to the Ying Qi. This nutritive qi can be extrapolated to include all things that nourish us, the ability to nourish and nurture ourselves, the health of our emotional life. The Ying Qi is the level of conscious choice and awareness. We have choices about our lifestyle, our diet, and our relationships. We can make decisions about where we are going in our life and the meaning of events in our life. We may not necessarily be able to choose our emotions but we can choose to learn to be aware of them. In Chinese Medicine, Mood is reflected by the Wei Qi, Emotions are reflected by the Ying Qi and Temperament is reflected in the Yuan Qi.

How we assimilate and integrate, how we digest the food, emotion, and events of our lives happens at the level of the Ying Qi. If we are able to keep moving, learn from and let go of the past, we have health. When we get stuck, can't swallow something or bite off more than we can chew, we begin to hold onto things that we can't get rid of, thus contaminating the blood. Our Small Intestine, which is paired with the Heart in Chinese Medicine, is shown to be our "gut-brain" according to science. We experience emotions and intelligence that bypasses the brain.

The Small Intestine is being shown to have all the same neuro-transmitters as the brain and appears to be the master control of brain chemistry. It is not merely a matter of food, but of emotional, psychological and spiritual digestion and nutrition. Any unprocessed emotions and events remain in the gut as an involuntary contraction in the smooth muscle, a freezing of the Wei Qi. What happens when we are unable to digest the factors of our life takes us for a ride through the process of latency involving all three levels- Wei Qi-expression, Ying Qi- suppression, and Yuan Qi- repression.

As the level of post-natal qi, the Ying Qi is very much involved in adapting to the social pressures of conformity, morality, and responsibility. We are forced to adapt on an individual level to the suppression and repression of the collective organism as recorded into the morphogenetic field and manifests as our social structure. The collective experiences its version of the disease process as well. War could be seen as an auto-immune process whereby the collective starts attacking itself.

Learning to manage our emotions is the key to experiencing the spiritual level of connection. The navel and the solar plexus are the organizing centers for the connection of our pre-natal energy body into the collective organism of humanity and the planetary mind, which appears to be deep in the throes of a disease process. As we awaken to this reality, hopefully we can heal our selves, humanity and the planet.

Yuan Qi- Differentiation

At the Jing-Essence level of our being, we have the level known as the Yuan Qi, or Source Qi. This is the level intended for the survival of the species. It is the level of our heredity, our DNA, our inherited energy, our ancestry. It is the energy of reproduction, of creation and pro-creation. This is the level that evolution takes place on, the level more concerned with perpetuation of the species than with individual survival(Wei Qi). This is the fuel for spiritual transformation and the meeting ground between Heaven and Earth in the individual. This is the pre-natal qi.

Pre-natally in utero we see the recapitulation of evolution take place from a single celled organism to an aquatic being to our birth as an air-breathing self-conscious land creature.[13] Our pre-natal self, our original nature can be revealed to us through our own spiritual evolution, our willingness to accept ourselves and participate in self-discovery. In this exploration of the Yuan Qi, we participate in, or at least bear witness, to evolution, healing our ancestry, the ancestral issues recorded in our DNA and uncovering the gifts that lie in latency. At this level we are shedding light on and cleaning up the genetic skeletons in the closet, the "sins of the father," the generations of species-level decay and preparing the Yuan Qi for the future. This is the re-discovery of our original nature, the return to innocence, before the traumas of life, the survival mentality and the social pressure to conform.

The Yuan Qi is accessed when survival and perpetuation of the species are concerned. In the ancient days it was basically only epidemic diseases that affected the Yuan Qi, and often the Yuan Qi would adapt to, say malaria, by creating immunity through another disease such as polio or sickle-cell anemia. This is known as Disease-Nemesis theory. You may get maimed by a lesser disease process but at least you will live long enough to pro-create. Nowadays, many things reach the Yuan Qi, such as vaccinations, radiation, xenobiotics(plastics), and other environmental contaminants. Scientifically we are at the genetic level and militarily we have the atom bomb. The Yuan Qi has been categorically breached by technology.

The Yuan Qi is now much easier to access with the increasing availability to ancient esoteric spiritual traditions such as Taoism, Shamanism and Yoga, the scientific ability of neurological and genetic mapping and engineering and the widespread availability of LSD, Ecstasy and other powerful natural and synthetic entheogens is precisely because it is a matter of survival of the species at this point in human evolution. We are mutating rather quickly to avert the potential disasters of our technological achievements. This work comes from the perspective that it is essential that as many people as possible have the opportunity to access their pre-natal energy body if they choose to. On a more cosmic note, information from the stars has always informed Humanity's genetic code. This is the nature of astrology and the consciousness program of reality that guides evolution. This is mediated through the

---

13. *Kiiko Matsumoto's Hara Diagnosis has an excellent section on embryology.*

quantum process of mass/energy, particle/waves such as neutrinos[14] that are the breath of stars and pass through us at some colossal rate like a trillion per second. This takes place at the level of the pre-natal energy body.

The Harmony of Ying and Wei

The harmony of Ying and Wei, of the Ying Qi and the Wei Qi is one of the goals of Chinese Medicine and of the Spirit. This is the harmony of feeling and action, when movement and expression have become natural and the filter of suppression and repression can be dropped because our natural self understands how to be. We have learned. Our Earthly soul, the Po has become the willing vessel of our Heavenly Messenger, the Hun. This is a version of the Taoist ideal of "Wu Wei"- often translated as "doing/not-doing." This could also be called "right place/right time," the harmony of the Hun (time) and Po(space), as we shall discuss in future chapters.

The Harmony of Ying and Wei is the harmony of the internal and external. When we have balanced these two, we become aware of our self and how we are connected to the ecology of mind and spirit that is the world and the Universe, the Web of Life. This harmony creates a clear window of communication in the feedback loop between inner and outer. We can receive information from the world in an undistorted manner and we can be received by the world in an undistorted manner. This is similar to some aspects of the idea that the spirit seeks the completion of the Zang-Fu Organs, the internal organs. As we shall discuss in later chapters, if each organ system can hold the higher vibration of its associated virtue, its channel and sensory orifice will open to the external allowing our two-way transceiver to function clearly.

When we are in the Harmony of Ying and Wei, we have created the ability for our pre-natal qi body of the Yuan Qi and 8x Vessels to communicate directly to the external world of our post-natal experience. If we function from this state of clarity, connection and knowing we are on the path of our Destiny, the union of our Will and Purpose.

---

14. *Human Design System.*

The Spirits of the 5 Elements

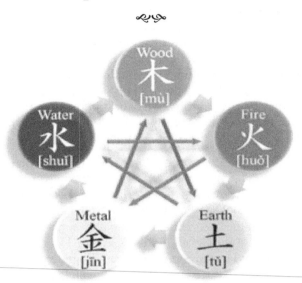

Figure 2.6: Engendering and Controlling Cycles of the 5 Elemental Phases

Ling and Shen[15]- Soul and Spirit

Before we look at the system of correspondence known as the 5 Elements or the 5 Phases, let us stay grounded in the fundamental way of organizing the Universe, by differentiating it into two poles, yin and yang. Each of the organs houses an aspect of spirit that informs our character development, the shaping of our soul on its earthly sojourn. In Chinese Medicine, the Shen-Spirit represents Heaven, that part of us that embodies the light, the light of the Heart, the light of consciousness. It has a yin pair that is called the Ling, which is most conveniently translated as the soul. The Ling is that viscous part of our self that is one with the natural world and the forces of nature. The Ling is sometimes seen as the yin aspect of the Heart, or as the infinite darkness and potential of the Water element. If the Ling is at peace, the Shen of the Heart will sit in its rightful place. If the Ling is troubled, the Shen has no place to reside in the body. In either case, it is through working with both these forces that we participate in alchemy. One sees time and time again traditions that emphasize one aspect at the expense of the other. Our goal is to shed light on the nature of Chinese Medicine as a spectrum. It is always about the relationship between things. If you think you have the world figured out, you have probably wound up at one end of the spectrum or the other and left the dynamic zone of relationship, the space in-between.

---

15. *Dechar, Jarrett, and Yuen's Hun,Po,Ling,Shen and Michael Winn's "Fusion of the Five Elements" class are the biggest influences on this section.*

Wu Xing- the Rhythms of the Five Elements

One of the most fundamental systems of correspondence in which everything is categorized in such a way that it can be meaningfully related to everything else is the system known as Wu Xing, the 5 Elements or the 5 Phases. They are elements in that they are fundamental building blocks and phases in that they are dynamically changing into and interacting with each other, representative of constant flux. The 5 Element System allows everything to be related on a continuum. We can then relate internal organs to seasons to constellations to body parts and functions and other natural processes. This is the ability to perceive the world in patterns and make sense of this web of connections in meaningful and useful ways, such as medicine, martial arts, cooking, astrology, spirituality, etc.

The elemental systems do not seem to be superimposed on reality in so much as they seem to be inherent in the fabric of the universe, a sort of holographic lens. For our purposes of exploring the spirit of the 8x vessels we want to take a further look at what are known as the Five Shen or the spirits of the 5 Elements and the "de(virtue)" or character traits associated with each element. Cultivation of the self allows these virtues to become character traits. These are lessons learned, simultaneously integrated from the post-natal level of experience and re-awakened at the pre-natal level of our original nature. We learn to trust that our original nature is innately good.

> *"First we walk the horse with a yoke, then we ride it with a saddle, then we let it go free."*
> — Ancient Chinese Saying

One of the goals of the spirit as it shapes the soul is to cultivate the virtues of the internal organs. This is referred to as the Completion of the Zang-Fu. When the organs are pure in nature they can reconnect through their meridian pathways and their related sensory orifice to the external world. The senses are the windows to the world and when the windows are open we can connect and communicate clearly between internal and external, between self and the larger self of spirit that is one with everything. We do this through cultivating the higher vibrational aspects of the organs until second nature and original nature are one.

The first two elements we will look at represent the most primal relationship of the sequence, that of Fire and Water. In alchemical terms this relationship is known as the Congress of Heaven and Earth, the Union of Fire and Water, or the Marriage of Kan and Li. They are interchangeable translations of finding the axis of our Destiny.

Element	Water	Wood	Fire	Earth	Metal
Yin Organ	Kidneys	Liver	Heart	Spleen	Lungs
Yang Organ	Bladder	Gall Bladder	Small Intestine	Stomach	Large Intestine
Season	Winter	Spring	Summer	Indian Summer	Fall
Gestation	Seed	Sprout	Flower	Fruit	Reaped
Color	Blue/Black	Green	Red	Yellow	White
Sense Organ	Ears	Eyes	Tongue	Mouth	Nostrils
Tissue	Bone	Tendon	Blood Vessels	Muscle	Skin
Emotion	Fear	Anger	Joy	Worry	Grief

Figure 2.10: Properties of the 5 Elements

Fire- the Light of Consciousness

The first spirit we will look at pertains to the Fire Element. The spirit of the Heart is known as the Shen, the light of consciousness. The Heart houses the Shen, the Spirit, the Mind. The Heart is the Emperor or Empress at his or her throne, the upper altar. It is the home of the primordial child that is beyond reach of the traumas, shocks, and suffering of existence. The Heart is where the observer consciousness resides, the observer that affects the experiment, the experiment of your life. This is the passenger, the wanderer, the stranger in a strange land. The Heart governs the blood and circulation.

The Heart is meant to experience its own capacity for joy and when out of balance it is related to shock, anxiety, shame, and guilt. All the emotions originate here. The Heart can be cultivated to feel at peace, to have empathy and compassion. It is the light that reflects off the water, the water of the self. Calm water can allow the Shen a constant home to shine out from. The Heart is our heavenly nature. The Heart opens to the tongue and reflects in our ability to speak our truth as well as understand how those words will affect the person we are speaking with.

The Heart is the coherent organizing principle. If the energy of the Heart is calm, all the energy of the body will entrain to this coherent pattern, as the Heart is the strongest magnetic field in the body. The Heart-Math Institute has done beautiful research showing how Electro-Encephalo Graphs(EEG's) will entrain to Electro-Cardio Graphs(ECG's), not only within the body but within those within the range of the magnetic field. Such is the power of the heart to promote peace and love in those we encounter.

Water- the Pure Potential

The next spirit we will look at related to the Water Element. The spirit of the Kidneys is known as the Will, or Zhi. It is responsible for our drive and ambition. It houses our Jing, our ancestral energy, our reproductive energy. It is related to the aging process. If we use our Will and primal drives recklessly we will use up our Kidney energy quickly. Similarly, if we suppress or dampen these energies we will damage the kidney energy as well. The Kidneys are the fertile ground of the self with the freedom to make choices, of free will. It is one of the most powerful energies of the universe. The Kidneys also house the virtue of wisdom, also translated as Zhi, although an entirely different Chinese character.

When we have pulled the essence out of our experiences we develop wisdom and can then become the calm water that reflects the illumination of the Shen. This concept is related to the Ling, or the soul. This is the yin, viscous aspect of the spirit. When we have done the hard work of crafting the Ling-Soul into a steady container, it will naturally attract the yang Shen-Spirit of heaven. The ancients would use cinnabar, or mercury, as an agent to sink to their Lower Dan Tian and anchor the Shen of Heaven into the body. This is one reason why the Dan Tians are often referred to as the "cinnabar fields."

The Kidneys are related to our bones. The bones are the earthly record of the shaping of our soul. The tensions, pressures, and wounds of life are written into the bone matrix. This is our crystalline record, recorded at the mineral level via the collagen and quartz nature of bone. Bone conducts piezo-electricity which can then charge our aura. In this way, our spiritual nature is a direct reflection of our physical existence. We become polished and fractured, humbled and tumbled as we awaken to our spiritual self. The bones represent the Ling, the charged aura represents the Shen. They are inseparable when activated. The Kidneys open up to our ears and our ability to hear clearly and pick up clear sound vibrations. The ears also relate to the bones and our ability to balance based on the vestibular crystals.

The emotion of the Kidneys is fear. Fear is the primal guardian at the gate of accessing the Yuan Qi. Fear is the driving force behind our survival instincts, our Wei Qi. This Wei Qi is rooted in the yang aspect of our Kidney energy, referred to as our Kidney Yang. Our left kidney is related to yin and is referred to as a "true kidney." Our right kidney is related to yang and is said to be more related to our Ming Men, our Life Gate or Gate of Destiny, which we discuss in the following chapter. It is interesting that our survival response and our Destiny share the same home. In order to activate our Destiny, we must reckon with our fear. These fears represent a whole lineage of survival energy that has been expressed violently and also suppressed and repressed. Our relationship to this lineage gives us an opportunity to clean up our lineage's relationship to fear. As we work through these ancestral issues we activate the potential of our Destiny.

The next pair we will look at are the spirits of Metal and Wood, of the Lungs and Liver respectively. These two have many interesting relationships. The earthly soul, the Po, is represented by Metal, and the ethereal or heavenly soul, the Hun, is represented by Wood.

Metal- the Sensation Body of the Earthly Soul

The yin organ associated with the Metal element is the Lungs. The Lungs house the Po, the corporeal soul, the earthly, plasmic aspect of our body and sensations, related to space(as in time or space). The Po returns to the Earth when we die. The Po are responsible for the lessons that we have been entrusted with in this lifetime. The Po are also related to the bones, the part of us that remains behind. The bones are white as is the color associated with Metal. Metal also opens up to the nostrils for breath and to the skin for contact. The Po is our sensory body and the Wei Qi that circulates through our skin and perimeter.

The Po is the consolidating force, the centripetal energy of material form that attracts experiences to us. The Lungs are responsible for judgment and discernment, of the detail that is so important to the experience of form. These traits facilitate the learning of lessons. Metal cuts through, but in so doing can be harsh, because part of the cultivation of the self is to achieve non-dual, neutral space in our self. Our relationship to this trait of judgment, necessary for safety, is one of the biggest challenges to creating a neutral space for the spirit.

Metal provides the virtue of clarity, when we can see things as they are, when we know the essence of a thing or event. Metal also provides the courage to face our fears here on Earth. Often courage is the only option when faced with fear. Metal represents inspiration, the taking in of a deep breath out of sheer exhilaration, of being imbued with the spirits of the ancestors that ride on the 8 winds. Metal represents letting go, of relaxing, of exhaling, of eliminating what no longer serves us as represented by its yang organ, the Large Intestine.

Grief is the emotion associated with Metal, the reaper. Grief will affect the Lungs and the grief of loss and death is one of the greatest challenges to the human spirit. The ability and inability to let go of the experiences that weigh us down is associated with Metal. The Metal element carves our life lessons deep into our quartz bone record to be used by later generations to communicate with our spirit. This is the shaping of the soul. When our Po is clear enough, when we are in right relationship to our lessons, it is a natural antenna for our heavenly aspect, the Hun.

Wood- Growth and Evolution
Guided by Our Heavenly Messenger

The spirit of Wood is known as the Hun. The Hun is housed in the Liver and is referred to as our ethereal, or eternal soul. It is the immaterial, heavenly aspect of our being that is related to time. It is responsible for the story of our life and goes back and forth outside of time retrieving information that may guide us on our journey, of our life plan, or destiny in the form of dreams, visions, art, etc. The Hun is connected to the cosmic library, the akashic records. It is the collective unconscious. The Hun is an expansive energy that drives us to connect outwardly. It is a centrifugal force. If too expansive it can cause a person to be ungrounded, disoriented, or simply uncontained.

Wood houses the energy of anger and when not related to properly can show up as irritability, frustration, depression. Healthy anger can protect us and defend our boundaries. The Liver is responsible for the smooth, free-flow of qi and emotion and any obstruction can challenge its healthy function. The Liver stores the blood and in order to anchor the Hun from its mystic travels requires healthy blood volume, healthy emotions which make the liver a happy home to return to. The Wood element opens to the eyes, the windows of the soul. The Wood element is involved in having vision, in having a plan to achieve that vision, and the ability to make the choices and decisions that will lead to its fulfillment. Wood is also related to the chaos of the infinite potential of Heaven and can be prone to disorganization and day-dreaming that keep us from accomplishing our dreams. Wood is the energy of growth and the energy of creativity.

The virtue of the Liver is benevolence. It desires fairness for everyone and functions best when it can embody this. It is a transpersonal energy of the collective, seeking to awaken the collective super-consciousness of man, whereby we are capable of going into the conscious trance of entering the collective unconscious together and steering the direction of Humanity. This is awakening from the nightmare of history as James Joyce said. The modern Westerner has lost this ability. Existential shock has driven the hyper-development of the linear, logical, rational aspect of the brain to seek solutions. This part of the brain has generated some amazing technology and improvement in the quality of life, but has been killing the planet and Humanity. It is wholly incapable of solving the problem it created. That solution must come from a different mindset than the one that created the problem.

This new mindset that houses the solution is the union of the two hemispheres of the brain through the corpus callosum. This is also the ability of the brain to reduce electrical activity and allow itself to sit peacefully suspended in the pre-natal aquatic matrix. This is the ability to be in dual consciousness and unity consciousness simultaneously and the ability to go into and out of either state of consciousness. Together the Hun and Po are like the Psyche and Soma, the Right and Left Brain. When they are balanced they create the opening of the central channel and the neutral space for spirit, similar to the Ling and the Shen, or the calm Water reflecting the Firelight of Heaven.

Earth- Central Equilibrium

The fifth element is the Earth. It is often depicted as the center. Its spirit is that of the Yi, of intention, attention and focus. The Yi is rightfully at the center. It is the only aspect that we can really choose. We can guide and focus the others but it's our ability to use our intention that allows any of the cultivation to be possible. Intentionality allows us to put directionality onto our life, or to align with a directionality. The Yi, supported by the Gall Bladder as we shall see later, allows us to guide our lives through the choices we make. Worry and over-thinking tax the earth element. Native American wisdom says that worry is a prayer for what we don't want.

The Earth is related to the Spleen and Stomach and is our digestive energy. The Earth element opens to the mouth and our ability to take in the world and to feel nourished by what we take in. Our ability to digest our life's events allows us to be present. The Yi functions properly in the Now, the present moment. When we are distracted by the past or future, part of our focus is there, too, being unavailable in the present. The qi follows the Yi. We can learn to guide our qi or we can be at the whims of our nostalgia, trauma, and desire and have our Yi too spread out in the past and future to be of much use to us.

The virtue of the Earth element is that of being centered and satisfied. It is the virtue of being in our integrity. It is our central equilibrium. When we are in our integrity it is clear how not to be knocked off our center. If we have doubts and gaps in the development of our character, the winds of change will provide the situations that give us an opportunity, or in other words, test our character. This integrity, this center, is our axis. It is how we manage the spinning vortex of energy that is our axis between Heaven and Earth. As we learn to live in this axis it will spin us off, or spin off our karma. It is learning to live in the fire of transformation. It is the Fire of Heaven transforming the Earth and Water of our clay in its kiln, its crucible.

Water	Wood	Fire	Earth	Metal
Zhi- Will	Hun- the Ethereal Soul	Shen-Spirit/ Mind	Yi- Intention/ Focus	Po- the Corporeal Soul
Wisdom	Benevolence	Compassion	Integrity	Discernment
Cleverness	Planning	Peace	Centeredness	Justice
Ambition	Vision	Propriety	Reliability	Courage
Drive	Dreaming	Clarity	Support	Righteousness

Figure 2.11: Psycho-Spiritual Aspects of the 5 Elements

 festina

Part 2 Chapter 7

Gates of Destiny

༷

The Ming Men- Our Jet Pack

In preparing us for our journey into the 8x, we should also look at a core aspect of our Human Battery, known as the Ming Men, the Life Gate, or the Gate of Destiny. It is also called the Moving Qi between the Kidneys.[16] Physically, there are transverse fascial bands that connect the kidneys to each other. It is located around the area just below Lumbar Vertebra 2. Aurically, this area connects us to the larger organism of Humanity, what we experience when we function from the pre-natal qi body. This is the battery, the motor, the dual jet pack of our kidneys connected to the larger source of the Universe. This is our Kidney/Jing-Essence energy and is associated with the Self and our Will.

This primordial energy of creation is disseminated up the spine in a Tree of Life expression(see picture) to nourish the internal organs. This is done via the Triple Warmer mechanism. It is the image of creating more of our self, of our Yuan Qi, either through procreation or action in the world, or through the self-replicating transcription of RNA creating proteins that sustain life. This dissemination becomes imbalanced and/or dampened very easily when we begin to function more and more from our conditioned self, our acquired mind. If we are willing to engage in the process of self-discovery we can optimize this primal function of life. If we are willing to accept and love ourselves enough on a core level and to trust that more of our self should be shared with the world. This is learning to trust and love our self as a gift to humanity.

The Kidneys are the seat of our Yuan Qi- Source Qi, of our inherited energy, of our Jing-Essence. They have the adrenal glands sitting on top of them with a strong relationship to how our survival energy functions(Yang Qi supports Wei Qi). Fear is the Guardian at the Gate of our vitality. In order to strengthen our Ming Men we have to transcend a certain amount of our autonomic relationship to fear. These are species-wide patterns that have evolved over millennia. This is our survival energy being stuck at our genetic level. Shining the light of awareness into the over-compensating nature of survival energy and liberating the DNA from these habituated over-reactions is the potential of the 8x Vessels.

The strength of the Ming Men emanates from the naval area of the Lower Dan Tian and this is how we manage this force, a version of Earth controlling Water in the 5 Element cycle. Trauma causes the rectus abdominis to retract at the naval, which functions like a valve that reduces the expression of the life force. As we learn to heal our fear and trauma, we can re-attach the energy of our umbilicus directly back to the source.

---

16. *Matsumoto, Hara Diagnosis has excellent further study on the Ming Men.*

The 8x Vessels, the Curious Organs and the pre-natal energy body are our evolutionary record. An interesting aspect of the Ming Men is that, like we shall discuss about the Chong Vessel and the Ren Vessel, it is pre-verte-brate in nature, an expression of the hydrostatic skeleton. Its energy is the pre-cursor of the formation of the Du-Governing Vessel and the spine. It is embedded in the implicate order of things, obscured from the eyes of those that only see the explicate order. The power and connection of the pre-natal energy body is embedded in our form, in our DNA, in the relationships between our Curious Organs, in our connective tissue matrix, just waiting to be re-awakened.

Evolutionary Enfolding of the Ming Men

This is the lumbar-sacral plexus that still contains reflexes from earlier stages of evolution. In this case it is related to the Jellyfish motion.[17] The Jellyfish motion is the arcing of energy that brings the mouth towards the anus during orgasm and causes a motion that arches the lumbar spine during orgasm. This is the channeling of the primal energy of creation that has existed forever. We evolved a spine to help manage, contain and direct this energy. However, it cannot be managed by the nervous system and spine exclusively. The fascia/connective tissue has to circulate this energy as well.

The fascia circulates this energy through its entirety and perimeter with the assistance of the hydrostatic pressure of the body fluids and the gaseous pressure of the respiratory system. This creates the pressures that allow fascial buoyancy. In this way we can learn to circulate and carry a charge indefinitely. This fascial buoyancy throughout the system creates a tenseg-rity structure that functions as a whole unit, responding to outside pressure without resistance, absorbing theses forces and grounding these forces throughout the entirety of the structure. This movement of mechanical charge throughout the organism can be perpetuated solely by breath and/or gravity and this energy begins to bring awareness into the potential structure of our auric body, allowing us to use this feedback for our cultivation. This takes place through the 3 Wai Qi Fields, or 3 External Qi Fields. This self-per-petuating primal energy of the pressurized system is the potential power of the Ming Men, the motor that puts us on the path of our Destiny without engaging the forces of resistance in our self or in others.

The Heart-Kidney Axis

The relationship between Jing-Essence and Shen-Spirit is known as our Heart-Kidney Axis. Our Heart-Kidney Axis is the core of our connection between Heaven(Shen-Heart) and Earth(Jing-Kidneys). It is our orientation towards our Destiny. This is the spirit having a material experience. This axis is sometimes called the Tai Chi Pole or the Primordial Chong Meridian. This is seen as a layer of our being that can only be accessed by our self. It is

17.   *Reich. 1960*

not something that can be done for us, but something that can be facilitated. In Chinese Medicine, Heaven's influence is seen as astrology and Earth's influence is seen as morphology, or genetics. It is the union of the two that creates life.

In spiritual alchemy this starts as the Primordial Chong, the seed of our soul, which grows to include the Ren and Du Meridians of the Microcosmic Orbit which can then be expanded into a column as large as our body and out into our auric field. This is the process of working with the 8x vessels in internal alchemy. This process can be greatly facilitated by understanding their medical usage as well, which is seen in the 8x acupuncture tradition.

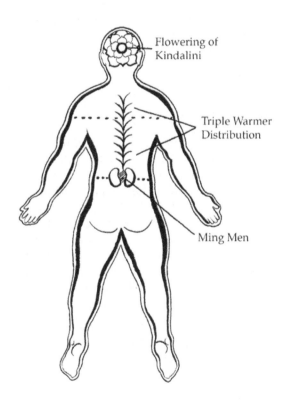

Figure 2.12: Ming Men with Triple Warmer Mechanism and Flowering of Kundalini

This alignment of the Heart-Kidney Axis is also known as the Union of Fire(Heart) and Water(Kidney), or the Marriage of Kan(Water) and Li(-Fire). Another name for this alignment is our Destiny. If we can align our Will(Kidneys-Self) with our Purpose(Heart-Humanity) we can achieve our Destiny. This is conscious co-creation, conscious evolution, participating in the vibration of life. The pursuit of Destiny is our birthright and the key to participating in the self-organizing principles that govern our species.

The Pericardium- Our Heart Protector and Shock Absorber

The Heart is the Emperor or Empress in Chinese Medicine. It holds such a revered place, that not only does it have its paired yang organ, the Small Intestine, but it also has the Pericardium, known as the Heart Protector, or Heart Constrictor. These names are very appropriate as its job is to protect the Heart from shock and trauma, and if it overdoes this, it will constrict the Heart, causing a variety of medical, emotional, social and spiritual problems. The Pericardium is a powerful sheath of connective tissue surrounding the Heart and whose central tendon connects directly to the diaphragm. The Pericardium represents our boundaries, especially our emotional boundaries and issues of intimacy and trust. The Pericardium represents the inward movement through the semi-permeable membrane of our auric egg. It is the wrapping of the "fragile egg-shell mind." As such it helps maintain our sanity and our perspective, it "sanitizes the emotions," like a filter.

Body Armoring and the Pericardium

The Pericardium holds our "body armoring" patterns,[18] psycho-emotional holding patterns frozen into the liquid crystal record of our connective tissue, facilitated by the blood, by contraction in the vascular system from emotional pain. The body armoring is a way to keep us from feeling our pain. Physically we accomplish this through the breath. The Pericardium's protective mechanism keeps the diaphragm from allowing us to breathe into the body regions that hold painful memories from our story. The Pericardium registers the contraction of the organism and often gets stuck in this contractive state and unable to return to the state of relaxed expansion. The organism becomes unable to exhale and let go of the tension that is being held as a protective mechanism that is back-firing by reducing the valve on the life-force.

The Heart is the natural expansion towards the world. It is our self and original nature. The Pericardium is conditioned by our experiences, shocks, and traumas, and is our acquired mind, our ego, our masks. It is related to our feelings of vulnerability and inadequacy. The Heart is the parasympathetic, relaxation response and the Pericardium is our sympathetic, "fight or flight" response. The Pericardium has a strong relationship to our sexual function, as it is responsible for intimacy, emotional health and blood circulation.

In utero, we are connected to all things. In order to individuate, to experience life as a separate organism requires a certain amount of imprinting. This is generally experienced through shock and trauma.[19] At birth we deeply contract as we adjust to the atmosphere, beginning the process of perceived separation, taking our first breath and setting patterns into place that may indeed last a lifetime. It is said in Chinese Medicine that we will experience a trauma, or perceived trauma, at sometime in the first couple years

---

18. *Reich term.*
19. *Jarrett, Clinical Applications has great information on this.*

of our life that will cause a deep imprinting. We transition from the unified consciousness of being part of all that is, to the potentially shocking reality of also being separate from all that is. At this point we lose our holistic perspective on the Universe and schism into seeing the world through a limited lens, these lenses are the archetypal aspects of the Five Element types. As we grow spiritually, these mechanisms, these early imprints registered in the Pericardium, the Heart Protector, are the challenges we face to opening the door of our Heart.

The Triple Burner- the Tree of Life and Creation of Our Self

The Triple Burner is the paired yang organ network of the Pericardium. It is imaged like a water wheel through the 3 burners of the torso. The chest is the Upper Burner, the area between the navel and the chest is the Middle Burner, and the area below the navel is the Lower Burner. Medically, the Triple Burner is responsible for the fluid metabolism and circulation through the body. This gives it a relationship to the lymph, hormones, and extra-cellular fluids such as the ground substance. As a physical structure it is analogous to the peritoneum and all the fascial wrappings of the organs. As science has shown, the connective tissue is a very dynamic system and one of the most important systems in the body.

The Triple Burner is responsible for the "dissemination of the Ming Men Fire." It is responsible for the conversion of Yuan Qi, of pre-natal Jing into post-natal Qi. This is shown in a Western sense through its role of circulating the hormones through the body. In the Eastern sense, this is represented by its movement from the Ming Men and the Kidneys up the spine to be distributed to the back transport points of the internal organs. This is the Tree of Life represented in Humanity. This is the dissemination of the Yuan Qi, our family tree into the post-natal resources of our individual life, a branch in a tree that goes back deep into the mystery of creation. This is the self-replication of DNA through RNA transcription.

The Triple Warmer represents the outward movement through the semi-permeable membrane of our auric egg. This is the ability to express, to extend our authentic self outward, to create and share more of our self with the world. The Triple Warmer is related to the expansive energy of yang Qi, and the strength to reinforce our boundaries so that we don't constantly feel impinged upon by the pressures of life. In this way it works hand in hand with the Pericardium, in that if we don't have enough buoyancy to our structure we may feel extremely vulnerable. If we are too retreated into our safe place, we may not be able to sustain any outward movement towards connection. This ability to connect outward is the outlet for our Ming Men, our Destiny. Our Destiny is meant for the betterment of others and the energy of Heaven inherent in our Destiny requires not only a grounded individual but a community to receive the message, the gifts of the spirit.

The Kidneys Anchor Lung Qi-
Creating the Pressurized System

Every organ system interacts with every other. The nature of these interactions is documented in extreme detail. It is beyond the scope of this book. For this book, we are mainly looking at the Heart-Kidney Axis, the relationship between Heaven and Earth as it takes place through us. The other relationship I would like to describe is that of the Lungs and Kidneys, for it is directly related to our principle tool of self-awareness, our breath. In Chinese Medicine, the Kidneys anchor the Lung Qi, they participate in the inhalation, especially any deep inhalation. If the Kidneys are challenged through tension or weakness or both, our breath will be compromised. The Lungs descend the Qi back to nourish the Kidneys on the exhale. The inhale is more yang, and sympathetic nervous system, the exhale is more yin, more parasympathetic.

In Chinese Medicine the meridians connect the organs to each other. The Heart has no innate descending connection to the Kidneys. This must be trained, must be cultivated. This is done through the breath, the breath and the intention. Much of acupuncture and cultivation is about creating, activating, or re-activating the potential of our circuitry, our meridian matrix. The deep beauty of our meridian matrix is that ultimately it connects us to each other. We have free will as to how to configure these connections to some degree, but we are one organism.

The descent of the Heart into the Kidneys, is the parasympathetic achievement, the relaxed acceptance of our nature and the sense of being breathed. In training for this in a more yang manner we discover our ability to use breath and posture to circulate piezo-electricity and how we can use this to shape the field around us and take responsibility for our piece of plasma in the Universe, our peace of Mind. The Kidneys anchoring Lung Qi also represents the Willingness(Kidney) to take in the breath and be present with the lessons of our incarnation, our Po.

Part 2 Chapter 8

The Lessons of Life

≈ঙ৯

The Format of the Curriculum[20]

"Spiritual therapy can be seen as working with unfinished business"

- Jeffrey Yuen

Our spiritual curriculum relates to the lessons of life and the unfolding of our blueprint over the cycles of 7 & 8, the rhythms and seasons of our life's big transitions, of destinations in life that we gravitate to like strange attractors that we programmed into the blueprint of our curriculum. Fate. Destiny. Free will. Wu Wei. These concepts are integral regarding our journey in life and our journey into the 8x Vessels.

We just discussed the 5 spirits or the 5 shen. The Shen equates more with the concept of spirit while the Ling resonates more with the concept of the soul. The Ling is the process of substantiation of the spirit, of learning our lessons over time and how that spiritual wisdom becomes part of our nature, becomes embodied, becomes embedded into our essence. The Hun is the coming and going of the spirit, the communication with spirit that is outside of space and time. It is the expansive nature of the Shen, our yang, centrifugal force that seeks to connect us with others and with all things. It is the movement of the Shen towards unity. It is more insubstantial in nature.

The Po is the building blocks, the raw materials of our Ling, of our soul. Through working with the consolidating, centripetal nature of the Po and the lessons involved therein, the lessons of being incarnate in a material form, we refine our nature. We craft the soul in the image of the spirit through patience and perseverance. We are humbled and tumbled into our own unique gemstone, from the complexities and obstacles of life into the simplicity of our original nature. If we were able to remove all the stressors from life we may miss out on the very fuel of our transformation.

There are many things that need to be reckoned with in life, many lessons that can be learned. We can always learn. We can always improve, become more efficient, refine our focus, love more, become an embodied prayer of devotion and service in everything that we do. In short, there is no shortage of room for growth. Within this open-ended potential for improvement, there is also acceptance, acceptance of who we are, where we are at in our process and where we are going. Essentially these lessons will break down into knowing thyself, understanding directionality and purpose, and understanding the myriad levels of conditioning fields we are subject to in order to be incarnate. These are distilled in Daoism to a trinity of 3 basic questions to reflect upon:

---

20. *Yuen's transcript "Hun, Po, Ling, Shen". This section is mainly drawn from this source.*

1. Who am I?

2. Where am I going?

3. Who's in charge?

These questions are embedded into the fabric of our lessons. The Po is our earthly or corporeal soul. They are related to the Lungs, space, to the physical body, to the bones, the skin, to sensation, to the breath. The Po are often said to be divided into 7 types. Each of these 7 aspects is considered a Po, a relatively autonomous earthly plasmic substance that is the fuel for our existence. These Po are embedded in, are written into our Jing- Essence. We are responsible for the lessons they embody and we are accountable to these lessons. That is the price of admission, for having a body, an avatar to work with.

We are said to have up to a total of 7 lessons that we are working with in any one lifetime. 7 is a number used in many mystical traditions. Though not entirely the same, the 7 lessons of the Po are somewhat resonant with the 7 chakras and that will be our working model. Each of us is said to have chosen 3 or 4 Po to work with in this lifetime, up to 7. Each Po of the 7 is active throughout a cycle of 7 and 8. That Po, that lesson will be active during that period and then that switch will be turned off and the next Po activated. Certain cycles may not contain any pivotal Po that we signed on for. As we move from one cycle to another, we condition our bones around the way we carry our self through that cycle in relation to our lessons. The lesson of the Po, if not transcended, will be embedded in our bone matrix, brain marrow and DNA in a state of latency, as a divergence in our life, unre-solved karma.

As the next cycle is entered this Po will become less active, more latent and the next lesson will become more active. As we go through our cycles the unlearned lessons, the untranscended Po, will remain as repressed or suppressed emotional and psycho-social issues, manifest as layers and layers of latency recorded into our calcified bone matrix modeling. As we age and gain the wisdom of experience, we may be able to go back and work on the lessons left unlearned that will have shaped our bones and our stance in the world, our gait and the way we move in the world. If we cannot achieve this at the level of the skeleton we always have the opportunity to redeem these lessons from the brain or blood record.

1st Po	2nd Po	3rd Po	4th Po	5th Po	6th Po	7th Po	Work on Unfinished Business
Age 1-7/8	7/8-14/16	14/16-21/24	21/24-28/32	28/32-35/40	35/40-42/47	42/47-49/56	49/56 & up

Figure 2.13: Po and Cycles of 7 & 8

# of Lesson	Quality of Lesson
1st Lesson	Unconditional Love. Identity, Gender, Ethnicity Issues. Self-Acceptance.
2nd Lesson	Conditional Love. Creativity. Reproduction. Dissemination of your Yuan Qi- Making more of your Self. Accept responsibility.
3rd Lesson	Moving into Individuation. Role in Society. Judgment. Morality. Rites of Passage to join Tribe. Shame. Embarrassment. Accept responsibility to the Social Agenda. Indoctrination.
4th Lesson	Heart is on a Quest. Putting thought to the feeling process. Faith. Faith in what you feel irrespective of society. Miracles. Heart Chakra opens often from chaotic qi. Faith is born from chaos. Opens door to spirituality.
5th Lesson	Honor who you are. Honor your own experience. Stepping into spirituality. Confidence. Respecting everything about who you are and what the world is without the configurations of conflicts and guilt. Everything coming together. Acceptance. Responsibility. Creativity. Sovereign ruler is comfortable with where he or she is moving. Verbally you honor what you believe in.
6th Lesson	Compassion. Empathy. No need for reality infringement. You don't see left and right. No judgment. Light emanates from the eyes. Light upon yourself. Awakened to your own enlightenment.
7th Lesson	Tao. Ascension. Rebirth. Being born into heaven whereas when you come into post-natal life you are head down. Redemption of spirit from that matter that we call essence. All things.

Figure 2.14: 7 Lessons of the Po

Qualities of the Lessons of Life

Here is a list of qualities associated with the 7 lessons of life. Be aware that there may be an infinite number of types of lessons, or 33, or 64, the main idea being that there may be more lessons than a soul can learn in a single lifetime and therefore, many lifetimes may be required to learn to navigate these spiritual waters. These are presented in linear fashion with the 1st Po representing the first cycle and so on and so forth.

# of Lesson	Organ Relationship
1st Lesson	Kidney-Lungs
2nd Lesson	Kidney-Liver
3rd Lesson	Kidney-Spleen
4th Lesson	Heart-Spleen
5th Lesson	Heart-Liver
6th Lesson	3rd Eye
7th Lesson	Crown Chakra

Figure 2.15: Organ Relationships of the Lessons

Problems occur when we arrive at a level before we have finished the previous ones, such as when one forces the premature opening of the 6th or 7th chakra through reckless practices. This kundalini movement is associated with the Liver and may cause Liver patterns and wind symptoms in the patient, and may cause brain stem issues as the body safeguards the energy rush into the brain. Spiritually we may be thrust into a state wherein our Po enter the realm of all Po and the body may be seized by fear as it enters a realm usually reserved for the dead. However there are many mechanisms of Grace in the universe to assist in these spiritual awakenings that occur before the individual has gained the necessary understanding and before humanity has developed nervous systems that can easily accommodate higher flows of energy. It serves as a reminder that there are no short-cuts, but we are free to seek the most efficient ways of growing spiritually.

Part 2 Chapter 9

The Three Spirits

The Goals of the Spirit[21]

The spirit seeks certain things in life. It seeks harmony. It seeks harmony with itself because it is all things, harmony between internal and external, harmony between the ying and wei levels. This is the pre-natal potential of harmony within chaos. The spirit seeks to be unobstructed. "Where there is obstruction there is pain and symptoms. Where there is free flow, there is no pain and symptoms." Spirit seeks expression of its own creativity. When this expression is blocked or obstructed, we have stagnation, stasis, static. Spirit seeks liberation. Spirit is the remover of obstacles. Spirit seeks completion. Spirit seeks completion of its creativity, completion of its union with matter, completion of its curriculum, completion of the Zang-Fu Organs. The Spirit seeks its destiny, its purpose, evolution.

The 3 Spirits of the Hun are known as the San Qing or the Three Pure Ones, and they are the Heavenly counterpart to the Earthly 7 Po. The 3 Spirits come down from Heaven, rain down from heaven into us through the 3 orifices: the Crown, 3rd eye, and anus(Po Men, the Gate of the Po). Sometimes the mouth and nostrils are seen as part of the 3 orifices. The anus, mouth and nostrils are where they would put jade in the dead as a symbol of longevity or eternity for the soul. Placing jade in these orifices helps keep the Po from escaping back to the Earth before the Hun has an opportunity to move towards Heaven through the Crown and the 3rd Eye. The 3 Spirits come down to explore lessons and to transcend them. Trance-end them. The spirit is also here to generate experiences, to experience life, to tell a story. It seeks to experience its own joy, to share its own joy, to tell the story of the glory of spirit, to live life as a prayer of devotion to itself, as a prayer to creation and creator, to redeem light from matter. We have an opportunity to differentiate our self within this mission, to be of service to the whole without losing our sense of self, to live our purpose, our Destiny.

Enlightening the First Layer of the Auric Field

The Hun are the messengers that communicate between the Big Shen of Heaven and our Little Shen-Spirit. The Hun are associated with our Liver. They are related to creativity, benevolence, planning, vision, and dreaming, all things that we need to intuit our Destiny and the road that will take us there. The 3 Hun have a direct resonance with the layers of the energy field or aura, the 3 Wai Qi Fields, or 3 External Qi Fields. The 3 Hun are called the San Qing, the 3 Pure Ones. They are Tai Qing- Great Purity or Great Clarity, Shang Qing-Upper Purity, and Yu Qing- Jade Purity. The 1st External Qi

---

21. *Yuen's transcript "Hun, Po, Ling, Shen", 2001. This section is mainly drawn from this source.*

Field has resonance with the 1st body of Tai Qing- Great Clarity, which represents polarity, yin and yang, and relates to physicality. It is related to the Physical Body and the Astral Body.

These levels represent that we reincarnate to feel what it's like to be loved again or to be abused again so that we can graduate from that lesson. We come back to take a breath, to experience the senses and the desires. This first body of the ethereal field is in the realm of the sensory organs and because at this level there is yin and yang, we have judgment. We will view it as a good lesson or a bad lesson. This is the spirit exploring matter and it comes with all the challenges and beauty of the physical world and the astral body, the home of desire and fear. This is where angels fear to tread, but fools rush in. The Hun is reporting to the Shen-Spirit via the 1st External Qi Field, and providing information as to whether we are moving towards being a lighter being, or if our states of consciousness are becoming darker, more consumed by fears and desires displacing our consciousness from the present, from our presence.

Generally, at this level we are identified with our ego, our post-natal configuration, our social game face, our masks and all they entail. We are functioning from the pericardium, from the protective mechanism, the caged-in seats, rather than the heart. This is a state of stasis. We are braced against change, resistant to moving forward, resistant to growth. Often at this level we are frozen in fear and self-protection or indulging in desires that eat away at our integrity. In this state of armoring, we cannot be receptive to the cues from spirit, to the messages of the Hun that guide us on our path. In the body this will create stagnation and accumulation. In the aura, this creates static, noise, and a dampening of the signal coming from the Hun, the truth being communicated to the Shen, to the Mind, to the Spirit, to the Heart.

The field and the body are in direct reflection of each other. The field is like an eggshell, a seed for our growth into an awake member of the collective of Humanity. Our resistance is like the eggshell barrier on our membrane. In the body this will be experienced as tension. Our field is like amniotic fluid, healthy yin. It has the nutrition for us to grow and it also buffers us from the changes, the bumps in our path. This viscous yin can easily turn into damp or phlegm that we use to stay protected from the truth of ourselves, to dampen and mute the messages from spirit. We can do this by keeping our attention from the present moment. To grow spiritually is to live life in the present, to allow more presence, being a clear channel to the transmissions of the Hun, the collective conciousness, with less noise and distortion in the system.

These levels may be able to be transcended as we learn to navigate from the higher frequencies. These higher frequencies, when grounded, give immediate feedback if we attempt to function outside our integrity. This makes it important that we have learned our lessons. Attempting to function exclusively from these higher frequencies, while in denial of our lower chakras and the fuel of the soul, what is sometimes called the shadow, is a sure recipe for interesting lessons, karma and distorted communication with the universe. While in the body you can learn how to be in relation to the feedback loop of the field, the Field of Constantly Changing Phenomena. We can learn to be in right relationship to fear and desire. We can learn to take care of our self and to be of service, to be benevolent.

1st Hun	1st Wai Qi Field	Tai Qing-Great Clarity	Polarity	Judgment
2nd Hun	2nd Wai Qi Field	Shang Qing Upper Purity	Transcend Polarity	Intentionality of Spirit
3rd Hun	3rd Wai Qi Field	Yu Qing-Jade Purity	Unity	Beyond Intent

Figure 2.16: Hun's Illumination of the Wai Qi Fields.

Reception and Identification with Spirit

The next layer of the External Qi Field resonates with the Shang Qing and is related to the Mental or Causal Body. The External Qi Fields are like a transistor radio for the Hun, spirit radio transmission, W-HUN. At the level of the 2nd External Qi Field, there is an intentionality of the Shen. This is related to the level of the Heart and the ancestral qi. This is where the message of spirit has become personally identified with. This is the level of the Heart Chakra and is where we transcend polarity. We have found right relationship to judgment in order to elevate our awareness to this level. Spirit cannot exist in polarity and judgment. Emotionally identifying with judgment is one of the quickest ways to chase away the Shen. Here we have found a neutral space for our Shen to reside in our heart, with a clear window on the world. We communicate clearly to the world and we receive clear feedback from the world. This is the Shen fulfilling its purpose. Then when you die you don't have to hold onto anything. There is no need for regrets.

The 3rd External Qi Field resonates with the Yu Qing, the Jade Purity. This level is beyond intent. This level is the pure spiritual realm beyond separation. Stones are said to be evolving to jade, and we are always evolving towards purity and clarity. This is the aspect of our consciousness that is one with the impersonal forces of spirit, the chaos of the spirit winds of change. This Field lies beyond the veil of the of the 2nd External Qi Field. Here we are in the 5th dimension and beyond. This is our intersection with the transpersonal consciousnesses of the Universe, represented by the Wheel of the I Ching, and the Crosses formed by the I Ching Wheel.

The Hun are the messengers that inform us of our spiritual nature through the feedback mechanism of the External Qi Fields. The Hun are our Heavenly Messengers that bring us information from the Collective Archives regarding how to stay light, gravitate towards our Purpose, work with transcending our curriculum, and achieve our Destiny. Achieving our Destiny is the most benevolent thing possible for it is from the self-organizing intelligence of the collective organism. Our External Qi Fields are relatively unconscious. As we cultivate our awareness we shine the light of consciousness into the External Qi Fields, whereby they brighten. This is the substantiation of the Shen. This is accomplished through the containment and shaping of our plasma body through the articulation of the magnetic field at our perimeter as generated by the piezo-electric charge of the bones and the liquid crystal collagen matrix. Magnetic fields are able to shape the 4th element of plasma. Cultivating and generating a coherent and consistent magnetic field occurs through the bones and the heart. The shaping of the plasma is the analog aspect of our antenna that we can tune in order to pick up the digital transmissions of the Hun.

Thunder on the Ghost River

꙳꙲ꙩ

The Ghosts of the Subtler Levels of Polarity

The Po is the configuration of the Earthly Soul and the Hun is the Heavenly Soul. The Po is related to Jing, the densest configuration of plasma. The Hun is related to the coming and going of Shen back and forth to the Akashic Record, the Cosmic Library. The Po represent space, the Hun represent time. We get stuck in space through shock, such as an accident or physical trauma and we get stuck in time through emotional trauma and emotional attachment. When we die, if we cannot transcend these issues, if we cannot liberate the Hun and the Po completely from the vessel, if we are stuck, then we have reincarnation. We have lessons that spirit still needs to transcend, and they will be passed on in some way. They will be reckoned with.

If either the Po or Hun cannot transcend, Gui-ghosts, parasites or entities, may be left behind. Both the words Hun and Po have the picture of a Gui-ghost, of a disembodied head floating as part of their Chinese language radical. The word Gui is commonly referred to as ghost or parasite, an interesting parallel in itself, similar energies but one is more substantial and one is more insubstantial. These Gui are then attracted to people whose lessons have an affinity with their own, whose lessons resonate with their own. The tendency of the Gui is to make the person more attached to the physical body, the yin. This allows the dense, dark nature of the entities a reliable home as we become less aware of the light of spirit. The idea is that when people die the Gui that they have been hosting can use the momentum of the person's death to "piggy-back" out of this realm, a plan that sounds rather unlikely to succeed, if the energy became a Gui to begin with.

The Po house our lessons and the Gui-ghosts sort of amplify these lessons and distort our ability to receive and act upon the guidance from our Hun. The plasmic density of the Po is similar to the vibrational resonance of the Gui. The 3 Hun are tempted into denser and denser levels by what are known as the 3 Gui, the 3 ghosts, or the 3 worms. These temptations begin to eat away at our character, our integrity, our self-esteem, siphoning away the yang energy necessary for present moment awareness. Through cultivation and working with the guidance of the Hun, we can make our External Qi Fields lighter, clearer, and more coherent. The 3 Gui work on the opposite principle, keeping us from picking up our connection to Heaven and the light, reinforcing doubts, fears and self-indulgences related to a world without meaning.

Hungry, Horny and Prone to Wander: The 3 Ghosts

The 3 Gui or 3 Ghosts are often called the Hungry Ghost, the Horny Ghost, and the Wandering Ghost. On the physical plane these are seen as Gu- accumulations associated with food, often related to worms or parasites. On the astral plane, these are ghosts, aggravating our attachment and resistance issues, our fears, desires, and leading them into addictions and obsessions. This is Pandora's Box. In a sense these energies shut us down and lead us into a darker place. The sooner we die the sooner they have their misguided opportunity at transcendence. At the mental level, these are negative thought-forms. They can be seen as autonomous ideations in the infinite thought-stream of the collective unconscious, plasmic embodiments of unresolved negative energy. These are the myriad negative thoughts that humanity has the free will to participate in, being hosted by the unresolved issues of our ancestors, our dead. Guilt, shame, violence, blame, you know the list.

From the shamanic perspective we are trying to reconnect with spirit and there are all these relics in the energy realm that interfere with the direct participation in this process. The less people are willing to engage in life with spiritual awareness and maturity, the more random noise and negative thought-forms that wind up in the vibrational matrix. In order to connect with the divine, we need a clear channel, undistorted by the negative forces. The Gui are often seen as the malevolent energies, and the divine is seen as the benevolent energies. As we open our self to spirit and to the opening of the connection to the other side, to the wisdom of the ancestor field, Gui-ghosts are one of the of the aspects of polarity that we will encounter regardless of the terminology, if any, that we use. Disempowering language and perspectives that feed polarity, such as ghosts and possession are slippery slopes. It requires a certain level of maturity to hold space for these models of consciousness without becoming merely superstitious. Essentially, ghosts and humans are not intended to interact. As an old Chinese song says, "Ghosts live below the ground, and Humans live above and that's where they both should stay."

Parasitic Influences and Resonance

Our tendency to attract darker forces into our aura is based on resonance. There has to be something within us that has an affinity with these darker forces. The more accumulations, the more attachments, the more repressed and suppressed negative emotions, the more toxicity, etc. in the body, the more tendency to attract the equally heavy and negative forces in the auric realm. It is the holding onto the past, the haunting of our past that carries these parasitic energies of questionable value. It is the energy of decay, of rotting. In alchemy we let these processes flow through us and support the processes of self-preservation, of essence preservation. This is the digestion process of the post-natal, applicable to food, emotion and experiences. This is the process of choosing what we take in, separating the useful from the useless, and eliminating and letting go of what no longer serves us.

Any information has to be metabolized, so reducing the amount of toxic information taken in would be a first step. However, learning to process toxins efficiently is a traditional alchemist undertaking, sometimes referred to as "the path of poison," a process that involves an understanding of the Divergent Meridian process of guiding poisons, including toxic emotions, away from our vital organs, and learning how to detoxify the constitutional level. By reducing the amount of unnecessary rot and decay occurring in our body, we reduce the amount of energy of rot and decay that we attract into our lives through resonance. But we should understand that rot and decay are natural processes, we just need to tend to them as we would our garden, our house or our car.

"The majority of men are but walking corpses..."

– Ge Hong, alchemist, Ge Hong 283-343 AD

The above observation is along the lines of "he not busy being born is busy dying." If we decay faster than we renew, the outcome is clear. We can assist the renewal process by becoming efficient at assimilating the experiences in our lives, at digesting our lives. The degree to which we become unable to process, to digest events in our lives and to eliminate and let go of them is the extent to which our body will be overloaded. In alchemy, we learn to extract the essence of whatever we take in whether or not it seemed negative or positive. And in this way we feed our essence. We learn to differentiate self from not-self.

The not-self program that we attempt to identify with is financed through the striving of our internal resources, thereby not allowing these resources to be available in the present moment. The more inadequate we feel about our true self, the more we will attempt to function solely from our ego. This builds barriers to the light of Heaven, mirrored by accumulations in the body that finance this dampening of the signal. The body will attempt to keep these accumulations inert, but all these physical accumulations are the medium for holding onto unfinished business and create a breeding ground for Gu and Gui- parasites, worms, longings for the past, regret, unfulfilled desire, fetal toxins, ancestral issues, etc. These stagnations create a resonance for external energies to get stuck in our energy field.

In this way, excess toxins in the body attract Gui from the astral plane to the body. These Gui have unfinished business that is a good match for your unfinished business. This becomes a broad aspect of spiritual work: knowing yourself well enough to recognize you from not you. How much of your program did you put there and how much was put there by outside forces? To the degree that we are unaware of our self, to the degree that we have not differentiated our self and explored our essence, to the degree that we are merely unconsciously participating in the homogenizing quality of the post-natal consciousness program is the degree that we are not occupying our self. In that scenario, who is? Who's in charge?

If we are clear enough about working on our lessons, we don't attract Gui from the collective unconscious. If we are coasting on auto-pilot, the Gui serve as reminders, forcing you to look at your curriculum or deal with a world complicated by static cling in your aura. As we begin to develop spiritually we open our self to multi-dimensional energies. There are benevolent and malevolent forces. Our greatest protection is the ability to be present in the moment. Our presence lives in the light of the moment.

Parasitic Influences and Flow Psychology[22]

There is an interesting parallel to the concept of parasitic influences in the psychology of Flow. A parasite is anything that causes us to be distracted from the present moment. Any influence that requires our energy to keep it at bay in order to sustain our focus on the present is considered parasitic. In a state of Flow we are naturally invested in the present. When we are not in Flow we have to use a high percentage of energy to quell the energies that eat away at us, to keep these energies in a state of latency. These are the energies of doubt, worry and anxiety caused by the uncertainty of the world. These influences are considered to be acquired influences, placed there by our social conditioning. These are the influences that keep us from the experience of being our self and of creating more of our self in the world.

22.   See "Flow Psychology" as a field of study.

Latency and Ancestry

☙

Latency is part of the natural adaptogenic nature of life. If something is too much to deal with and is affecting our ability to "get on with our lives" our body will put it into a state of latency if possible. If it can process 90% of something it may maintain the other 10% in latency. This happens with viruses, bacteria, fungi, and parasites, with physical trauma in the form of "energy cysts" and with emotional trauma in the form of body armoring. The flip side is true as well, for latency can exist at the genetic level, not based on any actions of the individual in this lifetime, and pathogenic factors may come out of latency at any given moment under the right or wrong circumstances, especially during a Cycle of 7 & 8 when access to the Yuan Qi is at its highest.

This is seen scientifically at the genetic level whereby we have a host of inherited traits that we do not want to wake up from their latency. An interesting thing that we are seeing in the science of epigenetics is that gene expression is controlled not by the nucleus itself, but by the messages sent to it from the cell membrane based on the health of its relationship to its cellular environment. I believe that this will be seen to be a direct reflection of the health of our External Qi Field, our etheric cellular membrane, based on our sense of community with our environment.

Latency is tied in to the memory process and the inability to adapt to change. This resistance to change or inability to deal with change causes latency. In this sense it is analogous to karma. Latency, like karma, can be the fertilizer that helps us cultivate our garden, the dark matter that distorts our reality but has great power for transformation. Latency holds us accountable for learning our lessons of life and provides much of the conflict and the tension, of our story.

Latency is divided into the three levels of our energy. At the Wei Qi Level, latency expresses itself either as a crisis, a healing crisis, or at times both. At the Ying Qi Level, latency is a process of suppression, maintained through holding patterns in the blood and overflow reservoirs of the Luo channels as blood stagnation and emotional stagnation. This is at the conscious level so these are events that we could be somewhat aware of if given a moment to reflect. This is also the level of social interaction and much of the stress it takes to adapt to the pressures of social convention and morality occur here.

At the Yuan Qi Level, latency exists in the form of repression. This is financed by the Jing and is unconscious to us. These could be pre-verbal memories, in utero memories, traumas too intense to process, or even genetic traits from recent ancestors or from the planetary collective. This is the concept of the "sins of the father...take 7 generations to be seen." Plant life has a phenomena where stressors or nutritional deficiencies take several generations to show up. With this model, we are all in the middle of a great experiment, with no way of knowing what sort of generational decay is afoot as the Yuan Qi processes and mutates over several generations creating diseases that save us from worse diseases as a species. Ultimately the body will keep using resources to finance the latency until the resources are all gone. Then we have the disease process, the loss of latency.

Financing Latency Requires Resources

Latency requires financing. Some physical resource, such as blood or Jing, will be used to hold the External Pathogenic Factor(EPF) or Internal Pathogenic Factor(IPF) latent. This requires energy to do, and ties up the commodity we are using to finance the pathogen. Generally, latency involves the Wei Qi, the Defensive Qi, trying to protect us from some tangible or intangible threat, either externally or internally generated. If it can't get the threat out it takes it inwards to store it, the goal being to not let the pathogen reach the organs because that can be fatal. If it goes to the joints or somewhere it just causes us pain and buys us time.

Wei Qi is warm, analogous to inflammation, and the body will generally have to respond by cooling it and/or dampening it by surrounding it with some mucous or fluid, what we call damp or phlegm. Over time this heat, this inflammation, damages the tissues, scorches the mucous, and as we age we lose the energy to maintain latency and meanwhile the degeneration process has been running rampant, so when the latent EPF or IPF erupts, it can be pretty advanced along the disease process.

Latency finances living outside of the present moment. It uses blood to hold onto emotional events from the past. Ruminating or dwelling on the past is a way of stagnating your blood. Latency also uses dampness to hold onto the past, to slow things done, to keep us from moving so fast amidst the winds of change. A tricky thing about dampness is that, as a body fluid, it has no inherent consciousness of its own. If we have a build-up of dampness and insulation in the body, all we can successfully do is to let it go. If we are using dampness as insulation and we choose to ruminate about it we will wind up merely recruiting blood and causing blood stasis in an effort to remove the damp. We can also have heat if we are feverish for change and future-oriented. We can have damp-heat as we are stuck in the past and striving towards the future, whereby the yang qi of movement creates heat but is not enough to move through the stasis of dampness. This situation can result in the feeling of being "tired and wired."

Latency and Ancestral Contracts

Latency is often directly related to the unresolved issues of our bloodline, of our lineage, of our ancestry. As we begin to clear out some of the issues of this lifetime, we begin to process the latent issues of our ancestry. This is the energy that needs to be liberated for the energy of the light to become embodied, for the energy of Heaven to be present upon the Earth. We are not the cause of all the latency or karma that we experience. As the *I Ching* says, "No Blame." The body comes with a several million year history, and in some ways even going back to the "Big Bang." However, we are responsible for our response to the adverse situation. We always have a choice. We can leave the world a better place than we found it. We can do our best to take responsibility for the contaminants that we incur in this lifetime and to be proactive about cleaning the genetic code that we chose to embody. Or we can repress everything at all costs. It is not ours to judge how others deal with their karma, for we have not walked a thousand miles in their moccasins.

One important thing about latency is that it's not all bad. Our spiritual gifts, talents, and amazing instincts are all in there too, so as we shine the light of awareness into our process we are fueling the fire of our creativity and uncovering aspects of our self that we never knew we had or had forgotten we had. We are disentangling our self from generations of coping mechanisms. We are "un-wounding" our spirit's entwined fractal bonds. Not so that we can fly away, but so that we can truly be present.

Winds of Change

❧❧

The Field of Constantly Changing Phenomena

Our Shen-spirit is exploring Jing-essence. Being in the manifest world puts us in the world of the constantly changing phenomena- the winds of change. The winds of change embody the principle of uncertainty in the world, in our lives, in our health. The ever-present reality of uncertainty breeds doubt, among other things, such as fear and anger or surprise and excitement. This doubt becomes the habituated approach to reality and then reality affirms it. With doubt we have a tendency to hedge our bet, to always have a contingency plan.

Our contingency plan often requires just enough energy to keep us from being effective with our actual plan. It can be a daydream that compromises our focus. Or often we have no real plan at all. Successfully navigating the sea of uncertainty requires faith, the natural antidote for doubt. However, a manic faith that is not built upon experience will be unsustainable. Deep faith that is based on experience and unattached to outcomes is a product of cultivation, of learning. We can learn to pay attention to our surroundings and be efficient in our survival, while maintaining deep faith in the process of life, of creator and creation.

Our Wei Qi-protective qi, and our Po- Earthly Soul, both related to the Lungs and Metal Element, comprise the sensation aspect of our being. We interact with the world through sensation. If we can freely sense and interact with the world without being attached or becoming attached to the sensation, without resisting or becoming habituated to resisting the sensation of being vibrantly attuned, vibrantly alive, we can be free. The field of sensation, being part of the Wei Qi, is autonomic. If we want to participate consciously, we have to pay attention, use our Yi, our focus, to tune into our sensations, otherwise, we will autonomically filter out information, habituate around this, and live as if this information did not exist.

If we desire more of a type of sensation, a pleasure, we may chase it and habituate around this desire. The longing it brings can displace our focus from the present moment. In this scenario, we will consume our essence at a more accelerated rate, burn our candle more quickly. Often our senses are dull from surrounding ourselves with man-made objects and creature comforts. Our senses are also dulled by our repression of primal fear. The full onslaught of sensation is something we no longer experience, it is a charged-state that can cause the fight or flight response. Our body may say, "if we are this highly alert, we must be in danger." Also, if we are this highly charged and sensually attuned we may enter into sexual/social transgressions that can cause us guilt, shame, remorse, or physical danger. Or we may resist the field of sensation, say due to body armoring, to physical/emotional pain, and become resistant to feeling the sensation body directly at all. In this scenario, we dampen, and numb ourselves, bracing ourselves against any potential change and become stuck, experiencing the tension of resistance and stagnating the resources required to finance this chronic tension of resistance.

Displacement from the Present Moment

In either case, our attention has been displaced from the present moment and the actual opportunity it brings for change. Swimming in the present moment requires all of our energy and focus, commitment and faith to sustain. All things are possible in the clarity of the present moment. Over time the existential phenomena of the present moment becomes but a vague memory and as it involves the autonomic process of Wei Qi, we are unaware of the process of filtering out so much information. So it is that "wind," the inability to adapt to change, is the root of the 1,000 diseases. Not only can the wind breach our defenses, generally because we have become too distracted, perhaps too past or future oriented to maintain integrity in our Wei Qi, but wind can also allow other EPF's to come in with it. This is where we have cold(often a metaphor for frozen in fear), or damp(often a metaphor for being insulated from raw experience- dampened) that can enter the body. Again, in Chinese Medicine, there is no separation of mind and body so wind can mean any number of things, from actual wind weakening the Wei Qi at an area such as the neck, or it can mean a virus or bacteria causing a flu or common cold, or it can mean anything that moves around a lot or moves quickly, chaos.

The winds of change are a form of primordial chaos, the creative force that allows life to come into existence. The Chinese have a story about Hundun, the mythical figure who represents chaos, and how the winds who loved him so decided to give him a gift as a way of saying thanks. Hundun had no sensory orifices, no windows to experience the universe. The winds decided to give him holes, to give him sensory orifices. Over the course of 7 days they gave him an orifice per day, 2 eyes, 2 ears, 2 nostrils, and 1 mouth and upon the moment that he had the 7th orifice, he died. Chaos was killed not through order, per se, but through sensory perception. Sensory perception allows us to create order of the world. We can create coherence via the heart orifice as it's called. Opening the sensory orifices, opening the heart orifice, opening our eyes, these are all metaphors for the way we see the world, changing our mind, changing our belief, changing our marrow, having a change of heart. By changing our marrow, disease can be cured. By changing the marrow, we change the world. Be the change you want to see in the world.

The *I Ching*- Sailing in the Winds of Change

The *I Ching* is the Book of Change and shows how the 8 forces, the eight directions, the winds, combine to form the 64 changes or the 64 situations, representing all possibilities, the 10,000 things being reduced to their essence. The eight forces are represented in a wheel, a Bagua(literally meaning 8 sides). There is a pre-natal Bagua and a post-natal Bagua. The pre-natal Bagua is known as the Heaven cycle and the post-natal Bagua is the Earth sequence. The pre-natal arrangement is harmonious, while the post-natal is not evenly balanced and is not intended to be. It is perpetual motion, not necessarily harmony or meaning. The arrangements of the *I Ching* hexagrams are similar. Much in their arrangement is elegant but by the time all is said and done, they are another representation of the life process, the constant change, the perpetual motion, the chaos. The 64 hexagrams have many parallels to the genetic code and the way that DNA sustains itself through RNA creating proteins is analogous to the way the Spirit-Shen sustains itself through situations that create experiences.

Qián	Duì	Lí	Zhèn	Xùn	Kan	Gèn	Kun
☰	☱	☲	☳	☴	☵	☶	☷
Heaven/ Sky	Lake/ Marsh	Fire	Thunder	Wind	Water	Mountain	Earth
Tiān	Zé	Huo	Léi	Fēng	Shui	Shān	Dì

Figure 2.17: The 8 Trigrams.

Our inability to process, metabolize, or digest these experiences will leave us stuck in a moment, a situation will have gone into a state of latency, we will have karma and this will register at the Jing-level, potentially affecting our genetic transcription, decaying the telomeres, i.e. aging. The 64 Hexagrams of the *I Ching* are also represented as a wheel, which, similar to the pre-natal Bagua, represents the harmony that can be attained by humanity when it is able to participate with the multi-dimensional forces of Heaven.

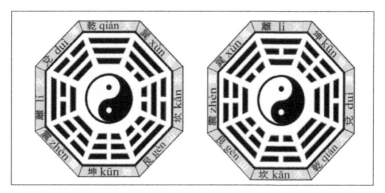

Figure 2.18: Pre-Natal Bagua(on left) and Post-Natal Bagua(on right).

121

It is impossible to keep up with change and chaos. In order to allow this relationship to the Field of Changing Phenomena to be sustainable one must get to know oneself, to find one's center, or else the winds of change will knock us off our game sooner or later, again and again. It is like playing the Tai Chi game of push-hands with time. It is a game meant to be played, not won. As the Fool set's out on his quest in Hexagram 4 of the *I Ching*, he has one tool in his bag of tricks: choice. Choice, the willingness to learn from these choices and the willingness to persist and persevere in the quest. We can choose our response to any event, we can choose an action, or choose non-action.

In order to have a choice about anything we first have to have awareness. Awareness that there is a relationship between things allows us to make a choice, a choice likely made to influence the outcome favorably. The *I Ching* guides the user in evaluating his responses to a situation, and aims to allow us to see through, to penetrate to the essence of any given situation including our part in it. In so doing, it allows us to work on our karma, to improve the characteristics of our ancestral traits through learning. It is a tool for developing one's character, one's "De." Through participating in the decision-making process with heightened awareness we can learn. Once we have learned a lesson, we can let go of the minutiae of the brain marrow record that consumes so many of our precious internal resources.

Character- a Constant Amidst Uncertainty

Through this process we learn to approach life from our center, from a place of awareness, and choose our actions from the proper intent, refining our intention and the motivations behind our intentions more and more subtly. However, as we learn, there is always some spin on a situation that throws us off and there is always more to learn. Life, the master, will win the game of push-hands, pretty much whenever life decides to call you on your blind spot, your character flaw. Here we have the same premise as in all Chinese cultivation, "learn the form, forget the form," or "let the horse go free." We can let the horse, the body, run free once we have learned our lessons, once we have trained our Wei Qi at the Jing level through knowing, once we have internalized all the myriad virtues into one thing: our self.

Through trial and error, self-acceptance and forgiveness, humility, patience and perseverance we have transformed the chaos of complexity into the simplicity of our innate being. At this point we have been thrown enough curveballs and can function from the natural way of wu wei with right action and right timing. Our character is beyond context and will hold at any level of proportion, any level of pressure, of trials, along the energetic fractal spectrum. And so the process goes. Transcendence can be achieved without abandoning responsibility, accountability, and morality. Remember, one does not simply have to seek the spirit at a loss of self. We can participate in a union between Heaven and Earth that creates the third thing, the trinity, the dilation of neutral space that allows Heaven on Earth but includes awareness of both the individual and the collective, of being able to embody both the Newtonian and the Quantum, or go back and forth between the two.

SW	S	SE
W	Center	E
NW	N	NE

Figure 2.19: We are the Center of the Magic Square

The 8 forces are the constant change. They are the perimeter of the magic square. They interact and shape our essence, shape our character. The center of the square is the constant beyond change. We are always free to choose the path with the most heart. This is the constancy of the spirit, our Heart, in the ever-present moment.

Palaces of the Heart

The 9 Heart Palaces represent the ways that our Shen, which resides in our Heart, can get lost or distracted on its earthly sojourn. Each Palace is an archetypal aspect of life and if the Shen becomes overly fixated or stuck in these palaces, this will have to be financed by the body's resources of qi and blood. Any sense of incompletion at each of these domains disturbs the spirit and can injure the Heart on many levels including the physical. In this manner the 9 Heart Palaces are referred to as the 9 Heart Pains. Our ability to be at peace with all these palaces and to let go of any regrets that we have related to these palaces can set our spirit free. The energy spent on these palaces becomes habitual, more like a neurosis or an obsession, or even an addiction of the mind.

Entanglement of the Spirit: the Palaces

4	9	2
3	Home/Heart	7
8	1	6

Figure 2.20: Magic Square as the Forces that Pull Us Off Our Center

The 1st Heart Palace is Health. How much energy and attention is being consumed by health problems, dealing with and worrying about illness? How often does your mind return to a symptom or pain or potential problem with your health? How much of our energy is consumed by the illness of a loved one? While this is natural and may be appropriate, this is energy that is being consumed out of the moment and is not available for use.

The 2nd Heart Palace is Finance. Here we may have abundance issues and "lack" consciousness. Are we able to manifest what we need to feel abundant, to feel financially supported? Are we able to feel abundant regardless of what manifests? Intensely focusing on making money, wishing we had more money, daydreaming about having money, any stress about money is more energy being used out of the moment. Fears and inadequacies that we have regarding finances tax the Heart. It is all about how we are in relation to each Palace.

The 3rd Heart Palace is Prosperity. Here we can develop compassion burn-out as we attempt to allocate our resources for the good of others. How much is enough, how much is too much? Why do people want this or that from me? How do we choose the way we assist or who we assist? Do we give the people a fish? Do we teach the people how to fish? There is no answer outside of oneself as to the solution.

The 4th Palace is about Relationships. Do we have regrets towards the way our relationships are? Do we hold grudges and resentment? Can we forgive others and forgive our self to others? Can we create relationships built out of respect, self-love, authenticity, and even devotion?

The 5th Palace is Parenting/Creativity. This is the honoring of the family name, the extension of our Yuan Q, our Jing into the world. Here we have the interesting combination of creativity and pro-creation. Both of these are the concept of creating more of our self, more of our Yuan Qi and extending it into the world. Parenting generally creates a situation where our Yuan Qi is going to support another being, perhaps several. Are we in full alignment with that or is a part of our creativity feeling stifled? With the creation of children and family we have the responsibility of maintaining the "family name" within the social feedback loop of society. Are we OK with the job we are doing?

The 6th Palace is the World or Adventure/Travel. Here we have the wonders of the world, the buffet that life has to offer. Sometimes this is the "bucket list." If we don't cross those things off the bucket list will we have regrets, or can we let it go? Is it an endless list and we cannot be satisfied regardless? Have we been too afraid to accomplish any of the wonders we wanted to as children, when we could still remember?

The 7th Palace is Career/Knowledge. Here is where we make our mark in the world, outside the home. Has our profession served us well? Has it served others? Have we achieved any sense of mastery or accomplishment in the domains of our passion? Have we lost our identity to our profession and forgotten who we are beyond the social titles and the role? Did we satisfy our curiosity regarding the banquet of things we can know deeply, the things we wanted to know deeply at some point? And, if not, can we let it go?

The 8th Palace is the Wisdom of being comfortable with yourself. Have we developed our virtue of understanding? Did we pay enough attention to understand the essence of life's experiences, mystery, wonder and manifestation? Did the suffering it took to refine our jewel leave us too wounded to feel joy and wonder? Did we recover from failures and setbacks, which the Tao says are so much more beneficial than successes? Did we arrive at the place where we know that everything happened the way it had to happen for us to be here now with the understanding that we have? Were we able to let go and accept our self?

The 9th Palace is our Home. This is peace in the Heart. The calm lake in the eye of the storm. The water of the soul, the Ling, reflecting the light of the spirit, the Shen. We have learned to let go. We have come to terms with regret. We have released the configuration of the conditioned protective mechanisms of the Pericardium and opened our eyes to a new way of seeing, of being. We have learned to listen with our Heart. We are ready to return home, because we are already home. Would we be at peace if we were to die right now, or would responsibilities weigh on our spirit?

Reincarnation Insurance-
Regrets, Nostalgia and Unfinished Business

Any regrets or unfinished business will keep us from completion in our life. We will be clinging to life instead of allowing life to be lived through us. If you want to know what it's like to die, take a look at how you live right now. The way you relate to life is the way that you will relate to death. However, there is a component of grace that may come to us before the great transition and allow us to work through our regrets before we die. This is the story of our Heart, our blood. This is recorded in the 8x Vessels, namely the Yin Wei or Yin Linking Vessel. This is the movie of our life, played out before our eyes by the Hun on the Akashic Record Player.

As we see the movie, we will learn why it all happened the way it had to happen, but we may be disappointed in the choices that we made and the "debts" that we have to the Heart Palaces, or we may have deep compassion for having done the best we could with the understanding that we had. Generally, we wish we lived with less fear and more love, and tasted life more deeply and loved others even more. If we are nostalgic, the "wings of desire" will bring us back again and again. If we are compassionate, we may choose what are known as the Bodhisattva vows that will bring us back again and again until everyone has reached enlightenment.

The Heart is the center of the magic square and the Heart Pains are the way we deal with being incarnate, the way we deal with impermanence and change. If we choose to function from resistance, we are coming from the stress response, the ego, and are subject to the laws of entropy, disease, decay and aging and the random chance of fate. If we function from the Heart with emptiness and peace, we naturally invite the spirit, the Heavenly aspects, the Higher Self to intervene and allow us to know our purpose. We can move towards our Destiny, in the meandering miraculous mystery that is the Tao.

∾

Awakening to Our Self

❧

Presence and the Ever-Expanding Moment

We can point to the solution of this situation called Life. The solution, if there is indeed a problem, is to be present. The more of one's awareness, of one's attention that is available, the deeper we can experience the Now. There is no other time, it is always Now. It's just that we may sleep through it if our awareness is on the past or future. Everything is possible in the Now. It is continually a clean slate. The more energy that we present with in the moment, the more we realize that eternity is at the heart of the now, the Eternal Now. The spirit can only exist in the now. It is polarized by concepts of past and future, and then we must function from the Pericardium, from our conditioned self, our acquired mind, and then we are on our own, missing out on the support and magic that spirit infuses into life.

Differentiation Evolves from Unity

"Individuality is only possible if it unfolds from wholeness." - David Bohm

From here we can see that everything has mind, that the vibrational matrix of the universe has a component of Shen, of mind. Each flower, each being, each celestial object, each individual, each animal and the collectives of each have a mind. Each thing in creation also has an Essence, has Jing. Everything that is, is anchored in form, in essence. This form naturally attracts a corresponding aspect of mind, of Shen. This is the energy body, the vibration, the frequency. As we come to know our self and differentiate our self, we can come to know the world and differentiate the essence and spirit of each thing, the living Shen.

It is through our own authenticity, our own willingness to embody our natural vibration that we can resonate with all things. When we can be in this space we are simultaneously individual and collective. In this Mind-field, we can begin to communicate through resonance, to harmonize. This is the energy of the solution consciousness. If we cannot access this expanded level of consciousness, all our memories and resources are in suspension in our matrix and unavailable to be uploaded and shared with the collective. They will not be uploaded by the Hun until death. We will be unaware of this ecology of mind, this unified field of diversified consciousness, this mandala of consciousness.

Coherence- the Foundation for Entrainment

Peace in the Heart allows for coherence in the field of the Heart which then causes the brain to entrain with this field, a pattern that, once trained into the marrow, affects the DNA. Peace in the Heart results through self-acceptance and acceptance of the world, of life as it is. Even though we can try to improve it and it may be important that we do, there may be very little we can do aside from bring in more love. We can let our Shen reside in the Heart, giving a window to the Big Shen on this sensational ride through the material world. This is the non-dual heart energy of empathy and compassion, where we are paradoxically one organism, re-learning and un-forgetting how to let ourselves be breathed. Polarized mechanisms such as judgment and all the myriad protective instincts on all levels can be free to protect us from danger but do not have to trigger reflexive responses unless split-second response is needed. This frees the diverted Wei Qi from the blood and emotional response(Ying Qi) and from the evolutionary/creative response(Yuan Qi).

The Shen and Jing have gifts to share with us, evolutionary traits in our marrow that may or may not have been awakened or were only partially awakened in the bloodline we have been born into. These gifts of the spirit, empowered by the liberated energy from no longer desperately financing these habituated patterns regarding our relationship to survival and Wei Qi, now can be expressed, be voiced by the Upper Dan Tian, the Sea of Marrow, the Seat of the Brain, the creativity and authenticity of the Throat Chakra.

We can open the eyes of the teacher within, the knowing that you are your best teacher once you trust and allow yourself to be. This is the energy of the 6th Chakra and the transpersonal Crown Chakra. These gifts can now be anchored and expressed through the Heart as a gift to humanity, when they are balanced by the Kidneys and the lower earthly chakras of our Root. The organism has learned to let its vitality hum, to let its engine run without the compulsive need to constantly act out. We have learned to let the motor of our Wei Qi idle, with the spirit seated in our Heart, windows wide open to the world, living in the ever-expanding moment surrounded by the world of constantly changing phenomena.

☙❧

Part 3

The Terrain of Our Journey:
The Meridian Matrix and the Curious Organs

The Meridian Matrix:
Circuitry of the 5 Channel System

৵৩৯

This section provides a brief and dense snapshot of the 5 Channel Systems of acupuncture. These channels are for lifelong study and embody the elegant complexity of nature the moment that we try to understand her myriad details. These channels are maps to metabolic function and psycho-social function of species evolution, personal ancestral lineage, and spiritual growth. They are the spirit's journey of embodiment, the crafting of our soul. Each section could be a textbook in and of itself and the cross-referencing of each section with modern science and bio-medicine would generate at least another textbook for each section. They are part of the infinite inquiry into human understanding.

Each channel system can be directly experienced by the individual. The acupuncture channels are part of the alchemical practices and deeper knowledge and better technique only serve to deepen the mystery. The goal is not to remove the mystery. The wisdom of the alchemical practices is how to *relate* to the mystery. In the meantime, through our alchemical inquiry we may learn a lot of facts and techniques that can be duplicated. Science is a by-product of the art of alchemy.

"The job of the artist is always to deepen the mystery." - Francis Bacon

This chapter has a lot of information in a short amount of space. It is not expected that the reader be able to absorb this information easily without a background in Chinese Medicine. Chinese Medicine is meant to be experienced and its understanding comes from reflection and application over time.

In order to further appreciate the perspective of the 8 Extraordinary Vessels, we must give them their context within the larger meridian matrix. The meridian matrix contains distribution and communication circuitry that has been broken down in amazing detail. There are meridians and networks to connect anything and everything in the body, and, of course, there has to be. Meridians chart the principle pathways for distribution of everything from nutrients, blood, body fluids, qi, yin, yang and the mechanisms of pathology and distribution of pathogenic factors, such as wind, damp, heat, cold, stasis, IPF's(Internal Pathogenic Factors) and EPF's(External Pathogenic Factors), deficiencies and excesses. These maps have powerful philosophy deeply and elegantly intertwined within every detail and have proven effective over 1,000's of years and practitioners of this medicine span the entire globe.

This deeper understanding of the wisdom of ancient medicine can easily and happily absorb and contextualize the knowledge of western medicine, because there is only Medicine. Medicine is a tree back to the dawn of

Humanity, and we just keep adding branches. Branches and fruits are good. Problems start when a branch is naive enough to call itself the tree. When this is believed by the people, this is a warning sign of a culture deeply out of touch with its roots. When the fruits are bloated with their own arrogance and the nourishment of the roots is forsaken, there is danger. Our modern medical system is in just such a perilous state. This is why we are beginning to re-discover our roots: the pre-natal energy system.

The Meridian Matrix essentially connects everything in the body and distributes between the three levels of qi in the body: Wei Qi, Ying Qi, and Yuan Qi. These three levels of the body have 5 channel systems connecting them(not counting the Cutaneous Regions as a separate channel system). To better illustrate these levels, let's look at this diagram:

Channel System	Wei Level	Ying Level	Yuan Level
Sinew Channels	X		
Luo Vessels		X	
Primary Channels	X	X	X
Divergent Channels	X		X
8 Extraordinary Vessels			X

Figure 3.1: 5 Channel System and 3 Levels

This is an essential reference for the organization of the body in terms of the meridian matrix. Essentially, the Sinew Channels circulate Wei Qi. The Luo Vessel's are a reservoir for Wei Qi at the Ying level, in the Blood. The Primary Meridians circulate between all the levels, but their ability to access the Marrow is up for debate. The Divergent Meridians connect the Wei Level to the Yuan Qi Level, and the 8 Extraordinary Meridians are the reservoirs of Yuan Qi.

The following chart further delineates the way that the 5 Channel Systems circulate between the various layers of the body from the most superficial level of the skin to the deepest level of the marrow.

Layer	Sinew Channels	Luo Vessels	Primary Channels	Divergent Channels	8x Vessels
Skin	X		X	X	
Sinew	X		X	X	
Blood		X	X		
Flesh			X		
Bone			X	X	X
Marrow					X

Figure 3.2: Layers of the 5 Channel System

The Sinews

Working with the Manifest

The Sinew Channels are the most superficial and the largest group of meridians. They appear to be essentially wider versions of the Primary Channels with a few unique twists and turns here and there. They are the most substantial of the meridians. They are the manifestation of the body. They are our form and our morphology, our shape. They are associated with our survival energy. The Sinews circulate our Wei Qi, our protective, instinctual, reflexive qi. They are associated with peristalsis and immunity in the body. The Wei Qi is meant to stop any pathogens at the exterior, like a fence, to keep them from going deeper into the body where they can do more harm.

The Sinews and the Wei Qi are governed by the Lung's ability to move the Wei Qi and assist in immunity and by the Liver's relationship to the tendons. The Sinews are essentially our fascia, our connective tissue. Wei Qi is warm and is responsible for the warmth necessary for life and as such is a sub-category of Yang Qi which is warm. Wei Qi is responsible for all aspects of inflammation when it is stuck. Wei Qi is meant to circulate through the skin, providing a perimeter, a periphery of energy. The Wei Qi is related to the piezo-electric charge that circulates through the liquid crystal collagen matrix of our connective tissue.

The Channels of Contact and Movement

The Sinew Channels, being the manifest part of our being, are designed for contact. They are our vehicle. This contact takes place through touch and the skin. Contact also takes place through the eyes and the other senses. The Sinews are represented by "ashi points," points associated with wherever it hurts. The Sinews use the local painful points in order to honor a person's suffering, to honor their pain.

The Sinew Channels are also associated with movement. Movement helps us survive. We get impulses from the Earth that activates our Wei Qi and we respond through the movement of our legs. We go where our eyes go. The Wei Qi is activated upon opening the eyes in the morning. The aspect of movement is represented by the Jing-Well points, which are the points by the nailbeds where qi comes into and exits the body. The Sinew Channels, being associated with touch and movement have traditionally been the domain of Bodyworkers and Massage Therapists and of Martial Artists and Movement Artists.

The Sinews represent our movement in the moment and how we move through life. Are we always going forward? Are we standing upright? Are we tilted? Are we hesitant? Do we have the brakes locked on? Can we reach out to the world? Can we bear our own weight? The Sinew Channels do not represent the emotion behind the movement, which would be financed by another meridian system and resource. The Sinews demonstrate that the body never lies and is an open book. The ways in which we hold our body show our resistances. There is always a position, posture, or movement that can help us put our awareness on our patterns.

By bringing our awareness into our movements, we are accessing the autonomic nervous system, the Wei Qi. This is yoga. We learn to have awareness and perhaps control over processes that are usually unconscious in people. In this way, working with the Sinews and posture and movement can be a path to liberation. If we rectify the form, the structure, the exterior, the internal functions will regulate themselves. In Chinese Medicine this is saying that if we have strong Wei Qi on the exterior, the body will be able to have strong immunity to anything from the outside and will be strong enough to purge anything from the inside. As the Wei Qi goes internal when we sleep, once we have liberated its flow, the body can accomplish deep healing while we sleep.

The Sinews organize our charge in relationship to gravity and pressure. It is this charge of the Wei Qi that allows us to make contact with the world. This charge also allows us to connect with the universal flow as can be seen in the smooth flow of natural movement. The Wei Qi also protects us from the world. The Wei Qi is our reflexes and we can always become more natural and more efficient. This is training the Wei Qi. Functioning exclusively from the Wei Qi is overly simplistic. It does not account for emotions, social interactions, purpose or spiritual curriculum. It is the pure existential awareness of the material form.

When working with Wei Qi we have to relax our conscious awareness and engage our peripheral awareness. If we focus too directly on any one thing we will fix our consciousness and lose track of the overall flow of movement and events. This is often done through relaxing the eyes, the gaze, to enter into proprioceptive awareness, the cellular awareness of the muscles. This is great training for recognizing the difference between particle consciousness and wave consciousness. Once we fixate our awareness, we enter particle consciousness. This is important training but it does not tell us about the part of us that is aware of being aware. For that we must look deeper.

The Wei Qi is about survival and self-protection, but it does not acknowledge the vulnerability of being receptive, especially emotional receptivity. For this we have to look at the Ying Qi, the level of nutrition, emotion, and blood. Wei Qi also does not acknowledge the usefulness of things that have no immediate application to survival. This can be clearly seen in how it usually takes military exploration to discover new technologies. Often the usefulness of evolutionary traits are not immediately discernible to the individual or society because they are intended for neither. Evolutionary traits are for the benefit of the species. However, the individual manifesting these traits will be tested for their ability to sustain survival. The challenge here becomes not to merely suppress or repress the traits in order to survive, but to express the traits and survive. These traits tend to be expressed first by artists and such. They are the canaries in the coal mine working through different levels of perception, empathy and consciousness, test-driving and forecasting the directionality of the collective at the level of the Yuan Qi.

The Longitudinal Luo Vessels
Hydraulic Overflow of Our Story

୰ଡ଼ଡ଼

The Longitudinal Luo Vessels are the next buffer against the raw experience of life, of exposure to the external. The Luo Vessels are related directly to our blood and function at the level of the Ying Qi. Our blood houses our emotions and our emotions are tied into social feedback loops that mediate social function. Our blood also records the story of our life, including the shocks and traumas. Essentially, these vessels are created as needed as holding grounds, as reservoirs that can take substances or emotions out of circulation so they can do less harm. The toxic substance whether an emotion, a habit, a substance, or a pathogen such as a virus or bacteria may be stored in the Luo Vessels to be maintained in a state of latency.

This latency may be stored to be dealt with at a later date or it may spill over causing symptoms or it may go deeper into the body causing potential difficulties in different systems of the body. Latency has a priority list with the vital organs being the top priority to protect. As the Luo Vessels are functioning to protect the individual they involve the Wei Qi, the protective qi. In order to hold something inert, the Luo Vessels will hold both the offending agent(IPF or EPF) and a portion of Wei Qi in a state of latency. The blood alone could not protect us for it is the Wei Qi that protects us. This begins the process of compromising the integrity of our Wei Qi as well as beginning the disease process internally. Luo Vessels are visible or palpable in the body either as a varicosity at the capillary level or as a nodule in the body. They tend to follow the longitudinal trajectories that have been mapped out in books.

The Progression from External to Internal

First, let's look at the progression from external to internal. If an EPF makes it past the initial defenses of the Wei Qi circulating through the skin and sinews, the next line of defense is the Luo Vessels. These EPF's are generally thought of in modern terms as viruses, bacteria, fungus, injuries. These are seen more clearly as external causes of disease. The Luo Vessels are also responsible for maintaining internally driven disease processes caused by emotions, diet, and lifestyle. Diet creates excesses, especially with habits or addictions. Anything that is ingested in amounts or frequencies that are beyond the body's processing ability may be held in a Luo Vessel. Often if there is an emotion that the body is trying to maintain in latency it will use a physical commodity to store with it as well. In this way a virus that occurred at a highly charged moment in time may be stored with the emotion.

The storage of emotion is termed the psycho-social model of the Longitudinal Luo Vessels. The blood is at the level of suppression. Any emotion or impulse that we want or need to suppress is being done at the level of the blood. Suppression involves emotions or memories that we generally could become conscious of if given enough time. We may have forgotten, but it's a memory that we are aware of. Repression can be something that we were totally unconscious of and can also be genetic traits and ancestral issues that we had no idea of because they did not involve events from this lifetime, the story in our blood.

Suppression allows us to function in groups and allows us to maintain order. Suppression allows us to sit still in a classroom for long periods of time or do chores that we do not enjoy. It allows us to show up for work at a specific time, especially when there is something else we would rather be doing or something else we really need to deal with. Suppression is designed to delay our dealing with an emotion. It is a dangerous long-term strategy. Suppression requires resources to finance. We finance this latency with our blood, with our wei qi and over time this causes many potential disease processes.

In essence we are financing the past and this comes at the cost of our ability to be present in the moment. People with the inability to suppress their emotions, impulses, and needs can be very tiresome and unreliable or downright manic, pathological and/or dangerous. This moment-by-moment inability to suppress emotion is generally caused by deeper wounds that make average suppression difficult. The ability to be able to go through your life, to experience the mundane with minimal suppression is a cultivation practice. It requires a great deal of acceptance and requires a developed ability to process emotion.

Our Emotional Buffers

The Luo Vessels function as a buffer that helps us get on with our lives. If the Pericardium is a shock absorber specifically designed to protect the Heart, the Luo Vessels could be seen as guardrails that go all the way around the pathways where our story circulates. Like the Pericardium they will protect us from the shocks and traumas of our life. They finance our body armoring. However, life is for living. We have a curriculum and a story to fulfill. If we try to stop the flow of the story, we are trying to stop the flow of our blood and we are trying to stop the flow of life.

This is a danger of spiritual practices, in that they can detract from engagement with life through focus on the immaterial aspects of the Universe. Monasteries and such have traditionally been used to some degree to house those people that are too emotionally stagnant to engage with society. As we are all one organism of Humanity, we are designed to participate socially to some degree.

140

Emotions mediate our social games and the organization of our social structures. They reinforce values, norms, mores, status, rewards and punishments. It is in the best interest of our survival if we can adapt to the current social model that we live in, especially if we cannot find an alternative. In this manner we respond to subtle and not-so-subtle cues from the collective that tell us if we are staying between the lines, if we are following the program. This can take a great degree of energy to finance, especially the more repressed and outmoded the social structure becomes. Nature herself begins to want to change these resistant structures and we can feel this in our bones, in our Yuan Qi, but it is often not the right time to act. Suppression teaches us to wait until we can learn to accept the flow of right timing and learn the art of waiting, of actively observing until the right moment for action.

Relating to our emotions prepares us for more expanded levels of transpersonal communication, for spiritual communication. Our emotions are tied into the deepest challenges that our spirit faces in life. Emotions mediate our relationships to fear and desire. They mediate whether we recoil from the stimuli of life or we expand towards the stimuli of life. Emotions mediate our relationships to pleasure, to boredom, to obsession and compulsion. Healing is coming to a place of responsibility for our responses, including the suppression and expression of our emotions. As we work at this level of consciousness we may begin to see the relationships of our emotions and the emotions of others to the deeper programming of our ancestry and DNA, which is the level of the Yuan Qi.

The Primary Channels
Our Conscious Path of Life

ॐॐ

The Primary Channels are the acupuncture channels that are most pop-
ularly taught and used. The other channels are considered collaterals.
The usage of the other channel systems has gotten out of fashion in the
mainstream teachings of acupuncture. Historically, this streamlining process began 1,000 years ago and reached a quantum leap of homogenization
during the era of communism and the attempt to match Chinese Medicine
to Western Medicine. This homogenization may have facilitated the export
of Chinese Medicine to the West and to the entire world. However, this
homogenization did not honor the millennia of development of 1,000's of
highly skilled traditions. These are what we refer to more as "Classical
Acupuncture." Chinese Medicine is undergoing a renaissance in its world-
wide transmission and it is important that this dissemination includes the
depth of its roots, through history, through the classics, and back to the
spirit of the pre-historic ancients who first developed this medicine from
the collective consciousness.

The Pathways of Our Lives

The Primary Channels are said to communicate to all the levels of Qi in
the body to some degree. Therefore people decided it would be simpler to
focus on this one channel system. The Primary Channels are named after
the Zang-Fu Organs, the vital organs of the body. In the 5 Channel context
the Primary Channels are the level of our conscious awareness. They are at
the level of our interaction with others. They circulate the emotions, with
the implication that our emotions are within our conscious awareness. The
Primary Channels are the pathways of our lives. These are the roadmaps
to the choices we make and to the roads we travel. Even if we master Wei
Qi through Yoga or Kung Fu or we choose to experience the transpersonal
nature of our spiritual and species-level consciousness, as a human we must
reckon with the choices we make and how these choices relate to our interactions with others. We are one organism.

We learn to explore the Primary Channels and post-natal qi with more
awareness through recognizing the nature of the 5 elements. We tend to see
through a lens comprised of one or two dominant elements. We then experience the world through this lens and have our perspective validated. Such
is the conditioning of the post-natal. We can choose to cultivate our awareness to more evenly distribute our essence between different organs. We can
choose to experience the world a little more through a Metal lens if we are
more Wood and vice-versa.

In this way we can shine light into the way the properties of these elements influence our behavior and choices. We can work through the challenging, denser vibrations of these channels and cultivate the virtues of these channels. As we learn to clear these primary channels, we open more windows onto the world. We begin to communicate more clearly with the outside world with less internal distortion. This is the completion of the Zang-Fu. We begin to harmonize ying and wei, internal and external. We begin to liberate our spirit and allow our Heart to guide the choices we make in our life from a place of connectedness, instead of through a distorted window imprinted through the fracturing of our psyche into separation consciousness.

The Divergent Channels

A Detour in Distraction

The Divergent Channels represent the connection between the Wei Qi and the Yuan Qi, from the level of the Sinews to the level of the constitution. Their purpose is to divert pathogenic factors away from the vital organs, because it can be fatal if they reach the organs. Anywhere is a better place to store pathogens than the organs themselves. The Divergent Channels are related to the joints. The larger joints are an area that the body will tend to store pathogens. Any joint or bone hole can be an ideal place for the body to store latency at the bone level. The 8 bone holes of the sacral foramen are a perfect example. Any acupuncture point with the name "liao" in it, which means "hole," is an access point for storing latency at the level of bone.

The body can use bone to maintain latency through the process of calcification. It can cool down the Wei Qi- the inflammation- and also keep a pathogen inert through mineralization. This interferes with our self-actualization process in that we are adding parts that are not innate to us into the Yuan Qi of our bone matrix. This can then become part of our curriculum, our unfinished business. This also gives us clues to the "firing process" referred to in alchemical texts, a process of calcining the mineralizations through heat, thereby purifying the bone. This is something that occurs naturally in the fever process.

Divergence from Our Central Channel

All the Divergent Channel trajectories connect to the Heart, giving us clues as to their nature. If we rectify the Heart, we transend the divergences. The Divergent Channels represent being diverted from our path, from our axis, from our compass. They represent postural distortion and side to side imbalances. They are the connection between the brain- Yuan qi and the holding patterns of the skeleton, the connective tissue- Wei qi. This side-to-side disharmony is related to functioning from left or right hemisphere-dominance and not through the central channel, represented by the corpus callosum in the brain. The self functions through the neutral space of the central channel. This is our channel. If we start to function from polarity, we distort our channel, we lose our anchor. We are no longer connected to our destiny. We have taken a detour in the distractions of life. Destiny cannot be found by going deeper to the left or the right, but by finding our center, our self. This relationship between connective tissue and brain also points to how to change the marrow of the brain. We can change our brain marrow through shining awareness into our patterns of movement.

The Divergent Channels can bring pathogens into the Yuan Qi level which gives them access to the bone, the brain, the marrow and the DNA. Here the Wei Qi can begin attacking itself as is seen in auto-immune disorders. At this level we may pass on the latency to our offspring and/or to a future lifetime. This latency will interfere with our ability to create. The converse is also possible. Pathogens may come out of the Yuan Qi and manifest. This is most likely at the Cycles of 7 & 8. These may be pathogens that we put into latency or repressed. Or they may be latent traits that we inherited from our ancestry or the collective ancestry. As we begin to do more spiritual work, we open up the Pandora's Box of working on archetypal themes in the genetic code. This requires a more expanded level of awareness as it is fully transpersonal.

The Divergent Channels have a strong resonance with the Lymphatic System and lymph glands are often used to hold latency until their filtration properties are filled to capacity. The flow of body fluids such as lymph is deeply tied into the bones. Our bones should be in suspension in the body fluid. To the degree that we have lost this property of our relationship to gravity, our fluid metabolism cannot be optimal. Our hormones are also related to fluid metabolism and to Yuan Qi, so any hormonal difficulties will have a component of divergence. Optimizing our hormonal expression would be a form of coming back to our self, to the central channel.

The Divergent Channels are the process of poison, of anything that does not serve us moving through the body and the various strategies that the body employs to deal with it. The danger of latency in the Divergent Channels is that it goes to the Yuan Qi, to the marrow, to the DNA. Also, anything that is maintained in a state of latency requires resources to maintain. When the resources are gone, we experience a loss of latency. Meanwhile, we are weaker and the pathogen has been festering for years, even decades or lifetimes. The Divergent Channels offer a clue to humanity about how to clean up our genetic code through taking responsibility for the ancestry that we have been given. Evolving higher consciousness on the planet has required a great deal of repression of more primal character traits from lower orders of the animal kingdom. The problem we see is that those who have re-pressed their primal drives the least are often the most powerful. We can heal these wounds and unwind, un-wound our DNA. This allows the coiling double-helix to dilate and for the energy of spirit to come into the central channel and rectify our divergences.

The 8 Extraordinary Vessels
Mystery and Wonder

⋘⋙

The 8 Extraordinary Meridians represent the level of our constitution. This is the level of our Yuan Qi and our Jing-Essence. This is known as the marrow, the level of the Curious Organs and the 8x Vessels. This is the level of pre-natal energy and its conversion into post-natal energy. This is our inheritance, our heredity, our ancestry, our DNA. This is our reproductive energy and drive. This is the genetic template for our morphology. The 8x Vessels are our spiritual curriculum, our blueprint, the architecture of our program. These are our lessons, our story, our destiny and our destinations. The Yuan Qi is the level of our astrology, our heavenly influences. These influences condition our DNA through the constant streaming of quantum data in the form of neutrinos which are generated by the fusion process of stars. This is the larger program of consciousness, the consciousness of stars. We are a combination of morphology/Earth/DNA and astrology/Heaven/neutrino data. This is the interface of Heaven and Earth and it takes place within us, as the Shen-Spirit consuming the Jing-Essence. This process generates the experiences that feed our consciousness, the experiences that feed our soul. These are our lessons and our story.

The Vessels of Evolution

The 8x Vessels are our evolutionary energy. This is where the survival and continuation of the species takes place. Here is where the adaptations occur that protect the species from extinction. We are being invited to participate in our own conscious evolution, to help orient the species to a more sustainable way of living. This is happening through the evolution of consciousness, through changing our brain and our genes, both of which are being shown to demonstrate high degrees of plasticity. When we evolve our consciousness we awaken within a larger consciousness. This is spirituality.

In order to safely participate in this expanded mind we must know our self. This is the process of differentiation. When we choose to ask, "Who am I?" and learn about the self, we are undergoing the differentiation process. This process is both a personal and collective evolutionary process. We begin understanding that helping each other through this process, helping each other achieve our purpose, is the best way to benefit humanity. I envision the 21st century as the era when facilitating the pursuit of Destiny became a top priority. But humanity has to learn how best to flow with the self-organizing aspects of the collective consciousness. Humanity has to learn the right use of will and right timing.

The 8x Vessels record our lives. The marrow is consumed by the moments that impact us to the level of the marrow. The marrow is more available for such imprinting during the major transitions of our life, the cycles of 7 & 8. Our essence is consumed through the process of memory, similar to how computers function. Our Jing-Essence is consumed, combusted by our Spirit-Shen and this generates the experiences that feed the soul. This takes place on one level as the thermodynamics of matter and energy never being created or destroyed, merely transformed to another state. This is the one-way ride of the material world, from dust to dust.

However this law of thermodynamics is predicated on there not being outside energy available from other dimensions. In alchemy, this is exactly the hypothesis we are working with and science is showing that it appears that up to 90% of the matter and energy of the universe is located in other dimensions. Through the Yuan Qi we can learn to access some degree of this energy. This slightly changes the rules of the game and opens the door to outside possibilities for a sustainable energy source that does not decay so readily. Galaxies are shaped this way as is the evolution of humanity. We are the stuff of stars and our Yuan Qi is where this takes place.

The Curious Organs
The Evolutionary Record

ન્યૂજી

In order to provide the context for the 8x vessels we need to look at the components of the Yuan Qi level. These are known as the Curious Organs, curious being the same Chinese radical as extraordinary. These are the organs associated with the 8x Vessels, and their relationships and properties shed light on the bigger picture of Yuan Qi, the species-level medium for consciousness. There is not a great deal of traditional medical literature written about the Curious Organs. Their understanding comes in large part from the spiritual traditions who understood the relationship between the driving evolutionary force of sexuality and its relationship to the evolution of the brain and consciousness through the kundalini energy of the spine.

The 6 Curious Organs are the Bones, the Brain, the Marrow, the Uterus, the Vessels(either the Blood Vessels or the 8x Vessels) and the Gall Bladder (GB). These constitute the terrain of the Yuan Qi, the pre-natal qi. The Gall Bladder stands out as the only Zang-Fu Organ that is also a Curious Organ. Essentially, the Curious Organs are the mediators of human evolution. The Zang-Fu organs don't change much from species to species and certainly not from stone-age human to modern human. What does change are the Curious Organs, the bone structure, the brain structure, and what we now have the technology to observe, the genes.

The Curious Organs record the experiences of the individual and mediate the flow of creative energy through the individual. A person ages in direct proportion to their efficiency of data processing and memory storage. Can you still learn something new? Can you still learn how to see something differently, through new eyes? Can you still change? Are you still able to participate in the shaping of the marrow, of the plasticity of the Yuan Qi. This will also be affected by the constitution and the overall Jing-Essence endowment or inheritance of the individual.

The Curious Organs
The Uterus
The Brain
The Marrow
The Bones
The Vessels
The Gall Bladder

Figure 3.3: Curious Organs

Creativity and the Yuan Qi

As the level of the survival of the species, the Jing-Essence is directly involved in our creativity, both the literal ability to pro-create and the creativity to spur on evolution through trial and error and mutation. Creativity is the ability to disseminate Yuan Qi-Source Qi, to create more of our self in the world, both for its own sake and ultimately as the greatest gift we can give to humanity: the gift of our self. To the degree that we are in conflict and self-judgment, through our self-imposed morality, likely identified with through social conditioning, is the degree that our innate creative energy will be dampened or stifled. We may recruit Wei Qi to protect our social personality from our true self and Original Nature, from our instincts, drives and gifts.

To the degree that we are not taking responsibility for our lessons, for our incarnation, for our vehicle, is the degree that these unprocessed lessons will be directed to the Belt Channel to be passed on to the next generation who will have another opportunity to work on them. Or these un-transcended lessons may be written into the Marrow Record for another incarnation to work on, which is essentially the same idea: someone is going to do this work and that someone may very well be us so we might as well get started now. In the meantime this dampening or armoring of our vitality can keep us from our full creative and co-creative potential, from our full capacity.

The Curious Organs also maintain our morphology: our form, our structure, our posture, our gait, our stance. The seed of our geometry, our form, is mediated through the morphic resonance of our genetics with the morphogenetic field plus the post-natal experiences and choices that make us who we are. Much of this character development and brain and bone modeling and remodeling is from our genetic tendencies, the "mirroring" of adults around us, and by the effects on the post-natal qi of trauma, body armoring and social conditioning that we must adapt to for self-preservation. Through this process the collective organism of humanity test drives the evolution of traits for the future of the species and mediates species-threatening contaminants that reach the Yuan Qi, evolving lesser diseases for ones that threaten the continuation of the human race. Spiritual evolution is the willingness to be aware and present for the process of the unfolding of life. We can be willing to be aware, to learn and love and grow in the face of great pressure. To learn how to love our self so that we may love others.

Bones

The Crystal Records

᪑᪐

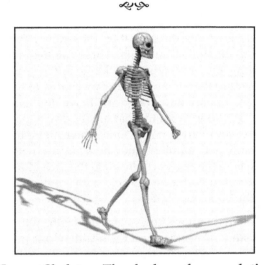

Figure 3.4: Human Skeleton. The shadow of our evolutionary record.

The Bones are the first Curious Organ we will discuss. The Bones hold the record of our earthly existence, the wear and tear, trauma, and habituated tensions that shape the bones through the pressure exerted by the connective tissue. The bones are the crystal caverns, the quartz record keeper, the emissary of the mineral kingdom, interested in evolving, being "humbled and tumbled" and polished and flawed. Through the constant pressure of gravity, movement, and breath, the bones conduct piezo-electricity, the electrical charge of the human body, in conjunction with the liquid crystal collagen matrix of the connective tissue. This allows a network of self-regulating information to be instantly distributed everywhere in the body regarding cellular shape, arrangement and integrity and the overall shape and integrity of the entire body regarding its spatial relationship to its own center. Our posture is the key to our potential to carry a charge, a charge held in the sacral chakra by the urinary bladder and conducted through the perimeter of the skin. This charge generates magnetism, creating a container for our plasmic body, the etheric part of our energy field.

The bones allow leverage and movement. They allow us to stand, to stand our ground and to stand up for our self, to our self, and to the world. They mediate the amplification of Wei Qi, allowing us more and more efficiency at survival the more charge we can hold. They are constantly molded through bone remodeling, to subtly change the quality of vibration they emanate, to amplify it to the collective or to dampen it from reaching the collective. An ecstatically charged being becomes an oscillator that is a catalyst for change, for evolution, and can transmit aurically the messages from their Yuan Qi regarding survival, mutation, creativity, novel traits, etc. In this way the Yuan Qi can work out the directionality of the species. As Chinese Medicine repeatedly warns, stasis, or stagnation creates symptoms, creates karma. The apparent solution would be to learn how to engender states that are not stagnant, or static, states that are literally ec-static. Vibrating. This is the nature of Yuan Qi.

The Bones are divided into three cavities, the Cranial, the Thoracic, and the Pelvic, related to the three Dan Tians. These cavities create resonance chambers for holding and organizing the charge of the vessel. Often we learn to create a posture that organizes the raw charge of life in such a way that we no longer experience any charge at all. We do this through "armoring" or resistance. We adopt a stance that breaks down the conductivity of piezo-electric charge and Earth energy somewhere along the chain. This energy will constantly get jammed somewhere and we will absorb it, generally in the joints, where the body will insulate the area of impact and dampen the conductivity through buffering the area with connective tissue which will cause changes to the bone over time.

The Bones are related to the Kidneys and the teeth. Our bone structure, especially our jaw and our teeth reflect the health of our Jing. Society often worships at the altar of good bone structure, adoring its specimens as models, movie stars, athletes, and sex symbols. The potential charge of charisma that emanates from some people and is looked upon as a sign of character often causes the manipulation we see in any arena of power, such as government or religion.

The bones are held together by the Sinews, by the muscles, fascia, tendons, and ligaments. The Sinews are related mainly to the movement of the body and the conduction of Wei Qi. The Divergent Channels are more related to the bone structure and posture. There is another grouping of Sinews referred to as the Ancestral Sinews which are related to the organization of Yuan Qi. The Ancestral Sinews are related to the muscles that govern our structure and it's relationship to our reproductive/creative capacity.

The Bones Record the Form

The Bones hold a record of the forms that have come before us and much of the latent energy of the animal kingdom that is dormant there. There is our tail, our tailbone where the kundalini energy lies to be awakened. There is our sacred bone, our sacrum, which communicates to the tribe the lead energy. There is our xyphoid process, the tailbone of our sternum, of our chest, protecting the solar plexus. There are the ribs, our gills out of water, learning to be pressurized as we were in utero, as we begin to swim in air, awakening

152

the pre-natal energy body in the post-natal world. There is the scapula, our wings, learning to fly with our feet on the ground as we spread the wings of our heart and survive at the same time. And there is our spine and skull, housing the Central Nervous System and the marrow since the first verte-brates evolved.

Evolution is recapitulated through us, as we can easily see in embryological development. We also have an extension of the phenomena of recapitulation, where previous echoes of form are "embedded" in the current form, kind of like building a pyramid over the previous one. This embedding process takes place largely in the relationship between the connective tissue, the brain and the DNA. It is hidden, part of what is called the implicate order, the internal order. As opposed to the more obvious and hypnotic aspect of the world, the explicate order.

Through cooperation of intent, posture, and breath we can awaken latent configurations that carry much potential power in the directness of their relationship to the field. Some examples of evolutionary embedding are mentioned by Wilhelm Reich, such as the single-celled amoeba, the segmental earthworm, and the jellyfish. Who knows how much more of our dormant energy potential is being resourced in the embedded connective tissue geometries? We will likely find out in that we do not merely evolve to higher states, we evolve to more expanded states. This means that for every improvement in the coherence of the configuration of our self we will expe-rience an equal and opposite exploration into the evolutionary tide pools of the genetic-connective tissue matrix.

The Brain

The Pure Potential of Plasticity

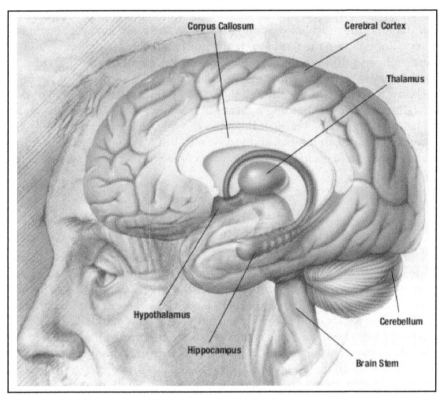

Figure 3.5: The Brain

The Brain is a quickly evolving component of our Yuan Qi. The brain is referred to as the Seat of Marrow. If we change the marrow, we change ourselves and the whole world responds to that change. We can wash our marrow, we can wash our brain to learn to see the world anew and return to innocence. The brain connects to the world via the sensory orifices, how we take in the world. The brain has neural plasticity and can change, adapt and evolve. The brain records through neural phase-locking all our experiences until its memory is full and it decays. The synaptical patterning of the brain is trained through habituation and we become hypnotized into identifying with our socialized personality. The personality tunes out, mutes, or dampens, some of its raw sense data in order to function socially and to the degree that it does this, its sensory windows can only give and receive partial data.

We no longer communicate with nature and it no longer communicates with us. The receptor sites in our sensory perception field are full. This is the divergent process.

The coherence of the electrical patterns of the brain are entrained from the much stronger electromagnetic field of the heart.The brains of others are entrained to the electromagnetic fields of our heart and vice-versa. The brain keeps the marrow record of all the choices we have made so that we can continue to learn from these experiences and make better choices in the future. In this way it has resonance with the Gall Bladder and we see the GB Meridian has the most points along the scalp. The brain tends to be hemispheric dominant in the world of duality and the cultivation of more and more pathways through the corpus callosum, the membrane that divides the two hemispheres, anchors the non-dual space that allows spirit to enter the body. This takes place through the Baihui point, Du 20 at the top of the head, the Crown. The holding patterns of the connective tissue of the body are habituated into the brain. If the brain can release its holding pattern, the connective tissue can release, and vice-versa. But for true brain change, true marrow change, to occur the change must come with a change in awareness.

The 3 Divisions of the Brain

Our brain is divided into three sections: upper, mid and low brain. These relate to the 3 Dan Tians and the 3 External Qi Fields respectively. The Lower Brain, sometimes referred to as the reptilian brain and the structures of the Limbic system, is related to Survival, to the Wei Qi. This area of the brain is pre-linguistic and is our power source, our access point to the Earth energy and the Lower Dan Tian. This is the area of the freezing of the Wei Qi for protection, the recording of trauma into the marrow, the brain. As such it becomes constitutional. This area is also the record of the species-level, and the embedded aspects of previous species and their relationship to fear and survival.

It is difficult, if not impossible, to have enough available energy for spiritual cultivation without rectifying this level, i.e. healing our relationship to the Earth. Wei Qi patterns that are not in alignment with the greater good will sabotage our growth through their inherent selfishness, not allowing the collective organism to trust the individual, due to the individual's fear-based operating system. Working with the Lower Brain is where we develop our character. It is also where people develop power and Will, both of which are seductive in their ability to manipulate others. This area of the brain is inherently amoral, which has created lots of colorful and questionable approaches to working with this "shadow" energy.

The Mid-brain is associated with Ying Qi and interaction. This is our conscious self and our social identity. It is sometimes referred to as our Mammalian Brain. This is where we experience bonding and the ties involved with bonding. The Mid-Brain is where we begin communicating in symbols and language adopted by the tribe. This is where we make our choices regarding our role and our responsibilities. We are all learning and as we judge our perceived failures along the way we undermine our ability to forgive our self, and be liberated within the collective organism. We become locked into our own self-imposed morality and sense of duty. These are the challenges of the Mid-Brain, the Middle Dan Tian and the Heart. Rectification of the Heart through forgiveness allows us to be healed.

The Upper-Brain is associated with the Shen and Differentiation. The Upper-Brain includes structures such as the neo-cortex. This is where we ask the questions such as "Who am I?" and "Why am I here?" In order to access this level we must be willing to accept our self. This is the Upper Dan Tian and the energy of Heaven. It is post-linguistic and telepathic. Here we can accept the paradoxes of life and not be limited by our polarized judgments. As we are able to access all three brain levels and their corresponding energy centers we can access the conduit of energy between Heaven and Earth. This has been called flow consciousness.

Scientifically they are able to show that we can enter flow states of consciousness where we have strong communication between these brain areas. This would parallel strong flow through the 3 Dan Tians. These flow states are generally defined psychologically as a complete immersion in an activity. There is an energized focus, and enjoyment in the activity for its own sake. Emotions are positive, energized and aligned with the task at hand. Experiencing depression, frustration, and anxiety is to be barred from flow. The hallmark of flow is a feeling of spontaneous joy while performing a task with a deep focus on nothing but the activity- not even on oneself or one's emotions. This is the flow of spirit and creativity into the world. It is the energy of pure potential and the miraculous possibility of Destiny. It is the energy that drives evolution.

It is our conditioned rigidity, conditioned by our own experience, reinforced and validated by our experiences, that keeps us from experiencing the transcendent beauty of the pre-natal energy. It is the experience of having been let down, criticized, or having failed and suffered the consequences of failure. This is the sacrificing of our dreams at the altar of adulthood. It is natural. This is the pruning of the neural potential of the mind until it reaches a place where it can be pruned no more, and we crystallize into who we think we are, a very natural process. We completely identify with our post-natal self and the pre-natal self becomes the whisper of a bygone dream, perhaps from our childhood. Somewhere in the pure potential of the plasticity of the neural webbing of the brain lies a return to innocence, a return to the pre-natal within an experienced vessel. A vessel that trusts that even if it washes its brain marrow clean of acquired information it would still have the wisdom to be itself

అఎఎ

The Marrow

Ancient Record Keeper

∽ঔৎ৽

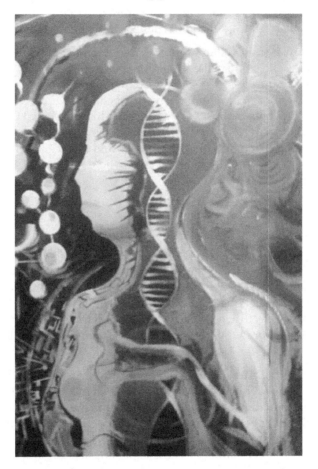

Figure 3.6: DNA/Marrow - *(Photo of a color painting by Robert Kromer)*

The Marrow is an extension of the brain and vice-versa. The marrow is our Jing-Essence. As it decays or dries up, we age and die. The 8x Vessels are directly related to how the life process consumes our Jing-Essence. The primal yang energy of the body is rooted in the Du-the Governing Vessel. The primal yin of the body is rooted in the Ren- Conception Vessel. Over time this deep essence is consumed through memory and experience in the Yin Wei and Yang Wei Vessels and is no longer able to accessed in the present moment, the Now, by the Yin Qiao and Yang Qiao Vessels. The Belt Channel provides a container for this process.

The blood is produced in the bone by the bone marrow. The post-natal commodity of blood is always transcripted from the Yuan Qi or Jing. To the degree that we are creatures of habit on many levels is the degree that this transcription rarely gets altered. If we need to alter our body's self-replication and growth patterns we need to change at a fundamental level, we need to change the story in our blood and we need to change our relationship to our genetics, to our ancestry. To change our patterns we must have a shift in awareness. This is the changing of the brain marrow, a change of belief or perspective which relates directly to changes in the bone marrow.

Bone Marrow is involved in immunity and the lymphatic system via the production of white blood cells. This is the production of Wei Qi-the Protective Qi of the Immune System from the Yuan Qi level of our bone marrow. This expression occurs through the Divergent channels that link Wei Qi and Yuan Qi, that link bone marrow to immunity. This is the level that we can affect our relationship to the ancestor field, thereby changing our marrow. We can let go of the decay of the genetic code and transcend the unfinished business of our ancestry. This is at the level where our Wei Qi may begin attacking itself, resulting in auto-immune processes.

The Marrow is Our DNA

The marrow includes our DNA. It is our heredity. The relationships that Chinese Medicine illustrates regarding the marrow and brain/Yuan Qi and Wei Qi/Connective Tissue point to some amazing possibilities for humanity to participate in the healing of its bloodlines. The 1st step is always acceptance. Humanity has to accept that it has a problem, perhaps a dangerous addiction to the ignorance of its true nature. It then has to be willing to change and grow.

Flow through the Three Dan Tians and the three levels of the Brain can be seen to be in direct relationship to the metabolism of energy in the DNA. The intercalation of the double-helix of DNA can be dilated to accommodate a larger bandwidth of energy flow. This can be demonstrated through monitoring the metabolism of certain exogenous(external) chemicals such as those found in the entheogen families. These exogenous chemicals are also formed endogenously(internally). We are wired for evolution and can learn to access this internal pharmacy.

This is the kundalini flow through the spine, the caduceus, the nucleus, rising upwards into the opening of the 3rd Eye and the Crown. We can interact with this on an experiential level through our 3 Dan Tians with yoga, qigong, shamanic practices, etc. The goal is to be in a state of sustainable flow with enough integrity of structure and character to handle the increased charge. Understanding the relationship between this state of flow in the Dan Tians, the brain and the genome is the key to understanding health and spirituality. This energy flow is the direct experience of the Tao, of the Field, and its bandwidth can be modulated through meditative exercise and optimized by finding our purpose, the activity that we can channel the most energy into without resistance.

As we have said before, our connection to Heaven and Earth is a macrocosm of the telomeres at the ends of the DNA strands. As we lose integrity and function in our connections to these poles, we set the stage for "sloppy" transcription at the genetic level causing aging and disease. Humanity is at a crisis point, a crisis in our relationship to the planet Earth and a crisis in our faith in relation to Heaven. As a result we are suffering a collective case of corruption of transcription at the genetic level. In short, our Yuan Qi is decaying through a complete lack of awareness that we even have a pre-natal energy body.

The Vessels

Communication between the Morphogenetic Field and the Manifest

8x Vessels and Blood Vessels

Historically, there is some debate as to whether these vessels are the blood vessels or the 8x Vessels. As a promoter of the fertile synergy of synthesis, we are happy to accept both concepts. If these vessels are taken to be the 8x Vessels, this makes perfect sense, as these are the vessels, the reservoirs, the canals, the channels that mediate the flow of Jing and Yuan Qi through the pre-natal energy of the Curious Organs. They are the story of the Shen experiencing the Jing, the mystery of how the insubstantial and the substantial interpenetrate. They allow us to flow back and forth to and from the primordial sea, at birth and death and every moment of creation along the way. The 8x vessels will be described in more detail in the following chapter.

If the vessels are taken to mean the blood vessels, this is slightly less elegant as blood is such a post-natal commodity in Chinese Medicine. But that could be their point, that the blood provides the link between the pre-natal and the post-natal. The Chong Vessel is our primal blueprint and it is called the Sea of Blood. The bone marrow produces the blood, constantly replicating the genetic information of the Yuan Qi into the blood. In this way the pre-natal dynamics are always providing the limits of experience, as we use blood to experience life and this blood is always defined by our blue-print, our marrow, our genes. It is a feedback loop in that our blood also in-forms our DNA, and any un-transcended experiences in the blood, any parts of our story that are disjointed or contain extreme attachment will eventually be written into the marrow record and written back into the blood and so on and so forth. This is the potential for the record of our story to become a broken record, a glitch that keeps writing itself into our code.

The Gall Bladder

The Great Mediator

࠾ঙ৯

The Gall Bladder is the only organ that is a Curious Organ(pre-natal) and a Zang-Fu Organ (post-natal). As such it is in familiar territory for the GB of being half this/half that, half internal/half external, involved in the either-or process of decision-making. Decision-making is a property the GB shares with the Du Vessel and the Brain. Life is an ongoing river branching out with each decision. Some lead back home, some lead further away from home. There are many different roads and our choices and curriculum create the type of journey we will have, gravitating to the strange attractors of our destinations over the rhythms of our life, the cycles of 7 & 8. The brain & marrow serve as a record of our experience, so that we can learn from these experiences how to improve our decision-making process for the future. This is accomplished in large part through the GB meridian which is responsible for side-to-side motion that allows us to go around obstructions.

This meridian also zigzags all over the head as a protective mechanism, as a ventilator in case of over-heating the brain. The record of the brain is kept in the GB meridian and the un-transcended experiences accrued over a lifetime will be transmitted from one Curious Organ to another, from the GB of the previous incarnation to the Uterus that shapes our next incarnation. The GB is the wood element, associated with creation, preparing us for our next birth or re-birth. Re-birth is the return to innocence, the transcendence of the marrow record, of our karma, of our lessons. More points are used from the GB channel than any other channel in conveying the 8x Vessel trajectories. The GB is also the Zang-Fu Organ most associated with latency, as bile can keep highly volatile/toxic things inert. Latency, as we have seen, will eventually affect the Yuan Qi level and the GB is a valve between the pre-natal and post-natal.

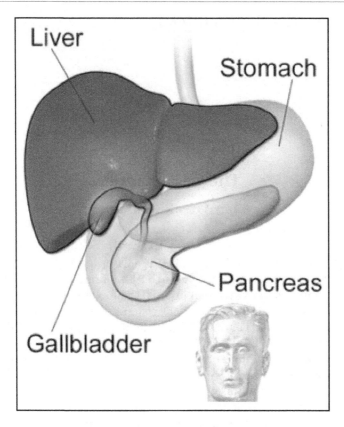

Figure 3.8: The Gall Bladder with Image of Head
(GB Meridian is the Ventilator and Record Keeper for the Brain).

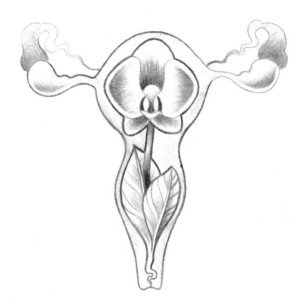

The Uterus
Transcendental Womb

∾

The Uterus is called the Bao. For practical purposes the Bao is said to represent either the male or female genitalia. It is through sexual creation that all Earthly life appears. All creation is the result of the copulation of Heaven and Earth. The reproductive organs carry the hereditary information, the marrow record for the next incarnation, dictating its morphology and its lessons, its Po. Un-transcended information will be shunted towards the genitalia via a vessel known as the Bao Vessel, which is part of the extended Belt channel mechanisms. This loads the Lower Burner, the reproductive organs with the information to be passed on to the next generation to work on. This is the way of evolution. We pass on the Jing-Essence of our ancestry through reproduction. This attracts spiritual energy that has an affinity with the lessons of the Jing, the body being created.

Ancestral Sinews

The body uses the Ancestral Sinews- its structure, its bones and sinews- to bring the energy of any lessons that the Heart is in judgment of, towards the genitalia through the process of retracting inward, or collapsing inward, returning to the fetal position. This will affect our creativity as well as our relationship to sexuality. It will affect our ability to create more of our self in

167

the world. The Ancestral Sinews govern our posture in relation to creativity and procreativity. They also hold the record and potential of our ability to articulate the embedded hydrostatic skeleton, of which sexual arousal is an aspect of. Liberation of the pre-natal energy system involves liberation of our creative energy, our sexual energy, which involves the liberation of our Ancestral Sinews.

The Ancestral Sinews are the structural muscles known as "Wu Shu"- the 5 Pivots. These are the muscles that maintain posture through mediating the relationship between the 3 bony cavities and our spinal curvature. These are often said to be the Psoas, the Diaphragm, the SCM's(Sterno-Cleido-Mastoid), the Paraspinals and the Rectus Abdominis. The psoas is directly related to our genitalia and is called "the soil of the soul." This is where we have the fertile compost of our karma to drive our evolution. The diaphragm is called the "spirit muscle." This is the muscle that we can bring awareness to in order to regulate our mind and body via the breath. It is our breathing that can allow us to heal, and to feel. The psoas represents the Kidney and Water energy of the Earth and the diaphragm represents the Heart and Fire Energy of Heaven. The Lungs are like a bellows to circulate the warmth of the Heart. These two muscles connect at the lower back in the area of the Ming Men, our Gate of Destiny. The ability to cultivate our sexual harmony is called the Union of Fire and Water and we learn how to be in right relationship to the underlying energy of all creation that is taking place between Heaven and Earth at every moment: sexual energy.

There are reasons that the pre-natal system emphasizes the Uterus, instead of all genitalia. Obviously, we are incubated in a uterus. The process of bringing life into the world, of bringing a seed to fruition takes place through the female. In working with the pre-natal energy body we are nurturing and growing the seed potential of our self. In alchemical terms, this has been called "creating the immortal fetus," a process that requires us to make space within our self for this gestation. Women, for clear reasons, have always been said to have an advantage when doing the alchemical practices, for the idea of creating space within one self is very foreign to the masculine. Masculine energy is designed for outward expression, outward pollination.

The term "immortal fetus" is a very fitting term. We are cultivating the aspect of our self that was active in utero, in the uterus. It has an etheric umbilical cord that is un-wounded and is directly connected to the organism of Humanity. We are cultivating the part of our self that sustains itself through adjusting its pressurized system to the atmosphere and drawing in subtle energy for nourishment through the same mechanisms as it did in utero. The Tao speaks of softening the bones so they bend and mend like a child. We can release the contrivances of the pruning of the brain and allow the full brain potential of higher organizational patterns as opposed to linear neural ruts. We can cultivate a part of our self beyond the senses and beyond language, a part of our self that listens to the heartbeat of the mother and senses the world through vibration. We can be connected to all that is. This is the flowering of the Chong Vessel, the realization of our self, the achieve-

168

ment of our blueprint. It is how the organism of Humanity awakens: through us awakening to who we were before we were born. How ironic. When we operate from our post-natal consciousness, the organism of Humanity sleeps. When we operate from our pre-natal consciousness, the organism of Humanity awakens.

Part 4

Story of the 8 Extraordinary Vessels:
Pathways of Our Destiny

The 8 Extraordinary Vessels:
Pathways of Our Destiny

The Pathways of Our Destiny and
the Vessels of Our Differentiation

The Unfolding of Our Blueprint

The 8x Vessels are the blueprint and unfolding of our life, of our fate and destiny. This is our curriculum and our story. The 8x Vessels represent the individuation process through which evolution can be experienced beyond mere generational change. It is the sea where genetic traits can be explored and aligned with divine purpose to catalyze the changes, adaptations, or mutations, which will most advance our species, our ancestral lineage and our own spiritual growth, for they are all one in the same. The 8x Vessels are the wilderness, the frontier of the Yuan Qi and the pre-natal qi. The 8x Vessels are the mediators of our direct connection to the source. They are where the Shen, the formless, explores the Jing, the form. This takes place on many levels. It occurs at the sub-atomic level within each cell. It occurs within the pre-natal architecture of the 8x Vessels. It occurs through the Curious Organs of the bones, brain, and reproductive organs. It takes place in the subtle energy body of our 3 Dan Tians and their corresponding External Qi Fields. It is one process.

It is the connection between matter and dark matter. We are learning to access 90% more energy or so than was previously thought possible. We used to say we only use a percentage of our brain, now we can say we only use a small percentage of available energy in the universe. It is the same thing, the marrow as mediator of multi-dimensional energy. We can become aware of this bridge between dimensions, the fractal tendril conduits of creation, the same energy that creates a galaxy, creates us. We are already connected to the universal architecture but we choose to experience form as a limitation, as separation consciousness, whereby shutting down access to the rest of the potential energy available to us. The 8x offer a framework for recognizing that life does not have to be an either/or situation. We can create space. We can hold spaces in-between. We can have all the benefits of being separate, our self, while simultaneously experiencing all the benefits of being one organism. This is the promise of the pre-natal qi and relates to the process of differentiation.

173

Destiny and the 3 Grades of Medicine

Chinese Medicine can be traditionally categorized into 3 Grades of Medicine: an Upper Grade, a Middle Grade, and a Lower Grade of medicine. This categorization comes from the first Herbal Material Medica, the *Shen Nong Ben Cao*, but its principle is as true for medicine in general as it is for herbology. The Lower Grade of medicine deals with symptoms. At this level we are trouble-shooting Wei Qi. The Middle Grade of medicine deals with wellness and preventative medicine. At this level we are managing the portfolio of the resources of the Ying Qi. The Highest Grade of Medicine involves Destiny, healing the Shen/Spirit, and getting to know one's own nature. This is the level of the Yuan Qi. It is my hope that we as a culture can evolve our understanding of Medicine to include this highest level of practice. This is where "Medicine" truly gets beyond pathology and signs and symptoms and begins to put purpose and awareness in their rightful place.

The wonderful thing about Chinese Medicine is that its framework includes how to physiologically support a seemingly intangible process like the pursuit of Destiny and how this process may be used to support physical health. Obviously, we need the two "lower" grades of medicine too, it's just that we should not be so short-sighted as to think that that's all there is. Even in the most impoverished situation, restoring an individual's connection to purpose and self is paramount. The consciousness that finds it too impractical or selfish to pursue Destiny is part of the main trouble on the planet. We are in a crisis of imagination. We often hold ourselves so hyper-accountable to the habituated experience of the mundane, to the transitory illusion of the material, that we never can see a solution and we just might laugh at it if it were shown to us. Such is the Tao.

Awakening as the Clean-Up Crew

At this point the challenge seems to be to clean up the karma and defensive energy that has been accumulated at the level of Yuan Qi and DNA, blocking us from our birthright of spiritual flowering. These protective mechanisms have become habituated and ingrained into our structural mechanisms. The rigidity of these navigational patterns has been outmoded. These outmoded patterns are a microcosm of the political, social, religious and economic institutional rigidity we see everywhere in the world. This is massive resistance to change, to nature.

These are natural survival adaptations that may have once been useful but no longer efficiently serve the purpose they were intended for. These individual and institutional resistances begin to function more out of habitual self-preservation than from serving their useful intended purpose. These protective mechanisms when functioning without awareness have an innate tendency to over-react and overcompensate, something that may have been deeply necessary in the evolution of our survival mechanisms, but does not serve to create balance or harmony. It just perpetuates mindless movement through habituated and internalized resistance. This is the nature of polarity, to maintain the motion of the manifest world. The 8x Vessels provide a window into how to create space within polarity for the spirit to be still, to be constant, within the endless motion of form consciousness.

These outmoded patterns of over-reaction are divergent, diverted, often deviant and decaying structures whether internal in our body-mind or external in our cultures, if there is indeed a difference. The challenge is to liberate the Wei Qi, the overactive self-preservation mechanism and return the structures to the efficiency of their natural state rather than their habituated state. What this means is that systems, both internally and externally, are meant to function as communication and distribution networks and do not merely exist to create stagnation through the hoarding of resources.

Life is meant to flow. There is no power shortage or resource shortage, merely a lack of connection, cooperation and imagination. It is no surprise that we can describe the systems of our health and the systems of our culture in the same terms. There is an old saying, "what we do to the world we have already done to our self." We cannot heal the world without healing our self, and we cannot heal our self without healing the world. And we cannot hope to solve these problems, whether political, economic, spiritual or medical from the mindset that created them. Humanity can learn to swim in solution and stop drowning in the problem mind.

So how do we break the cycle? If a structure solely functions by bracing itself against all change through resistance, it causes tension and stagnation in the organism, be it a human or humanity. The habituated fear regarding the past or the future takes us out of the moment where the charge of the life force actually occurs and puts us into the resistance mode. In this scenario, the organism holds the resistance as a negative charge of contraction that is being stored through tension. An inefficient method at best and one doomed to the entropy process of not having enough resources available to flow, to go around.

In this model, we are trapped in the dual consciousness of self-preservation, of predator/prey, consume or be consumed. This model is fine for the limited individual consciousness of animals but obviously a model that causes much unnecessary suffering on the planet when adopted by humans as the main mode of functioning. The Animal Kingdom, we are discovering, is actually much more cooperative than previously thought and furthermore participates in a self-regulating eco-system, a system that is more important than any one of its parts. When humans participate solely from a competitive model, which has been reinforced through short-sighted and self-serving scientific models like Darwinian Theory, such behavior makes us less than human. This competitive behavior has led to a potential destruction of the eco-system. This could never be the goal of evolution. But it is a strong motivation to evolve.

The Story of Returning Home:
Evolution through Redemption

The 8x Vessels tell the story of our original nature and the way back home. This is the story of the redemption of spirit from matter. It is essentially the story of learning about our own nature and transcending the aspects that are outmoded, the habituated survival resistances in our code. Humans have the awareness to function from a place of community, cooperation, and acceptance. The process of cultivation is being able to work with polarity in order to allow the spirit that unites us, the consciousness that recognizes that we are all connected, to guide us, or rather itself, in the self-organizing way of the spirit. As we achieve or approach achieving this we become the change we want to see in the world, perhaps even the miracle we want to see in the world. This starts within our self, within our local bonds, our family, our village. What we do to the world, we have already done to ourselves. Through self-exploration of the Yuan Qi level, we can clean up our own mess, harmonize our eco-system, and remember how to love and accept ourselves, each other and the world.

As a species we are in the process of making a step that is as big as the ability to create fire. Humans were very limited in what they could do and still survive before the dawn of fire. They were limited to living in caves and places that could hyper-protect them from the elements and from predators. We are doing the same transformation now. Our bones are our cave and they house the conduit of our spiritual connection to multi-dimensional energy, the marrow. As we work through our defenses, tensions, and resistances in our muscles, mental body and emotional body, we are moving towards removing the unnecessary tensions in our bone matrix, removing the resistances programmed in our marrow. This allows us to engage a flow of energy that we forgot even existed.

This energy flow through the marrow and the bone matrix excites the opportunities for its own realization of purpose through its powers of direct transmission, of vibrational resonance. It changes our reality. The "hollow bones" function as an amplifier for the message of spirit contained and conducted by our marrow, our DNA. The optimal approach to survival is changing as we begin to see the way this multi-dimensional energy can transform reality. We are learning how to thrive as a species. Just as we discovered how to use fire, we are learning to participate in the firelight of our spirit. We are learning to come out of our caves, out of our hyper-tense self-protective shell/identity and create a world with more light. This relationship between our bones, our DNA, our personality and our survival takes place at the level of the Yuan Qi and the 8x Vessels.

Destiny as a Conscious Choice

Fate represents the hand we are dealt. Destiny represents the choices we make and how those choices leave room for the flow of spirit to participate in our path. When we can harmonize the two and learn to make choices not based on resistance we can achieve our purpose. The pursuit of destiny is not only our god-given right, it is our god-given responsibility. We are a vessel for the flow of the life force between Heaven and Earth. If we can allow this force to flow through us, we begin moving along the trajectory of our destiny. This force is a multi-dimensional energy that brings in the energy that catalyzes evolution. We are learning to allow this force to flow through us without activating our conditioned resistances. This is the way of the spirit.

We can get out of our own way by getting to know our self, and trust our self, our original nature. In this way we all can bring in the energy of solution and transform ourselves and the world. Ironically, it is the individuation process that allows for the unfolding of spiritual consciousness. Evolution is accomplished through allowing enough life force to flow through us to activate the self-organizing principles of spirit. Through this we can achieve the spontaneous equilibrium that comes after a period of chaos caused by acceleration. It is like learning to ride a bike or learning to swim. It is natural. Let us enjoy the journey and explore the primordial ocean and wilderness of our nature. Remember, the map is not the territory, and you are your best guide, but here is a beautiful map to guide you in as much as it can. The choices are all yours.

The Chong Vessel - Channel of Our Blueprint

The Curriculum, The Architect, and the Design

Other Names - Central Channel, Uterine Vessel, Penetrating Vessel,
Thrusting Vessel, Core Channel

"The Chong is searching for one's nature, not influenced by culture"
- Jeffrey Yuen

Conception and the 3 Trimesters

The Chong Mai represents the most truly pre-natal of the 8x Vessels. It is the single cell, the embryo of the egg and the sperm meeting. The first mitosis will begin the formation of the Du and Ren Channels. This is the Jing of the Kidneys, the sexual energy moving between two people awakening/mobilizing the cosmic qi of the universe, represented by the Lungs. We see this in the changing of the breathing patterns during sexual union as we enter the realm of the pre-natal qi. It is the Kidneys anchoring the Lung Qi. This occurs through resonance and vibration. The ocean of the cosmic library of the Hun is activated to choose an incarnation, a collection of lessons, a form, a vehicle, a Po body through which to tell our story. The Chong is the circle of life, the Wu Ji, our access point to the pre-natal and the spirit. At the insemination of the sperm into the egg, the original axis is formed, the Tai Chi pole, the sperm's entry point becoming Du 20- the Crown and the mirrored point being Ren 1- the Root. The preparation for polarity has begun.

In the 1st trimester, it is the corporeal soul coming to terms with the incarnation. Is it the right time, the right place? Is the Po really up for the lessons, the gender, the ethnicity, the ancestry, the culture, the morphology, the parents, etc.? This first trimester is represented by the Earth element. It is the Earthly manifestation of spirit. It is also the anchoring in of the Po by the Jing, the Kidney-Lung relationship. This is the raw material of our blueprint and curriculum, of our morphology and our lessons. How many lessons are we going to emphasize? How many Po are we going to choose? At what times in our life will these lessons be most active or more latent? This is our contract with our ancestors.

The 2nd trimester is the Fire element of the Heart and begins the aspect of the journey of the Shen through Form. At this stage, we are developing the unfolding of the blueprint. What type of story are we telling? What type of experiences should we have? What destinations should we be drawn towards? What type of people will we meet? How shall the cycles of 7 & 8, the chapters, reveal the story? This is the Shen, the Heart, the sovereign of the vessel choosing a quest, a conquest, a question, a story. What we shall see is that although the Shen is the original storyteller, in life it is to be the passenger, not the driver. It is watching the movie. If it tries to take the reins it can create resistance in the program. As it learns its lessons, it can let the Horse run free and simply allow the story to unfold. It is the innate intelligence of the Form that is moving through space that is the driver, the emotions, the instincts, the gut response, the intuition.

The Shen can learn to navigate change through choice by observing the results of its intentionality. Eventually it can achieve the "choicelessness" of Wu Wei. It can achieve right timing, right place and right action. During the 2nd trimester we have the Shen editing and refining the story, adding and deleting as it programs the software of our story. Traditionally there is the great debate over how much of our life is pre-destined and how much is driven by free will. Paradoxically, they both appear to be true. A good model is that of having free will in our decisions, but also of having destinations, events, and opportunities that we will be strongly attracted to. These are considered related to the cycles of 7 & 8 when our Yuan Qi is in more direct communication with our day-to-day lives.

The 3rd trimester is the Wood element, the element of creation, of birth. This is the Hun preparing the nervous system for a smooth response to the ride. It is beginning to hold the vision, to hold the plan, to honor the story, to store the blood that the Heart has written the destiny into. This is the ideal time for the mother to be able to stay relaxed, while the Liver, and its relationship to the smooth flow of qi, is most active. Here we have the crown-first entry into life. The fontanelle, Du 20, where the internal trajectory of the Liver Channel ends, is how the spirit enters the Earth and also where it will exit. It enters crown facing down and exits crown facing up.

Birth and Birth Trauma

At this point we have birth. Ideally we are born into a relaxed, comfortable, warm, wet and sensual environment, so as not to aggravate the shock and trauma of birth. The child could be born into a warm, aquatic surrounding, it could retain the cord, if no emergency, until it slows down or stops pulsing. The child could have a smooth climatic transition and take in its first breath in as gentle a manner as possible. Obviously, we have as a culture created quite the opposite situation where pregnancy is routinely approached as a medical condition and birth is routinely seen as an emergency situation. Our worse-case-scenario approach almost guarantees a highly traumatic entry into the world, one of our strongest imprints. It is said that the Earth is the water planet, associated with fear and represented by the two frozen icecaps of the poles and as we first enter we are imprinting our relationship to the Water element. This is a continuation of the Lung-Kidney theme as the shock of birth forces the survival instinct into immediate high gear as it takes its first breath, creating an adverse relationship with the medium in which we exist, our atmosphere.

To compound this situation, we often have the added insult of pain medication and the over-sedation of the mother(and the baby). Often the child will be sedated upon entry to the atmosphere and shocked into survival, the earliest imprint having occurred in a drugged stupor. Add the frequent inheritance of drug and alcohol addiction in the genes, and it is no small wonder the degree of drug addiction that we have in the world. Then add the potential situation where the baby is not given to the mother immediately and we have the beginning of the challenging imprints to the next meridian we will explore, the Ren Channel, the Channel of Bonding related to the hormone oxytocin. We have an epidemic of iatrogenic birth trauma on our hands, of c-sections, forceps, machines, bright lights, and cold air. These are highly sterile environments that are an affront to the innate sensuality of a new-born. A portion of the world has gotten wiser, but the institutions are highly resistant to placing the proper value on nurturing and nourishment.

Karma, Shock and the Primordial Child

To soften the violation we may feel due to the current stage of development of our culture, spiritually speaking, it is best to remember that it all unfolds the way it was meant to(a theme that we will return to, due to its powerful and questionable implications). The responses and types of imprinting we have to these traumas are part of the programming, the karma. Some people shake off extreme situations, some people are traumatized by seemingly innocuous events. Our post-natal existence is born of trauma. It is said that we lose touch with our original nature, the tai chi pole of the Heart-Kidney axis, the Original Chong, through the adaptation to trauma.

In order to individuate, to separate from the entirety, we have to imprint ourselves to define our boundaries. This process parallels the cutting of the cord, the closing of the fontanelle, the weaning from the maternal matrix, the learning to walk and be independent and takes place to some degree through the first cycle of 7 & 8. Early on this process, we begin to see the world through a lens, through a filter, being unable to become embodied if we only see the totality. This imprinting causes us to see the world through the lens of one or more of the 5 elements. At this point the triple warmer/ tree of life/dissemination of pre-natal qi mechanism will begin to devote more energy to the back shu/spinal reference point and corresponding organ to that elemental lens. We are developing our acquired mind, our post-natal nature. We now can perceive ourselves as separate with all the advantages and disadvantages that that entails. This process takes place in the paired organ of the Triple Warmer as well, the Pericardium. The Pericardium is the Heart Protector, or Heart Constrictor.

The Heart is our throne for the Little Shen, our portion of the Big Shen, God, Tao, or the totality/unity of consciousness and spirit. The Pericardium protects the Heart from the shocks and traumas of life. The Pericardium becomes an aspect of the ego, of the acquired mind, that serves to function in the social milieu of post-natal life. The Heart is the Primordial Child, that aspect of spirit, of Heaven, that is beyond the decay and imprinting of the Earth. A nice image in that no matter how much trauma one has undergone, there is still a spark of the divine that has not been harmed in the process of life.

The alchemy process then becomes the ability to allow the windows of the sensory orifices and the window of the heart orifice to be able to receive and send, to communicate with the world, with nature. From post-natal consciousness the information we send and receive is always distorted in the filtering process, always having some information that is not tuned in, that is muted or dampened. As we learn to trust, honor and love our self, we begin to soften the boundaries that were frozen by fear and begin to move again with the flow of life, our post-natal nature aspiring to become resonant with the divine, so that whether we are in Newtonian(post-natal consciousness) or Quantum(pre-natal consciousness) we trust, honor and love our self, modulating back and forth as the situation requires.

Chong Vessel as the Seed and the Single-Cell Organism

The Chong Vessel is our seed self. It has all the potential energy of nature. It is the mystery. It houses the chakras, the adherence points to the levels of consciousness we must learn to relate to in a physical form. As such it houses our pre-natal karma and will house our acquired karma for use at some point in this life or the next. It is the pre-natal Jing becoming and supporting the post-natal resources. As we learn to operate from the Heart, and to heal the relationship between the Pericardium(post-natal) and the Heart(pre-natal) we move to having less baggage in our blueprint, less karma for the planet, the ancestry, and the soul. This concept is represented by the last point on the Heart channel, *Shao Chong*, the Lesser Chong. As we work through our lessons, we have less baggage in our Chong Vessel.

The understanding of the Chong Vessel is the axis between Heaven and Earth and the seed of our cell, of our self, in the organism of Humanity. How we relate to our karma, our experiences and our memories, of our pre-natal and post-natal nature is the nutrition for our soul. It is the thick and viscous amniotic fluid, the dampness that we use to buffer the raw experience of the union of Heaven and Earth. As we learn to ground the form, to be in duality, yet leave space for the Shen, reconnecting the windows to nature, we can begin to participate in our birthright of spiritual consciousness.

The Chong Vessel is the single-celled organism still present inside us. We have our skin, a connective tissue wrapping like a bladder, and an auric/psycho-social boundary(semi-permeable membrane). These single-celled aspects of our self function similar to the way an amoeba functions.[23] We respond to noxious stimuli by recoiling and we respond to beneficial stimuli by expanding. This instinct of expansion and contraction is the fundamental yin/yang pulse of life, equally present in our highly evolved design as in the most basic life form. If an amoeba experiences a noxious stimulus, for

23. *Reich.*

instance poking the amoeba, it contracts and becomes smaller. If we stop poking the amoeba, the amoeba returns to its original size and shape. If the noxious stimulus persists for awhile without a period of rest, rejuvenation and expansion, the amoeba only returns to a percentage of its original shape.

This is analogous to the traumatic imprinting of the Human Energy Boundary, written into the myo-fascial electrical conduction system. If the noxious stimulus persists continuously, the amoeba will die. Stress is contraction, relaxation is expansion. Stress is who we think we should be, relaxation is who we truly are. The Chong Vessel is working from this first aspect of life, the human as a single-celled organism. If we heal the whole, we heal the parts. If we heal the whole, we also awaken to the larger network. It is a matter of healing the traumas, the fractures, the frozen tension, the sense of always being stuck on the inhale. We do this through relaxation, through expanding towards beneficial and safe stimuli, learning to let go, to exhale. The Chong Vessel represents this primal imprint in relation to expansion and contraction and this imprint is largely responsible for the ability of the pre-natal energy to be converted to post-natal energy, one of the primary roles of the Chong Vessel.

The Sea of Blood

The Chong Vessel is called the Sea of Blood and the Sea of the 12 Meridians. It has a strong affinity with the aorta and the pulsing, pumping and rushing of the blood through the arteries. The imprinting of our seed self, our singularity is written into every aspect of our being including the blood. It is this record of how much blood volume we can hold and how much residual contractile tension we carry in the vessels that affects every aspect of our post-natal experience. Our DNA and bone marrow keep writing the same old story into our blood, the only story they know, and the blood returns back to the marrow affirming the reality of this story. Our spirit seeks liberation from this script of life as constant drama, preferring life-affirming surprises and miracles at every step along the way. Otherwise, it might just as well remain sleeping and wait for the synopsis of the highlights at death.

Chong Meridian Trajectories and Point Energetics

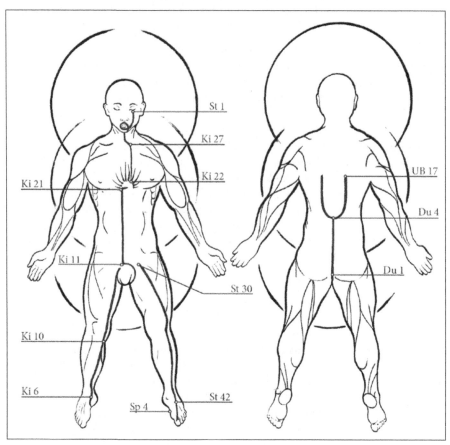

Figure 4.1: 5 Trajectories of the Chong Vessel[24]

Chong Vessel Trajectories

Primordial Chong *Du 20 Ren 1 Kid 1*

The Primordial Chong Vessel is beyond the reach of material intervention. It can only be accessed by our Heart-Mind, our Soul and Spirit. The points listed above are references to our conduit between Heaven and Earth. This aspect of the Chong is our Spiritual Axis, often referred to as our Tai Chi Pole.

---

24. *Trajectory from Cecil-Sterman, p. 238-252.*

5 Trajectories of the Chong Vessel[25]

Opening Point *Spleen 4*

1ˢᵗ Trajectory *Stomach 30, Kidney 11-Kidney 21*

This trajectory begins in the lower abdomen and emerges at the pubic bone giving a clear picture of the creative and reproductive pathways. It ascends along both sides of the mid-line to the navel, referencing our birth and our potential re-birth. It then ascends to the solar plexus where emotional energy can be focused into will and spiritual communication and then diffuses into the chest.

2ⁿᵈ Trajectory *Kidney 22-Kidney 27, Ren 22, Ren 23, encircles mouth, St 1*

Communicates between the Heart and Kidneys. Here we enter from the solar plexus into the chest, the home of the Zong-Qi, the Ancestral Qi, clearing out the cobwebs from our lineage and the ghosts of the past that have taken up residence in the palace and restoring the rightful heir to the throne of the Heart. This connection is mediated by the breath via the ancestral sinew of the diaphragm. This trajectory goes to the collar bone and connects to the Ren Channel and the ancestral sinew round muscles of the mouth and eyes.

3ʳᵈ Trajectory *Ren 2, St 30, GB 26, Du 1, Du 4, UB 17*

Begins at the pubic bone and connects to the tailbone via the Belt. Here we have the pelvic floor mechanism responsible for the ascension of Yang energy and supporting the tailbone. The trajectory goes up the Du Meridian to Du 4, Ming Men, and continues to UB 17, the Influential Point of Blood and the Transport Point of the Diaphragm. Physiologically, this is the Yang Qi supporting the production of blood. Mechanically, this is the ancestral sinew connection between the psoas muscle and the diaphragm. Ultimately, mechanics and physiology, form and function are one in the same.

4ᵗʰ Trajectory *Kidney 11, Kidney 10, UB 40, Kidney 8, Kidney 6, Kidney 2, Kidney Prime(posterior to Kidney 1)*

This trajectory travels down to create the Qiao Vessels. This is the evolution from hydrostatic skeleton to endo-skeleton. We are extending our core to the Earth and receiving its support through our bone structure so we can adopt the upright posture and participate in our own conscious evolution. Descends from pubic bone to the knee and splits at base of calves to Sp 4 and Kidney Prime, connecting us directly to our ancestry and to the Earth herself.

5ᵗʰ Trajectory *Stomach 42, Liver 1, Spleen 1*

This trajectory represents the nourishment of our post-natal qi. It is the Liver Channel as it descends to establish the roots of the Wood Element in

---

25. *Cecil-Sterman, p.238-252.*

preparation for growth. The nourishment provided by our roots is represented by the Earth Element of Spleen and Stomach. Descends from St 30 to St 42 at the dorsum of the foot and to Liver 1 and Spleen 1 at the big toe.

Traditional Paired Point *Pericardium 6*

Primordial Chong

The Primordial Chong Vessel is our original connection to source and to our self. It is the sacred ground of our original nature. This is our open conduit between Heaven and Earth, sometimes referred to as the Tai Chi Pole, formed at conception as the sperm enters the egg creating Du 20, the fontanelle, and Ren 1, the perineum, as the poles. In this Primordial Chong Vessel we are beyond polarity. As an embryo, we are the fusion of yin and yang, but paradoxically one cell, before the endless divisions that sustain the material aspect of life. This is the neutral space, the empty space which calls the spirit to spiral in. Nature does not sustain a vacuum, so we can use the vacuum suction created from the empty space inside our self to beckon the spirit. By remaining empty we awaken the spirit and begin to move on the trajectory of our purpose, our Destiny. The Primordial Chong is the original empty space.

The Formless Self: a Channel in the Field of Vibration

The Primordial Chong is where the formless connection to spirit occurs. Post-natally, and even in the 8x Vessels as they unfold the material body, we participate within the limits created by Du 20 and Ren 1. We are capped in our growth. Spiritual cultivation is the awakening of the awareness that we do not end there. We do not end at the edges of our body. We do not end at the edges of the layers of our aura. We do not end. It is the ability to safely sustain this awareness and the influx of potential energy that comes along with it, that leads us to look at the 8x Vessels. They hold the keys, as they are a canal system to help keep us from drowning in the flood from the formless ocean of the cosmos. The Chong is known as the Central Channel. It is our axis. As we learn to be able to ground the flow of universal energy, we begin to embody our station. Our frequency emerges from the universal field of vibration. We become differentiated through accepting more energy into our self. We can pick up our channel amidst the infinite frequencies broadcasting through the cosmos, the chaos of the creative force.

Cultivating the 8x Vessels leads to the awakening of the Chong Vessel. We are dilating the flow through the central channel until it forms a wider bandwidth, a column wider than our body, as wide as the External Qi Field of our Heart. We have awakened to our own womb, our own auric egg and we are ready to be reborn into the Universe. This is the enlightening of the 3 Dan Tians. This is the opening of the Yang Qiao Vessel, the vessel that communicates directly with the exterior world. This is the expression of the light in the present moment, seen in the eyes, connected and in communication with the universe, yet grounded in a strong skeleton. This sensual spirituality can be sustained when the Zang-Fu Organs are completed. When the virtues of the organs are manifested, the pathways of the organs are reconnected to the external environment through the opening of their sensory orifices. The light within has been illuminated by the ability of the Yin Qiao Vessel to look within and brave all the temptations, doubts, and isolation of the darkness of the self. This is the embodiment of spirit. This is participation in the Shen's crafting of the Ling, of the essence, of the soul in its own image.

Conscious Evolution: Exploring Our Hard Drive

Here we are exploring the hard drive, the factory settings and the operating software that run the programs of our experiences, instead of just playing the game. With time, we learn to understand the programs, and life becomes just life again, and the game is just the game again. We recognize that it is a game that is meant to be played, not won just as life is meant to be lived and not necessarily figured out. The Yuan Qi is the hard drive and software of the program. The Ying Qi is the experience of the program, using the program, playing the game, etc. The Wei Qi is the protective mechanism of your avatar in the program, and also of your hard drive and software.

The Wei Qi also has a deeper level of spyware, of encryption, that is connected through the Divergent Meridians to the Yuan Qi. We are programmed to protect against our self from realizing the program, and to just keep accepting and participating in life at face value. This is one of the major challenges on the path, the disturbance of the Wei Qi caused by the piercing of the veil. The Wei Qi attempts to protect the organism's identification with its life events, to protect its identity. It is merely another face of the same phenomena, fear. These are the safeguards of the Morphogenetic Field, the seals on our evolution. However, once we are grounded in our self, we have earned the privilege of opening these seals. Once we understand something we no longer need to keep unnecessary amounts of Wei Qi on guard. We can just be efficiently prepared instead of hyper-vigilant.

At the level of the Primordial Chong, we are the observer, the passenger. We bear witness to our lives in all their splendor, agony, ecstasy, tragedy and comedy. We affect our lives through bringing love to them, the spiritual energy of connection. We learn to accept our self and to play our role in life, be it that of a warrior or a saint. We pay attention and gauge our responses accordingly through active observing and active waiting. We learn to stay engaged in the flow, in right action and right timing. We can learn to be in communication with the Universe and to live in Wu Wei, letting our Wei Qi idle until needed instead of running our lives out of reaction to or repression of fear.

The Chong Vessel- The Sea of Blood

Opening Point

Spleen 4 *Gong Sun,* Grandfather/Grandchild, Grandmother/Grandchild

We enter the Chong Mai through the uterus connecting us to our ancestry, our bloodline, our lineage. We are participating in the growth of our lineage and the karma of our lineage expression. The opening point is located on the Spleen Channel, the Earth Element, the representation of post-natal qi. This point is located on the arch and is supporting life, supporting our weight and the pressure of life. This is the instep, the journey of 1,000 miles beginning with a single step. We are learning to walk 1,000 miles through the 10,000 things in our own shoes. It is a Luo point, representative of blood, the story of our blood.

1st Trajectory of the Chong Vessel

Stomach 30 *Qi Chong,* Pulsating Qi, Surging Qi, Sea of Nourishment

Here we have the Sea of Blood, the arterial flow from the torso and the conversion of pre-natal qi into post-natal qi represented by the Stomach Channel. The great transducer from the mystery to the manifestation, from the marrow to the blood. This is the pulse of life, the rhythms that connect us to nature, the connection of the torso to the legs and to the Earth at Kid 1. The Journey begins beneath your feet. This is the blood. The blood contains the stories of your lineage and your story will be written into the blood.

This is the conversion of DNA into RNA. This transcription process creates the proteins for self-replication. The transcription process requires healthy telomeres, the connections of Du 20 and Ren 1, and Kid 1 as the ground for Ren 1. This is the playing out of the story that we co-wrote in utero. The story that honors our ancestors, honors our self, and honors the spirit.

Kidney 11 *Heng Gu,* Pubic Bone

Here we have the genitalia, the continuity of our jing, of our family tree. As we honor our lessons, our story, creator and creation, we begin to become creators of our lives. As we clear out the karma of our lives, we uncover the gifts of creativity and the vitality of our self.

Kidney 12 *Da He*, Great Manifestation

This point is about fertility, yin and jing-essence. The yin and jing are what allow for the manifestation of creation. Manifestation occurs through the connection of the Heart and Kidneys.

Kidney 13 *Qi Xue*, Qi Hole

We are bringing light into the darkness of the water element of the Kidneys and bringing the pre-natal qi up to the surface to support the post-natal aspects of our life. This is the Kidneys supporting Spleen, the original nature infusing the expression of the social self.

Kidney 14   *Si Man*, Four Fullnesses

The uterus, the uterine palace, extending out to the ovaries. This is a gate to our original qi and our ability to store jing. Are we holding onto stagnation, to blood stagnation from our ancestry, or are we empty and open to creation? Receptive to creating an atomic furnace, a cauldron for the union of Heaven and Earth, of male and female.

Kidney 15 *Zhong Zhu*, Central Flow, Central Director

This point is about removing obstructions to the flow of our life, our yin, our blood.

Kidney 16 *Huang Shu*, Vital's Transporting Hollow

The representation of the Chong as the original birth imprint, the first wound, the first separation being played out post-natally. The cutting of the cord. The first scar. Dying to the pre-natal and being born into the post-natal. Leaving the amniotic water for the atmos-sphere and the upright posture to aspire and inspire towards Heaven, fueled by breath. We are cutting the cord again and being born into the conscious awareness of swimming in air, our breath being drawn by the natural function of our naval sphincter and the MingMen, the Sipapu between dimensions. The reconnection of the umbilicus to the mother.

Kidney 17 *Shang Qu*, Shang Bend

Between the navel and the sternum we are in the realm of the post-natal qi. Here we are working on supporting our digestion of food and life's events. We are integrating and transforming the dampness we have accumulated from unprocessed aspects of the past to be able to bring more of our self to our post-natal reality, our material life.

Kidney 18   *Shi Guan,* Stone Pass

Here we are removing obstacles and obstructions that have manifested as solid blockages(food, blood, qi, fluid, phlegm) thus interfering with the communication between our Heart and Kidneys.

Kidney 19   *Yin Du,* Yin Metropolis

This point is about re-establishing the integrity of the yin, of the fluid matrix of the body. As we dissolve blockages and obstacles, we liberate the essence that was trapped and re-establish the healthy flow of blood.

Kidney 20   *Fu Tong Gu,* Abdomen Connecting Valley

We are approaching the dark gate, the entrance to the valley of the spirit corridor of the chest. We are developing the faith in our purpose as we approach the unknown. Here the Spleen and Kidney Yang work together to support the inspiration provided by the Lungs. A good point for accumulations such as Gu-parasites keeping us from embracing our path.

Kidney 21   *You Men,* the Dark Gate

This is the entrance way into the Spirit Corridor, or the Valley of the Shadows of Death from Psalm 23. It is the gateway into the chest, into the burial grounds and cobwebs on the pathway to the Heart of Humanity. We are clearing the haunting of the past and our fear of the unknown. This is the beginning to clearing out the phlegm blocking the heart orifice, clearing out the amniotic buffer in our auric egg that blocks us from accessing Heaven directly, our true self, our Heart. It assists in allowing the Heart to descend to the Kidneys. The beginning of the awakening to the spirit of pre-natal awareness in a post-natal environment.

2nd Trajectory of the Chong Vessel

৵৽৽

Kidney 22 *Bu Lang,* Corridor Walk/Stepping Gallery, *Water*(post-natal)/ *Metal*(pre-natal)

We are exploring the mystery, the mystery of one's self. We are looking at our own intrinsic beauty and meaning. We are preparing to view the holographic slideshow of our life that is stored in our blood, in the Yin Wei and read at the time of our death/re-birth.

Kidney 23 *Shen Feng,* Spirit Seal, *Earth*(post-natal)/*Fire*(pre-natal)

We are invoking the spirit that resides in the chest. We are making an offering of our post-natal attachment to our ego and showing our integrity in asking for the seal that separates pre-natal from post-natal to be opened so that we may know truth and purpose and proceed on our quest. Promotes self-esteem and allows us to become grounded in our purpose.

Kidney 24 *Ling Xu,* Spirit Burial Ground, *Wood*(post-natal and pre-natal)

We are letting go. Putting our affairs in order. Taking care of regrets and unfinished business and coming to terms with our lives and our self. Letting go of the obstacles and putting the past to rest. Removing the obstacles to acceptance of our lives and self as feeling complete. Strengthens essence to provide the resources to manifest our potential.

Kidney 25 *Shen Cang,* Spirit Storehouse, *Fire*(post-natal)/*Earth*(pre-natal)

Here we are discovering the essence of our self. The true nature that was buried. The soul that got hidden beneath the layers. The crystal gemstone that has been buried and alchemically transformed through the pressures of the Earth.

Kidney 26 *Yu Zhong,* Lively Center, *Metal*(post-natal)/*Water*(pre-natal)

Here we are regaining inspiration. Recovering from the loss of animation of being frozen in post-natal forgetfulness. The Po is regaining sensory awareness with the reverence and wisdom of how to relate to sensation, to fear and desire and sensuality without simply crystallizing into the resistance, the limiting into one perspective.

Kidney 27 *Shu Fu*, Conveying Palace, Master Point

All the Upper Transport Points unbind the chest and allow the Lungs to be strong enough to cultivate forgiveness, the rectification of the qi and the ability of the kidneys to grasp that qi and bring it into the world.

Ren 22 *Tian Tu*, Celestial Chimney

This point is located just above the sternum, at the base of the neck. It is a Window to the Sky point, an opening to the Upper Dan Tian, our internal representation of Heaven. It opens our upper orifices, opens our eyes, so that we can see the world and our self in a new way. It resolves the phlegm, the dampening of the signal, the truth, from Heaven. Our prayers are sent from the Fire of our Heart through Heaven's Chimney to the heavenly transceiver of our Brain, changing the way we perceive and receive the world.

Ren 23 *Lian Quan*, Angular Ridge Spring

This is the Throat Chakra, the Heart as it is represented by the tongue. The ability to speak our truth, from the Heart. The ability to gauge the affects of our words on the Hearts of others. Our ability to manifest in the world through open communication, a clear channel. Our tongue quivers at the mere thought of words, of language. To find peace in our heart, we have to quell this addiction to language and find the truth before language, the pre-natal vibration. This is our swallowing mechanism. Have we swallowed our fears, our emotions? Have we bitten off more than we can chew?

Stomach 1 *Cheng Qi*, Supporting Tears/Tear Container

Allows us to see ourself and the world without judgment. The tears that wash the windows of the soul and open up the doors of our perception.

3rd Trajectory of the Chong Vessel

The 3rd Trajectory of the Chong Vessel serves to connect our torso, the core of our core channel, down to the ground through our legs. This is done through accessing the Yin Qiao Vessel points. Our Chong Vessel is more ancient than our ability to walk on land. The Qiao Vessels are thought to have begun developing when we evolved into the upright posture. It is from connecting our seed, the Chong, our torso down to the ground through the Yin Qiao, that we begin the process of growing roots. We need strong roots to Earth if we ever aspire to realizing the potential of our connection to Heaven.

These points on the Yin Qiao are from the Kidney Channel, the water element and demonstrate that we cannot begin to grow deep roots of our own until we can learn to relate to our fears. Until we have reckoned with the "fight or flight" aspect of fear which keeps breaking our root, we cannot fully settle into the unconditional support of the Earthly Mother providing buoyancy and venous blood flow back upwards. This is another example of the conversion of pre-natal to post-natal. Pre-natally we are the Chong Vessel but in order to manifest this in the post-natal world we need to connect to the Earth through our legs. Sitting meditation makes this connection directly through Ren 1 at the perineum. By adding the connection through the soles of the feet, we are establishing the ability to be autonomous and mobile while retaining our connection to the Earth.

4th Trajectory of the Chong Vessel

The 4th Trajectory connects the Chong Vessel to the Du Vessel. The Du and the Ren are both born from the Chong, representing the first meiosis of the embryo. The Du represents the substantial part of our vertical axis, the spine and the Belt represents the support and reinforcement provided by the horizontal axis. This trajectory comes around the Belt Channel and reinforces the Ming Men area and comes up the spine, the Tree of Life, and goes to UB 17, the Back Transport point of the Blood. This trajectory reinforces the integrity of the architecture of the Chong Vessel via the support structures of the Du Vessel(vertical axis) and the Dai Channel(horizontal axis) and how this structural integrity facilitates the function of the production of post-natal resources represented by the blood.

5th Trajectory of the Chong Vessel

The 5th Trajectory supports the Chong Vessel in a way that reflects the post-natal channels related to blood production via the digestion. It connects to the Stomach, the Spleen, and the Liver Channels. This is Wood and Earth. After the organism has connected down to the Earth via the Yin Qiao and Kidney 1, it begins to grow upward, creating the trunk of the tree that will grow roots towards Heaven, branches that will bear fruit and seed and continue the process of life. This post-natal nourishment occurs via the digestive capabilities of the Spleen and Stomach converting food into qi. We grow roots in order to bear fruits. This upward movement of the Liver Channel towards the flowering of the Crown Chakra at Du 20 is the kundalini energy of evolution.

Part 4 Chapter 2

The Ren Vessel- Channel of Bonding

Our Reception on Earth: Receiving Nourishment

Other Names - *Conception Vessel, Sea of Yin*

U pon our arrival on the planet, we are being received by the Mother
Earth, our birth mother and other figures who will bond to and nurture
the child. Here we have the Ren Vessel, the Conception Vessel, which begins
to become active. It is the meridian of the front midline of the body and
the Sea of Yin. It includes the Du Vessel of the back as they interpenetrate
each other and together become the substantiation of the body's axis. The
Ren Vessel is activated for bonding. When the child is born, it comes from
a place of complete connection to unity. Upon separation, the first thing it
seeks is to connect. At birth, both the mother and the baby have higher
amounts of oxytocin, the endogenous chemical most associated with bonding, than they will ever have again. As they begin the bonding process they
set imprints that will affect the child's ability to feel nourished and nurtured,
to feel receptive and open, yet contained. The changes made at the level of
the Ren Vessel could reduce the use of violence on the planet considerably.
Many warrior cultures knew this and would interrupt this bonding process to
insure premature activation of the Du Vessel, and the reduction of the ability
to feel empathy.

The Maternal Matrix

The Ren Vessel is the yin matrix of the maternal and is associated with
the development and coordination of the sphincter system, the involuntary,
parasympathetic, and peristaltic movement in the body. This is the natural
rhythms of the wave-like motions of the waters throughout the body, pro-
pelled by gravitational force, like the power of the Moon over the tides. It
is the development of synchrony and coordination of the round muscle
network. The image is of the baby suckling at the mother's breast with the
round muscle of the mouth engaging the suckling reflex, and gazing into
the eyes of the mother, round muscle of the eyes to the round muscles of the
mother. The baby has the entirety of the front of its body up against the soft,
round belly and breast of the mother. Its heartbeat is next to the heartbeat of
the mother and they will entrain to each other. The child will then associate
this heart rhythm with the comfort of the mother. This could create tendencies to seek out partners that help recreate this rhythm, even though this
rhythm may have been one of anxiety.

The sphincter of the navel gets to rest at the breast as the physical cord to the mother has been broken and the integrity of the etheric cord is being imprinted. If this relationship is difficult and the child's needs aren't being met, the child may become closed off or needy, creating a situation where it will be difficult for the child to bond directly to the maternal matrix of the Tao when it seeks spiritual individuation and worldly acceptance.

The development of voluntary sphincter control of the lower orifices of the anus and urethra begins to be set early. If a child is being weaned or if their cries aren't being met it will try to compensate for the lack of oral nourishment through controlling the orifices, causing the entire sphincter system, including the anus and urethra to tense up and activate before the introduction of toilet training. The toilet training period is another period of Ren Vessel conditioning as approval and disapproval aspects of sphincter control enter the picture, setting the stage for the child's sphincter response to the world, towards its control issues or over-controlling issues to be more accurate.

Sphincter Network

The sphincters create a network of the eyes, mouth, throat, cardiac sphincter, navel, urethra, and anus and more. Any disruption in one of these areas will disrupt the entire network, and so forth. The sphincters control peristalsis on every level and the movement of blood, food, air, and fluid is all dependent on our micro-sphincter network which is controlled by the major ones. The sphincters become an area of expression, repression, and/ or suppression. Through "body armoring" we impede the life force through over-controlling the sphincters, in order to not express the primal drives of the body. This learned and inherited social conditioning causes a disconnection to the life force that flows through us, these gravity waves of peristalsis. If unimpeded, this energy will flow through us, allowing emotions to flow, creating a harmony of the internal and external, of the Ying and Wei.

When impeded during the imprinting process, the socialization process, this energy will be experienced as stuck emotion and the Wei Qi will guard against it. In this manner we won't have to keep feeling or experiencing the negative emotion, be it shame, guilt, fear or whatever. The Wei Qi guards against the feeling of the emotion, of the life force, and as it does this it creates a cascading effect of chronic deep-seated tension. Now the emotion has been repressed or suppressed for reasons of perceived survival and this energy will be stuck as a chronic negative charge in the body until it can be discharged, either through expression or release.

The ring muscles of the body are a more primal system than the nervous system, predating the evolution of the nervous system. If we suppress an emotion, we may hold our eyes, or mouth, or breath, collapse our chest, clench our anus or retract our genitalia, or all of the above. Our master sphincters are arranged in horizontal segments. The eyes, the mouth, the esophageal muscles in swallowing, the heart/cardiac sphincter/solar plexus, the navel, the urethra and the anus are the 7 sets of master sphincters. There are others. What happens is that by armoring the eyes so that they don't express an inappropriate emotion, or by armoring the mouth so we don't say the wrong thing, through the general "swallowing" of emotion, the whole horizontal segment of muscle becomes tense and impedes the vertical conduit of energy. For instance, eye suppression will tense the temples, the forehead and scalp and so forth.

The fascinating thing is that it won't directly affect the muscles at the mouth level. Mouth armoring might be present, too, but the muscles are prioritized by their relationship to the sphincter segments, not by their relationship to the nervous system. This sheds light on the myriad distributions of muscle pain and tension and much visceral tension. Stretch your hamstrings all you want, but if it's an anal sphincter imprint, they will not go very far. Wear a tooth guard if you grind your teeth, but if its mouth armoring, it is only a band-aid. Also, the sphincters function as a network and therefore tension in the eyes could affect the anus, tension in the urethra could affect the mouth, etc. Blockage in any one of the horizontal segments will affect all of the segments and the overall capacity for flow of the life force.

The sphincters are part of our Ancestral Sinew network. Sphincter coordination is deeply entwined with our breathing, our diaphragm and psoas, and they are keys to voluntarily accessing the involuntary system. Smiling relaxes the mouth. Laughter relaxes the diaphragm. Slow movement coordinated with the eyes affects proprioception, or muscle awareness. Looking at someone or something with devotion relaxes the eyes. These early imprints are clues to releasing the body and its connective tissue matrix. No amount of physical rehab can be successful in the long-term without releasing the repressed and suppressed charges held in the physical body.

Much of the above work on body armoring, horizontal segments related to sphincters, and the vertical conduction of universal energy being blocked at these segments was rediscovered in the West by Wilhelm Reich. Many bodywork systems have been greatly influenced by his work. Reich posited that we have evolutionary archetypes still active in our current configuration. They are embedded in the implicate order. They are powerful in that they are much simpler and older parts of our organism. They are more primal.

According to Reich's research, the sphincter reflexes, coordination and horizontal segmental arrangement represent the earthworm being still present in the primal configuration of the human.[26] Just as we still function energetically like a single-celled organism, we still function energetically as a pre-vertebrate segmental organism. These are precisely the evolutionary remnants that we need to be aware of in order to harness our energy in the present moment and move forward to evolution. These remnants of the implicate order hold evolutionarily repressed charges that we need to remove in order to safely sustain the energy metabolism required for expanded consciousness. It is ironic that we need to recapitulate these ancient forms in order to activate the dormant evolutionary energy inside of us, to pre-capitulate the direction of the species.[27]

26. *Reich*
27. *Pre-capitulation of Ontogeny and Philogeny is from the works of Timothy Leary.*

Ren Meridian Trajectory and Point Energetics

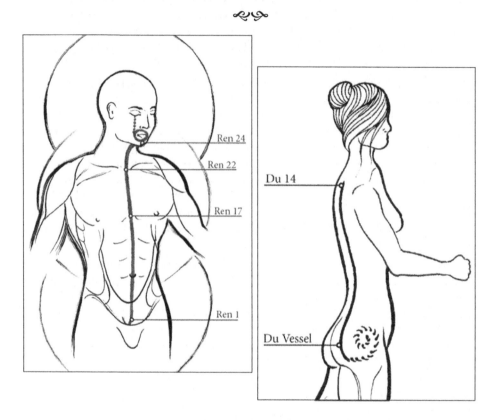

Figure 4.2: Ren Vessel Trajectory. Also goes to St 4(mouth) and St 1(eyes). (Right) Second trajectory interpenetrates Du Vessel and goes up to Du 14.

Opening Point   Lung 7   Lie Que, Broken Sequence

Ren Vessel Trajectory 1

Begins in the Lower Jiao behind Ren 3 and emerges at the perineum at Ren 1. Continues up the mid-line to Ren 24 just below the mouth. Connects to Du meridian when the tongue tip is connected to the upper palate where it completes circuit of micro-cosmic orbit. Continues to mouth and eyes to represent the complete sphincter system of the round muscle network.

Ren Vessel Trajectory 2

Begins in the pelvis and travels up the spine to Du 14. Demonstrates the interpenetration of yin and yang. Does not travel beyond Du 14 as this represents the protective mechanism of keeping accumulation from reaching the level of the brain with its karmic re-incarnation implications. Yin often accumulates at Du 14 forming the "dowager's hump" or "buffalo hump."

Opening Point

Lung 7 *Lie Que*, Broken Sequence

Broken Sequence, from "breathing" through the umbilicus pre-natally to the first breath taken by the Lungs upon interaction with the external world. The child has now broken from the sense of wholeness and will seek unity through connection, seek containment through bonding. The Lungs represent the Po and the sensation body and this point's ability to release the exterior points to our ability to be born again through releasing, through letting go and reconfiguring our Wei Qi to an ever-changing environment.

Ren 1 *Huiyin*, Sea of Yin

This is the seat of our connection to the Earthly Mother, to the Yin, to the manifest. This is the darkness of infinite potential, the lair of the sleeping serpent of the kundalini, the latent power of the perineum. This is the gate of Po Men, the anus from which the un-transcended Po returns to the Earth, dust to dust, and the strongest round muscle in the body.

Ren 2 *Qu Gu*, Curved Bone

The uro-genital sphincter and diaphragm. This is the pubic bone, the curved bone. It curves under tensegrity circumstances when there is optimal relaxed pressurization of the system. This creates the sealed basin of the two lower orifices, so we can have a foundation for our qi cultivation. We often use tension to prevent this leak, requiring discharge to accommodate the pressure instead of flow through the meridians. This tension/flow, charge/discharge balance is mediated by the Liver's relationship to Wei Qi, the Liver's ability to allow qi to flow like a "free and easy wanderer." A casual observer.

Ren 3 *Zhong Ji*, Central Pole

This point reflects the Bladder as it relates to our axis. The Bladder holds the charge of the organism. It reflects the charge of the Wei Qi circulating at the periphery, the skin being a "qi bladder" of the entire body. The ability to circulate this charge of the Wei Qi calmly through the surface of the body relates directly to our ability to hold this charge of Kidney Yang, in our Bladder, the Yang organ of the Water element. This is "orgastic potential" in Reich's terms, a seal that allows flow to go through all segments instead of "leak" at the gates associated with the 1st and 2nd chakras.

Ren 4   *Guan Yuan*, Gate of Origin/Gateway to Original Qi

This is at the level of the uterus, the container for human creation. This is the connection to the blood and the primordial qi and functions as part of the Lower Dan Tian. Helps root the soul, the Hun into the body via the blood. This is where we incubate the seed of our light body in order to give birth to the full expression of our self via our auric body's illumination.

Ren 5   *Shi Men*, Stone Gate

Helps the movement and dissemination of the Yuan Qi-Source Qi through the body for the creative expression of the self. Opens the flow through its connection to the Triple Warmer.

Ren 6   *Qi Hai*, Sea of Qi

This point is just below the navel and is the point that represents the Lower Dan Tian, the Sea of Qi. The Lower Dan Tian is called the Elixir Field, the Cinnabar Field and this is the incubator for spiritual rebirth in the body. The Lower Dan Tian functions like a spinning wheel, a spherical turbine pumped by counter-torsional dynamics creating a gyroscopic effect. It pivots between the triangular geometry created by Ren 1/Du 1 and Ren 8 in the front and Du 4 in the back.

Ren 7   *Yin Jiao*, Yin Junction

Nourishes the yin and the blood. In women, it helps regulate the uterus.

Ren 8   *Shen Que*, Spirit's Palace Gate

The umbilicus. This is our *sipapu*, to use a Native American word, our connection to spirit, to source and pre-natal energy. It is the first wound and represents how we are wound up in, entangled in post-natal energetics. We can unwind/unwound ourselves and cut the cord to our separation and re-attach our umbilicus to the maternal matrix of the Tao. This is the anchor of our breath, the healing of the first breath and the sphincter activity that allows us to be breathed by the Tao field. This is the Kidneys anchoring Lung Qi and the Earth element containing the Water. Physically this is mediated through the coordination of the diaphragm- the spirit muscle, and the psoas muscle- the soil of the soul, which come together at the lumbar junction behind the navel.

___

Ren 9   *Shui Fen,* Water Divide

An important point for any disruption in the flow of body fluids anywhere in the body. Body fluids are necessary to lubricate the stagnant phlegm accumulations in our body that create homes for the autonomous energies that no longer serve us.

___

Ren 10   *Xia Wan,* Lower Stomach Cavity

The points between the navel and the chest represent our Middle Jiao, our Middle Burner, and regulate the digestive functions. We need to digest our emotions and our experiences just as we do our food and this is regulated by the internal organs. Any unprocessed charges will be held as contractions in the smooth muscle of the viscera and will cause stagnation and accumulation. Ren 10 represents the lower part of the Stomach, the sphincter that connects the duodenum and the pylorus of the Stomach.

___

Ren 11   *Jian Li,* Strengthen the Interior

This is a tonification point for the Middle Jiao and promotes stronger digestion.

___

Ren 12   *Zhong Wan,* Middle Stomach Cavity

This is the post-natal qi furnace. It represents the Stomach's ability to extract energy from food and it is the internal beginning of the Lung Meridian and our ability to extract energy from air. Ren 12 represents the body of the Stomach.

___

Ren 13   *Zhang Wan,* Upper Stomach Cavity

One of the best points to subdue rebellious Stomach Qi, the events that we cannot stomach, cannot swallow. This is the upper part of the Stomach function, connecting the fundus and the esophagus. This is where the Middle Jiao begins connecting with the energy of the Heart.

___

Ren 14   *Ju Que,* Great Palace Gate

This point represents the Heart. It is located at the solar plexus, an area known as the Gao Huang, the Yellow Court. This is the area between the diaphragm and the pericardium. In embryonic development there is a brief rare occurrence in nature where there is an empty space here. As such we can cultivate this emptiness to allow a seat for our *Shen*-Spirit. It is a matter of clearing out the phlegm that mists the heart orifice, that mists the mind. This parallels the accumulation of buffer in our auric field, that we can metabolize to come out of our shell.

Ren 15 *Jiu Wei,* Turtledove Tail

We are still in the solar plexus area here at the tip of the xiphoid, the tailbone of the sternum. This is the source point for the yin of the body and the yin organs. This is the Luo point of the Ren Vessel, an accumulation point for karma that will be stored for the next incarnation or shunted through the Bao Mai to the genitalia for passing on to another generation. It is a switch for accessing the un-transcended lessons of the Po that have been sealed into the bone matrix at previous cycles of 7 & 8.

Ren 16 *Zhong Ting,* Center Courtyard

Helps remove accumulations in the chest, the undigested and un-integrated experiences that accumulate around the Heart orifice. These are caused by the Heart's own self-judgment of its experiences. This generates phlegm as the body "dampens" these feelings to be processed later.

Ren 17 *Tan Zhong,* Central Altar, Upper Altar, Primordial Child.

This is the front point for the Pericardium. The pericardium is our inner gate that allows communication to and from the Heart. It is the shock absorber for the Heart and crystallizes into our ego defense mechanisms. It functions from polarity, self-preservation and the sympathetic nervous system. The Heart functions from the para-sympathetic. The Heart is the primordial child that is never tainted from the traumas and shocks of this lifetime. It is the Observer, along for the ride, watching the movie unfold, bringing the power of love to what it witnesses. This is the ceremonial fire that we meditate on and sends our prayers up to Heaven. This is the Ancestral Qi of the Middle Dan Tian.

Ren 18 *Yu Tang,* Jade Hall

Helps with the respiratory effects caused by disturbed Shen-Spirit. Jade represents the highest level of purity. As we move upwards from Ren 17 towards the Uper Dan Tian we are embarking on this process of spiritual refinement.

Ren 19   *Zi Gong*, Purple Palace

Purple is the color of royalty and here in the sternum we are in the palace of the emperor or empress, the Heart. We have changed since ancient times and the role of the Heart changes, too. We are in the time of the New Mandala and the emperor has to learn how to live within the mundane and not be isolated in a Forbidden City or Ivory Tower. We are clearing out the divergent decay of hierarchical organization and the Heart must learn to accept, must learn to soften through the humility of being open to all of life's events and responding justly.

Ren 20   *Hua Gai*, Florid Canopy

The diaphragm is the florid canopy. We are learning to stop and smell the roses, to appreciate the grace provided in the moment through the inspiration of the breath. The beauty of spirit is in everything and very clearly seen in the beauty, scent and sacred geometry of flowers.

Ren 21   *Xuan Ji*, Jade Pivot/North Star

The North Star is our star of Destiny. It is the Pole star that helps us find our way. Our Heart orients us to follow the way of Heaven. In our body, this takes place at the junction between the Middle and Upper Dan Tians. We are learning to trust in our self and develop faith in our purpose, knowing that we can always find our way home.

Ren 22   *Tian Tu*, Heaven's Chimney

This point is located just above the sternum, at the base of the neck. It is a Window to the Sky point, an opening to the Upper Dan Tian, our internal representation of Heaven. It opens our upper orifices, opens our eyes, so that we can see the world and our self in a new way. It resolves the phlegm, the dampening of the signal, the truth, from Heaven. Our prayers are sent from the Fire of our Heart through Heaven's Chimney to the heavenly transceiver of our brain, changing the way we perceive and receive the world.

Ren 23   *Lian Quan*, Angular Ridge Spring

This is the Throat Chakra, the Heart as it is represented by the tongue. The ability to speak our truth, from the Heart. The ability to gauge the affects of our words on the Hearts of others. Our ability to manifest in the world through open communication, a clear channel. Our tongue quivers at the mere thought of words, of language. To find peace in our heart, we have to quell this addiction to language and find the truth before language, the pre-natal vibration. This is our swallowing mechanism. Have we swallowed our fears, our emotions? Have we bitten off more than we can chew?

Ren 24 *Cheng Jiang,* Supporting Tears

This is the mouth, one of the many ring muscle segments that we armor to block expression. As we learn to love ourselves and have deep compassion for our self and others, we can learn to trust the words we speak and trust our emotional expressions. It is the repressed emotions that others can see, that we cannot. The mouth is also where we take in nourishment, post-natal qi. Are we able to nourish and nurture ourselves? Do we feel contained enough to take care of our self or are we dependent on the social grid to define us, to fill us in where we feel inadequate? The Ren connects with the Du at the tongue and palate of the roof of the mouth, completing the circuit of the Microcosmic Orbit.

Traditional Coupled Point: *Kid 6 Zhao Hai,* Shining Sea

This is the Shining Sea, the deep potential of the unknown of the water element. We are shining light into the darkness, learning to awaken the Golden Flower, the light within. As we get to know our self, as we illuminate our self, we can learn to relate to this vast reservoir in the present moment through the Yin Qiao Vessel.

Du Vessel- Channel of Individuation

Moving through the World

Other Names - Governing Vessel, Sea of Yang

As the Ren Vessel is the Sea of Yin, the Du Vessel is the Sea of Yang. It is the channel up the spine, the channel that becomes the spine, from the tailbone to the skull and interpenetrates with the Ren Vessel to form the substantiation of our axis and our Microcosmic Orbit. The Du Vessel represents the ability of the organism to move from a strong pivot, to leverage off the spine, to be vertebrate, and to organize the charge of life in a sophisticated manner through a nervous system protected by a shell. The Du Vessel allows for the individual evolution of the organism through movement in the marrow, up the spine and into the brain. This is the Central Nervous System, the kundalini conduit, the upward movement of energy through the chakras, from the Root Chakra upwards, spreading its wings as it opens the 3rd Eye and the Crown Chakra. The Kundalini is housed in the perineum at the tailbone. This is the sleeping dragon, the spiraling energy of life, the double-helix energy of evolution. It is Earth energy, yin, that as soon as it enters the body at the feet or perineum becomes yang in nature, fiery, volatile, warm, fast, and upward moving. The yang energy of the Du Vessel is the raw electricity of life and as such it needs to be grounded to be useful. The Du Vessel is also responsible for the thermodynamics of the body, for generating the heat required to sustain life.

Kundalini Conduit

The ungrounded manifestation of the kundalini energy in the Du Vessel can eventually, possibly quickly, burn out the organism and consume its resources. This is frequently a Divergent Channel process as the body seeks to divert the excess energy away from the spine and brain in a person who is not grounded enough to sustain the charge. The root has been activated and the evolutionary energy begins to circulate in an organism that has not created the proper circuitry, ground and insulation to accommodate this charge. The organism can choose to break the root to short-circuit the energy from its source. This will leave the organism in a state of "fight or flight," or PTSD. The organism can attempt to divert the evolutionary energy along the axis to avoid injuring the brain, the Sea of Marrow. This can create strong blockages at the base of skull, the entryway to the brain as the organism tries to safeguard the marrow from such intense heat and energy. The base of the brain is associated with the visual cortex, which is deeply involved in the dynamics of the "3rd Eye," and inner vision.

This blockage can cause lots of Liver Wind symptoms. These are shaky and twitchy neurological symptoms related to the Liver Network which is directly related to the movement of the kundalini energy, the energy of growth, creation, and rebirth. The Liver is related to the eyes and opening the 3rd Eye, experiencing states of consciousness usually associated with R.E.M. states of sleep, which is one of the chief goals of evolution, the ability for spirit to experience itself directly. But experiencing itself without the wisdom of the rest of the centers of consciousness is unsustainable, and may activate different safeguard mechanisms.

These safeguard mechanisms can be seen as resulting from fear, often fear stemming from a spiritual level. The individual that opens its upper chakras pre-maturely may appear to have transcended its Po lessons by arriving at the top of the ladder of the spine and experiencing its own God consciousness. As such the organism may experience itself in the realm of the Po, with many Po coming towards them. This is very disorienting for it tends to only happen between incarnations, leading the organism to wonder if it may have died. These are the Bardo states, discussed extensively in the Tibetan Buddhist tradition. Generally if we arrive at these states through cultivation, through having learned our lessons, we will not be so surprised to be there. Traditionally, it was a teacher's responsibility to help their student if these sorts of things happened.

However, if catalyzed through other circumstances such as reckless practices, then the individual is on their own with the Tao as his or her teacher. This can be a tough situation as the individual may now be in a very weak condition to attempt recovery from a process that can be very difficult to integrate or understand. However, the evolutionary energy has to try new ways of experiencing itself, to test drive the viability of new traits for the collective, and spontaneously awakening of the kundalini is one of the ways it does this. It is a type of reverse-engineering and is a method unto itself, albeit a method that often meets with great resistance from the collective as the process of integrating genetic change deeply threatens the status quo on many levels. Interacting with the kundalini energy is one of the main drives of life, because it is the energy of all our drives. People's experiences in relation to this energy are deeply related to their spiritual curriculum. As we individuate through this energy it becomes all-important to know our self, for this energy will meet up with all the resistances we identify with.

In order to ground the Du Vessel, the Sea of Yang, we need the energy to be able to circulate and recycle and renew. This happens through the energetics of the Ren Vessel, the Sea of Yin. The relaxed peristaltic yin nature of the Ren is very insulating and shock absorbing. It is a downward energy of the parasympathetic energy, which is the energy of Heaven which becomes yin as it enters the body. These are the core aspects of polarity, of yin and yang. As such their interplay is one of the keys to the alchemy of the Chong Mai, the unity consciousness. Over time the energy of the primal yin and yang declines as we will see through the Wei Vessels, the organism's memory storage. Its availability in any given moment will be seen in the Qiao Vessels.

The containment for this process will be seen in the Dai Vessel also known as the Wrapping Vessel or Belt Channel.

Developmental Aspects of the Du Vessel

The Du Vessel becomes active as the infant prepares itself to interact more with the world through movement. It begins to stabilize its neck when feeding. It begins to fire Du 14 at the cervical-thoracic junction and Du 4, the Ming Men, at Lumbar 2. These are the curvatures of the spine which are mediated by the 5 Pivots of the Erector Spinae, Rectus Abdominis, Psoas, Diaphragm and SCM's. These are referred to as some of the Ancestral Sinews. The baby will spend much of its time while its lying down unable to move strengthening these reflexes and preparing to move, to crawl or walk. As it begins to walk it has quite a few considerations. First is, "where is the mama?" and "I want to be independent but I want the mama in sight." Second, this is the beginning of hearing "no!" quite a bit as it begins its explorations. Conditions on love begin to play a bigger role. And as far as movement is concerned, the child needs to learn to stop, to engage the antagonist/reciprocal muscle groups that allow braking. Also, it has to begin to make decisions, to move side-to-side, to avoid bumping into stuff, to manage the obstructions along the way. This is a strong Gall Bladder activation and its relationship to the decision-making process of Du Mai, Yang Wei Mai and the brain.

In its early development, the Du Mai is setting the imprints for our independence and our individuation. It is our ability to move and be free. It is the energy of bone and the brain. The yang energy is what we do, the yin could be said to be what we feel. The overuse of yang energy comes at the expense of the yin, and aggressive, extreme behavior will tax the yin. The secret to health and longevity is to know both yin and yang. The Dao De Jing says, "know the yang, but stick to the yin." This is another way of describing Wu Wei; act as needed, but don't overact. Learn the art of right timing.

Du Meridian Trajectories and Point Energetics

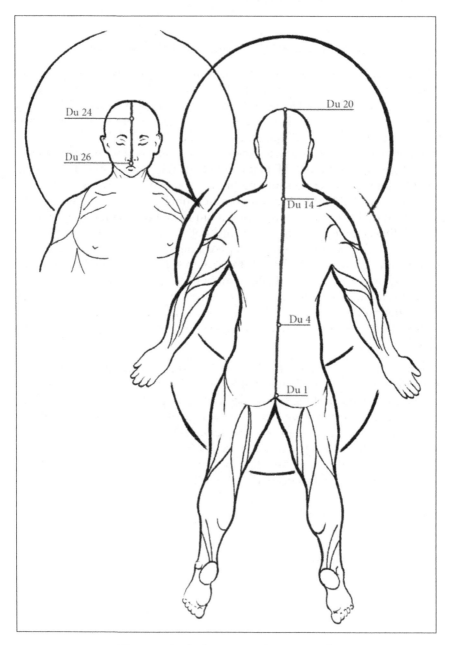

Figure 4.3: Trajectory 1 of Du Vessel.

Opening Point Small Intestine 3 *Hou Xi,* Back Stream

Trajectory 1 of Du Vessel

Originates from *Xia Ji*, "behind the pole." This could mean Du 1, Ren 1, the anus, or the Tai Chi Pole itself. Emerges at Du 1 at the tailbone and continues up the mid-line of the back via the spine. Enters the brain, continues to vertex at Du 20 and comes down mid-line of head to meet with the Ren Vessel inside the mouth to form the microcosmic orbit.

ॐॐ

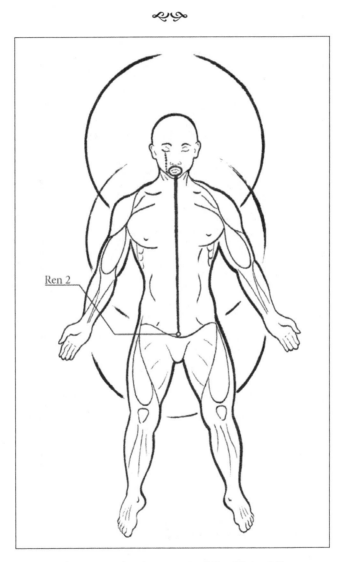

Figure 4.4: Trajectory 2 of Du Vessel.[28]

---

28.   *Trajectory from Cecil-Sterman, p. 273-277.*

Trajectory 2 of Du Vessel

Begins in lower abdomen and follows Ren Vessel trajectory. Demonstrates the interpenetration of yin and yang and the creation of the Microcosmic Orbit. Yang needs to temper itself not only through the yin but through its own active tempering, allowing us to express the instinct of moving towards home, towards our truth.

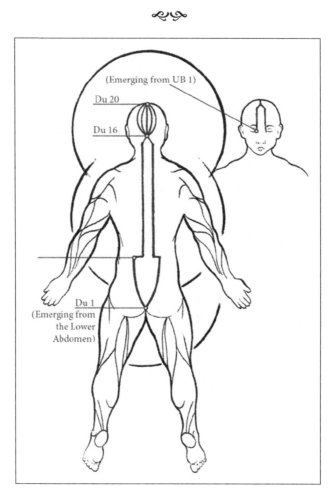

Figure 4.5: Trajectories 3 and 4 of Du Vessel[29]

Trajectory 3 of Du Vessel

Begins at UB 1 at the eyes and continues to Du 20, enters the brain and emerges at Du 16. Here it travels bilaterally down the spine along the *Huatuojiaji* Points to enter the Kidneys at UB 23. This trajectory governs the

29. *Trajectory from Cecil-Sterman, p.273-277.*

sensory-motor tracts. Its trajectory from the senses to the Kidneys shows the potential of "sealing our senses" to create more jing, more of our self.

Trajectory 4 of Du Vessel

This trajectory begins in the lower abdomen, goes to the genitalia, Ren 1 and Du 1. It then goes to the gluteus muscles, the spine and ends at the Kidneys, UB 23. This is like a reinforcement of the yang's role in supporting the tailbone, the reproductive function and the Will. Enables the sustained enthusiasm and exuberance of the yang qi.

Opening Point Small Intestine 3 *Hou Xi,* Back Stream

This point is located on the most yang meridian of the body, Taiyang, and is located at the point of contact for a karate chop. Not the only image for yang extending into the world, but still an appropriate one. The karate chop gains more power through the softening of the bones like a child, through the rejuvenation of the marrow. The rigid tree snaps in the wind, in the change, and the supple tree bends and endures. Change is inevitable, but growth is optional. This point is also translated as "Behind the Ravine" with the Kidneys being the ravine, where the Yuan Qi is disseminated or "streamed" from the back. Represents yang's extension into the world and the Small Intestine sorts out the information before it is received by its paired organ, the Heart.

Du 1 *Chang Quang,* Lasting Strength, Long Strong

The tip of the tailbone, the entry point for the kundalini energy to travel up the spine. A well-wishing for the endurance for such a journey and a reference to male virility. The tail is the docking station for the Earthly aspect of this circuit, as seen in James Cameron's *Avatar* movie. Du 1 is the Luo point of the Governing Vessel and is the accumulation point for the yang aspects of our karma. It is a switch that can activate the access to the ossified, untranscended lessons of the Po from our cycles of 7 & 8. Together with Ren 15(the tailbone of the sternum and Luo of the Ren) they create a fascial pulley that can only be maintained through willingness to maintain integrity at the deepest levels of our bone matrix and our self.

Du 2 *Yao Shu,* Lumbar's Shu

The sacral heatus. The sacrum is the sacred bone, the energy of the alpha that sets the energy of the tribe. This is the area of latency as unresolved issues settle into the Lower Burner and calcify into the bone matrix, written into the DNA. As we journey towards awakening, this is our power source, our engine. There are cobwebs to dust off to access the potential of this engine as we have repressed the shadow aspects of our dominance-submission issues of predator and prey. Here we have the ghosts of our ancestral past of surviving on the material plane. This energy is the energy of life. As we gain the ability to be a casual and compassionate observer of our own experience, we can let this engine run without mindlessly getting entangled in more karma due to basic drives. We can learn to let the engine idle until needed, Wu Wei, the idling of the Wei Qi.

Du 3   *Yao Yang Guan,* Lumbar Yang Gate

Treats the cold and fear that can get trapped in the Kidneys and weaken our connection to life and the Earth through our legs and movement.

Du 4   *Ming Men,* Life Gate, Gate of Destiny

This is the moving qi between the kidneys. As we open up this area of the lumbar spine we can begin to directly transmute energy from the ancestral field, the dark matter of the quantum zero-point field, the source energy of the Tao. Fear is the Guardian at the Gate that freezes our relationship to this field and locks our Pericardium into polarized consciousness. This is the energy of the other side, the connection of birth, life, and death into a continuum of awareness and ancestry powering us on our path of Destiny.

Du 5   *Xuan Shu,* Suspended Axis

Lifts yang energy to assist the Spleen and the upright energy of the axis and the central qi.

Du 6   *Ji Zhong,* Spinal Center

Clears heat and dampness that have accumulated through stasis and obstruction in the Du Vessel.

Du 7   *Zhong Shu,* Central Axis

Supports the whole digestive network of the Spleen, Stomach, Liver and GB. Supports the Middle Jiao and the upright qi.

Du 8   *Jin Suo,* Sinew Contraction

Helps change the habitual response to stress, the patterns of tension locked in the body. Treats the trapped winds in the body that manifest as tremors, twitches, spasms and neurological symptoms. Opens the patient to new possibilities, new ways of moving through the world.

Du 9   *Zhi Yang,* Extreme Yang

This is where yang energy reaches its height, where the upright nature of the spine must maintain an awakened pivot. Helps the diaphragm, Liver and GB.

Du 10   *Ling Tai,* Soul Tower, Pagoda of the Soul

The residing place of the soul as it relates to the Du Vessel, the spine, the tower that allows us to have a perspective on our experience of life. When we have worked through the lessons of our life, we gain this view. The Ling represents the soul, the more substantial, embodied, plasmic, yin aspect of spirit. Contraindicated to needle in some traditions as it may disturb the spirit.

Du 11   *Shen Dao,* Spirit Path

This regulates the Heart and is the residence of the Tao of Spirit, our connection to the Big Shen of the Universe. Contraindicated to needle in some traditions as it may disturb the spirit.

Du 12   *Shen Zhu,* Body Pillar

The beginning of the "buffalo hump," the accumulation of things we cannot change. Master point for pathology in the brain affecting the spine.

Du 13   *Tao Dao,* Way of Happiness

A point also known as "furnace of the Tao," the alchemical cauldron that assists going through changes and letting go of wind. Here we are approaching the entrance to the brain and have the opportunity to work through issues and lessons before they get deeper into the marrow and the chance of becoming curriculum issues in the next lifetime. This point also diverts heat into the scapula, preferring to store latency away from the spine.

Du 14   *Da Zhui,* The Great Hammer

This is the yang energy of the Heart as it expresses through the arms to reach out into the world and connect with others through its purpose. This is the busiest nerve intersection of the body and entanglement and distortion here keep the energy of transcendence from reaching the brain. Can cause accumulation and postural distortion as we shut down to the memory of the events of our own life.

Du 15 Ya Men, Gate of Muteness

The entry into the Low Brain as it regards the tongue. The tongue is attached to the cervical vertebra and related to the Heart. Even thinking in language makes the tongue vibrate. If your thoughts, your words, and your truth are in conflict there will be blockage hear. Du 15 and Du 16 represent the Atlas and the Axis, one is the "Yes" vertebra one is the "No" vertebra. When we say yes when we mean no and vice versa we jam the signals at these junctions, an essential dilemma between the acquired mind and our original nature.

Du 16 Feng Fu, Wind Palace

This is the entry into the brain the beginning of the flowering of the kundalini. This is the Low Brain, the deep reptilian record of survival and the emotional and traumatic imprinting of the Limbic system. These are the Delta waves that affect everything through resonance. This is where the un-transcended events of our lives are written into the marrow record, to be used for future decision-making and also to attract the situations for their own opportunity to be transcended either in this lifetime or the next.

Du 17 Nao Hu, Brain's Door

Represents entry into the Mid-Brain, the mammalian, socially interactive brain. Treats memory and wind symptoms.

Du 18 Qiang Jian, Unyielding Space

This is the beginning of the "ladder of the brain," as Du 1 is the beginning of the "ladder of the spine." We are embarking on the path to the upper brain, the flowering of the light within as represented by the neo-cortex of the Upper Brain. Consolidates our thoughts for less distraction on our journey.

Du 19 Hou Ding, Behind the Vertex

Calms the mind and treats neurological disorders.

Du 20 Bai Hui, 100 Meetings point

This is the "scenic by-way" of our connection to Heaven and the representation of the non-dual nature of the Corpus Callosum, bridging the hemispheres. Confusion activates this point, creating the dynamic tension for its own release. This is the fontanelle, the opening to spirit that is available as an infant and then entirely sealed at the end of the first cycle of 7 & 8. One-way kundalini circuitry can open this point, but often causing premature aging. The recycling nature of the microcosmic orbit circuitry being the antidote, allowing the descending nature of the yin and the para-sympathetic to return to Earth and be lifted back up by its own buoyancy.

Du 21   *Qian Ding,* Before the Vertex

Calms the mind and treats neurological disorders

Du 22   *Xin Hui,* Fontanelle Meeting

Represents the entry into the Upper Brain and its spiritual and extrasensory potential. Potent point for bringing energy up to the head. When our fontanelle closes we lose our direct access to spirit, through cultivation we re-awaken this connection with all the mystery, wonder and imagination that we remember from our childhood.

Du 23   *Shang Xing,* Upper Star

This is a Ghost Point. Here we are removing residual obstructions in the plasmic Po body. The Po are represented by our Lungs and this point opens up our nose and sense of smell. Our sense of smell is deeply related to the animal kingdom and a sense that has been deeply repressed to provide higher social order.

Du 24   *Shen Ting,* Spirit Court

Calms the *Shen*-Spirit and brightens the eyes.

Du 25   *Su Liao,* White Bone Hole

Opens the nose orifice and clears heat. A latency point due to its nature of deeper access to the bone matrix. This is seen in its name, from being a *Liao* point- a bone hole.

Du 26   *Ren Zhong,* Center of Man

This is a resuscitation point. Good for coma or for reminding those that are sleeping through their lives of their spiritual nature. A Ghost Point for releasing the static on the Wei Qi.

Du 27 *Dui Duan,* Extremity of Mouth

A resuscitation point. Treats loss of voice and throat obstruction.

Du 28 *Yin Jiao,* Gum Intersection

At the inner part of the upper lip, the only acupuncture point on a meridian that is on the inside of the body. Clears heat. Treats loss of voice and throat obstruction.

Paired Point Urinary Bladder 62 *Shen Mai,* Extending Vessel

This is our stance towards the world, written into our posture and skeletal structure. It is how we see the world. Is it a hostile place? Is it a place that we need to change? Is today a day to enjoy the world or to try to improve upon it? It is the opening point for the Yang Qiao.

Part 4 Chapter 4

The Dai Vessel- Channel of Consolidation

The Container/Pandora's Box- Consolidating the Astral

Other Names - Belt Channel, Wrapping Channel, Girdling Vessel

The Dai Vessel is also known as the Belt Channel. It is practically the only horizontal vessel of the acupuncture channel system(although there are the Transverse Luo Channels). This creates the necessary axis to allow for the coordinates of time and space to be woven onto. This channel wraps the entirety of our body and creates the container for our experiences. The belt reinforces the boundaries of the self, of the seed structure of the Chong. On the body, it has two channels. One channel is at the navel level, more associated with consolidating the Yuan Qi of the Kidneys and reinforcing the Ming Men for upright dissemination. Its better known trajectory in acupuncture manuals is along the Gall Bladder points of the iliac crest of the pelvis where it serves as a dumping ground in the basin of the pelvis. This is the closet, or perhaps the basement. This is where we put things that may have sentimental value to us, but really no longer serve us. This is the "to be processed or filed later" area, that tends to never get filed but maybe the filing cabinet fills up and moves to the basement. This is our garbage dump and needs to be emptied from time to time. Emptying the Belt is a strategy that can be very effective, but is not a permanent solution. The bigger picture has to do with: why is the person putting everything into storage? Why don't they look at and process some of these things?

The Belt Channel and the Heart

Along with these two trajectories, the Belt Channel is paired with another wrapping that goes around the chest which is called Da Bao, or the Great Wrapping. The Da Bao is at the level of the Heart, the home of the Zong Qi, the Ancestral Qi, the Pectoral Qi, the breath we share with our ancestors. The Heart is here to witness our valiant efforts at rectifying the ancestral energy of the lineage that we are born into. Whatever the Heart cannot process due to its own self-imposed morality, perhaps a socially-internalized morality, wherever it gets stuck in judgment and justice and regret, whatever it can't let go of, gets shunted away from the Heart into the Belt Channel, because it's better than having it affect the Heart. The secret to rectifying this situation is to forgive others and to forgive one's self to others, to free our Heart from the inner distortion and karmic entanglement of polarity and allow ourselves to evolve spiritually. Grace. The main thing standing in our way of this sense of liberation is our sense of responsibility. This is our sense of responsibility to that which we are bound, that which we have bonded with.

This includes being bound to the story of this body in this lifetime, to the ancestral agreements, to our bonds to our family, our culture, our country, our religion, etc. This is our honor towards our duty. Many cultures put their civic responsibility as the number one thing, without which you shame, disgrace and dishonor your family. How to grow spiritually and participate in social constructs is often set up as a paradox. It takes a lot of work to live in duality, and carry the torch, the grace of the spirit. We can do this by getting to know our self, by getting to know what is real to us. Being alive comes with a responsibility, but what is this responsibility?

Whatever we are unequipped to process gets shunted into the Belt via the Bao Vessel. This is the loop that connects the genitalia to the heart, the loop that connects the Da Bao to the Dai Vessel. This is another way of saying it connects the Heart-Kidney Axis, the Heart being the Da Bao and the Belt Channel being the Kidneys. The Bao Vessel participates in the process of how un-transcended curriculum goes into the Yuan Qi to be passed on to the next generation. In the meantime, we lose access to our creativity, our ability to create more of our self in the world.

The process of loading the Belt Channel parallels many processes in the body. It is a version of the process of latency. The shunting of unprocessed judgment away from the Heart is similar to the process of creating phlegm to buffer the Heart. We call this clouding of the mind and spirit, "phlegm misting the mind," or "phlegm misting the Heart Orifice." This takes place through the loading of the Gao Huang, the membranes that wrap the organs, especially the space between the Pericardium and the Diaphragm. This area is the original pre-natal empty space. For a brief period in utero, there is an actual empty space between the pericardium and the diaphragm. This is a rarity in nature and when it occurs it should be paid attention to. We, similar to nature, don't know what to do with an empty space, so we fill it. Seeing as nothing actually belongs there, we cannot fill this space with something useful, so we fill it with something useless. We can do this with the mucoid substance we call phlegm, a combination of fibrous tissue and fluid. This is our amniotic fluid. It serves as a buffer to the raw experience of atmospheric pressure.

There is a direct relationship between the amniotic fluid in utero, the phlegm in the Gao Huang, and the unconscious filler in our auric egg. This is the protective mechanism of the spirit, of the Heart, of the pre-natal energy body in relation to the shock of direct experience. If we can re-establish this empty space, we can learn to function post-natally, or socially, from the pre-natal energy body. We do this through the organization of our emotional body as articulated through the Solar Plexus. Of course, this is rather difficult if this level of cultivation is not the norm in the culture. Such is the tension that has driven evolution.

The Spin of Our Container

A related mechanism that mirrors the process of the loading of the Belt occurs through the Gall Bladder Channel and the Yang Wei Vessel, and this process is pointed to by the Belt Channel's trajectory of GB Meridian points and the Belt Channel's traditional pairing with the Yang Wei Vessel. These relationships are informing us of the process of experience, latency, and the record of our lives that is recorded into the brain marrow. This is another demonstration of how unprocessed baggage will make it to the Yuan Qi level, to the source qi, and provide the karma, the imperfection, the flaw that allows incarnation, either re-incarnation or pro-creation. In one scenario, it is written into the uterus, the reproductive organs, in another scenario it gets written into the brain and marrow, both of which are caused by the spirit and the Heart's inability to withstand the direct experience of polarity. To what degree can we return to innocence after the accumulation of experience, without having to die to do so?

As the reinforcement of the container of our auric field, the Belt Channel functions similar to Wei Qi, defending our boundaries from infringement on all levels. The Belt Channel maintains our structure in conjunction with our vertical axis. But there is one more all-important aspect to the Belt Channel: it spins. It is our spin, our unique and authentic energy signature. The Belt is designed to spin like a hula-hoop, like an orbit or a multitude of orbits. Once we remove the stasis that binds us into a state of resistance to our own spin, we have the ability to experience ex-stasis, ecstasy, or spin. This experience of our self as a vibrating, pulsating life form is joy.

"The soul is here to experience its own joy" - Rumi

This is our birthright. The spinning orbits of the Belt Channel can spin off layers of stagnation, static, karma, from our energy body. This spin can also have a strong effect on the energy bodies of other people as well. Our Wei Qi is comprised of a series of spiraling orbits and orbs. Each Dan Tian is an orb and each joint is an orb. Every imaginable relationship between these orbs is an orbit. These orbits have power. They are our instincts and reflexes and they are capable of martial applications and the ability to influence people's movements from a distance. These orbits, these belts, can be "loaded" like a rubber band, or coiled like a rubber band allowing for more power than speed and strength alone. This is an ability that can descend upon us, and an ability that can be cultivated through working with the natural torsion that coiling movements create in the body. This is known as "silk reeling" in Tai Chi terms.

Spin is the natural uncoiling of the body, of the spiraling motion of the serpentine energy of the kundalini, right down to the torsion that occurs in DNA. We can train this from the ground up, but this energy originates from spiritual states. Most of the sophisticated martial, medical and spiritual arts involve the endless detail that arises from reverse engineering multi-dimensional experience. Perhaps we should spend as much time awakening multi-dimensional experience as we do obsessing about the arts and sciences that these experiences have inspired.

It is our ability to spin that allows us to access our multi-dimensional self and the gifts that are innate to us. We spin most authentically by participating in the activity that allows us to experience the most "flow" consciousness. These energies are readily experienced through dance and music, two of the most socially acceptable outlets for these primal belt drives. Sex, violence, and drug use are all related to these unfiltered energies of creation. Neither repression and suppression or mere indulgence can provide the solution. If we suppress and repress, we begin to dampen our spin, until we have none. This is the accumulation of karma, of resistance, in the Belt Channel. If we begin to spin without restriction we "accelerate" our karma, attracting the lessons and temptations that we need to work through. Science is beginning to show that we benefit from a blend of "hedonic" and "euphonic" experiences. The former provides us pleasure in the moment and the latter provides us the long-term benefits of purpose and serving others, the experience of our self as part of a community.

Pandora's Box

The Belt channel offers a container to help us work with the transpersonal energies of the astral layers of our psyche. This is our Pandora's Box, our relationship to the oceanic primordial drives and images of the Earthly chakras. We do not own these aspects of our psyche. These energies are autonomous. We are responsible for how we manage these energies. By establishing a coherent container through the wrapping aspect of the Belt Channel, we can create space to bring up the images, drives and feelings of the collective unconscious. As we learn to accept our self and remain neutral, we do not have to project these archetypal forces onto others, suppress them deep into the psyche or act out on them as they process. We can maintain clarity and make the choices that are most in alignment with our integrity, whatever that means to us.

The Belt Channel provides the buffer for our experiences in our time/space continuum. The Belt Channel functions at the edge of our personal energy body and the transpersonal energy body. This occurs at the 2nd External Wai Qi Field of the Heart. The energy field of the Heart is relatively unstructured. We bring it into coherence through cultivation. As we develop and maintain a structure through coherence and integrity, we begin to connect and awaken within the 5th dimension at the edge of our container and the transpersonal realms of spirit. This boundary is not meant to be merely dissolved, which would be abdicating our personal responsibility, but to be articulated. We articulate our aura through expressing our Yuan Qi, the energy of our bones, the piezo-electric charge that circulates through our liquid crystal collagen matrix and creates the magnetic field that contains the plasma in our field. And through awakening the empty space pivots of the strange attractors of our blueprint beyond the 5th dimension, we can learn to let ourselves spin. But it is quite a responsibility.

❧

Dai Meridian Trajectories and Point Energetics

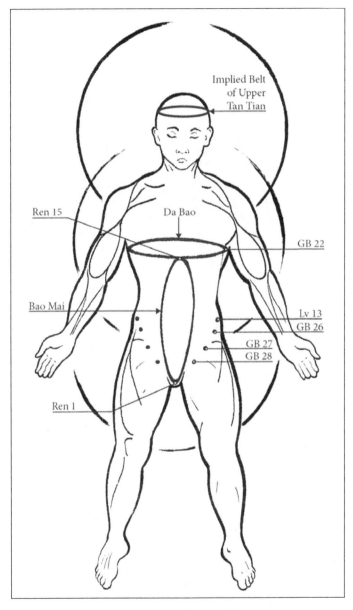

Figure 4.6: Dai Vessel-Draining Trajectory

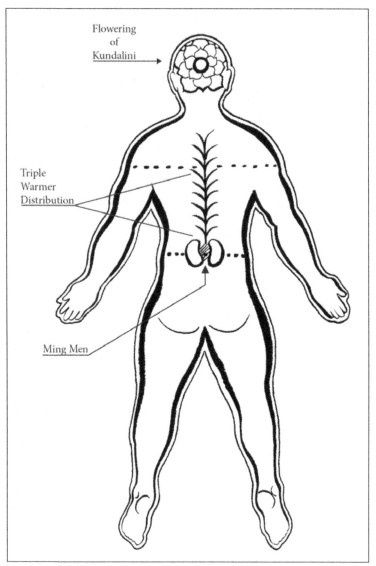

Figure 4.7: Dai Vessel- Consolidation Trajectory

Opening Point **Gall Bladder 41** *Zu Lin Qi,* Foot Palace of Tears

Draining Trajectory of Dai Vessel

The trajectory of the Belt Channel is complicated as it represents the main way that unprocessed events and emotions are stored into the constitutional level so we can be more available in the moment. Its trajectory is entered from several places such as the Qiao Vessels, the Divergent Channels, the Da Bao/Bao Mai to mention a few. As a trajectory it emerges at the 11th Rib at Liver 13, and follows the GB Meridian along the pelvic basin to GB 28. It dampens the charge of the Yang Qi, compromising our enthusiasm for life and our creativity.

෴

Consolidating Trajectory of Dai Vessel

This trajectory of the Dai Vessel consolidates the Chong Vessel, Ren Vessel, and Du Vessel, known collectively as the 1st Ancestry. The pathway encircles the horizontal axis of the body from Du 4(Lumbar 2) to Ren 8(the Navel). This supports the Ming Men function and the Triple Warmer function of bringing Yuan Qi to the organs along the spine at the Back Transport points.

Trajectory of Da Bao and Bao Mai

The Da Bao wraps the Middle Tan Tian from Sp 21/ GB 22 at the "forgotten muscles" of the lateral aspects of our chest and across the front and back to the solar plexus at Ren 15. Un-transcended issues are shunted away from the Heart via the Da Bao. The Post-Natal influences that have impacted our original nature can accumulate and enter the constitution both at Ren 15, the Luo Point of the Ren, and at Sp 21/GB 22, the Great Luo of the Spleen. The Bao Mai is a vertical trajectory from Ren 15 to the perineum at Ren 1 and provides the mechanism whereby these un-transcended issues reach the Belt Channel and affect our ability to support the anus/tailbone and extend more of our self into the world.

෴

Draining the Dai- Pandora's Box

***

Opening Point Gall Bladder 41 *Zu Lin Qi,* Foot Palace of Tears

We shed a tear to wash our windows, to renew our perspective, to change our marrow, to return to innocence. Today is the first day of the rest of your life and we can always start our journey with a single step in a new direction, or renewed awareness of each step in the direction we are heading.

Liver 13   *Zhang Men*, Camphor Gate

We are releasing dead issues that no longer serve us. The wood element is constantly growing and in order to put energy to the new, towards the living, we have to let go of the dead branches, remove the obstructions on our path. We keep our feet planted firmly on the Earth and remove the dead wood. It will make a great fire for our Heart.

Gall Bladder 26   *Dai Mai*, Belt Channel

Here is where the draining and consolidating aspects of the Belt cross. This point is very related to the psoas, the soil of the soul, the karma and fertilizer being eliminated and transformed into essence, into fuel for our transformation.

Gall Bladder 27   *Wu Shu*, Five Pivots

This is our horizontal axis as mediated by our pelvic floor. If this axis is open, the 5 Pivots that govern the 3 bony cavities will liberate our structure and vice versa. We are learning to know our bones, our ancestry and to let these issues unwind, surrendered back to the Earth, rebounding with gravitational buoyancy in our axis. Bearing our cross and being carried by the field.

Gall Bladder 28   *Wei Dao*, Linking Path

The settling of our untranscended baggage, our dampness, towards the deepest yin of the perineum. The lessons of the Po, of our ancestry, must be accounted for before we can access the energy of creation.

Paired Point   *San Jiao 5   Wai Guan*, Outer Gate

This is the ability to bring our Yang creativity to outward expression. To create more of ourselves. To allow our true self to be expressed and seen. Overcoming the dampness of the past, the heaviness and haunting of the past to break through our shell, release our exterior and allow us to be reborn in this lifetime again and again.

Consolidating the Belt- Our Cocoon

ༀ

Du 4   *Ming Men,* Life Gate, Gate of Destiny

This is the center of the back of the belt channel, which is all the points even with the navel. It is like a belt cinching up our skeleton to a more up-right posture. This is called consolidation. We tend to collapse our life gate, not allowing it to attach to the gravity axis. Why do we inhibit the life force?

Urinary Bladder 23   *Shen Shu,* Kidney's Shu

This is the representation of the Kidneys, the batteries, the seat of Yuan Qi as it begins to be disseminated up the Tree of Life to the shu points via the Triple Burner.

Urinary Bladder 52   *Zhi Shi,* Will's Chamber

This is the outer shu point of the Kidneys, associated with the Will, the Zhi. The will is associated with the self, essentially amoral by nature, due to its freedom. The will becomes wisdom as it learns to align with benevolence and the Heart, its heavenly purpose, its destiny.

Gall Bladder 25   *Jing Men,* Capital Gate

Point that represents the Kidneys. Not on the umbilical line, but it has associations with the pre-natal aspects of the Kidneys and GB. It is associat-ed with the quadratus lumborum, a muscle that opens and closes the space between the ribs and pelvis.

Gall Bladder 26   *Dai Mai,* Belt Channel

Represents the dynamics of the psoas as it interplays with the diaphragm, quadratus lumborum and rectus abdominis. Maintains space between the ribs and pelvis.

Spleen 15   *Da Heng,* Great Traverse

Post-natal aspects of the Spleen's Zheng Qi that lifts the organs and the posture. Treats tendency to avoidance and allows us to own our life experi-ences, to absorb and eliminate them.

Stomach 25   *Tian Shu*, Heavenly Axis, Heavenly Pivot

Front point of the Stomach. The Heavenly Pivot between above and below and the Hidden Beam of the rectus abdominis. The ability of the Hun to come and go freely as provided by the umbilicus that is reconnected to pre-natal energetic.

Kidney 16   *Huang Shu*, Vital's Transporting Hollow

The pre-natal aspects of the naval and the umbilical sphincter that inhibits the upright movement of Zheng Qi in the traumatized umbilicus.

Ren 8   *Shen Que*, Spirit's Palace Gate, The Navel

We retract inward from trauma and this is the first trauma and the first breath. The separation from source and the reconnection to source allowing us to be breathed by the larger organism of humanity.

❧

Da Bao and Bao Vessel

Ren 15   *Jiu Wei*, Turtledove Tail

The Luo point of the Ren. The beginning of the accumulation of the matters that the Heart cannot process due to judgment. This judgment is based on self-imposed morality. This is how the shunting process begins.

Gall Bladder 22   *Yuan Ye*, Armpit Abyss

This is the opening point of the Da Bao. Opens the diaphragm. This point is on the serratus muscle and represents how the Sinews hold the armpit and Heart 1 closed and thereby protect the Heart at the expense of the fluid movement of our chest, arms and breath.

Spleen 21   *Da Bao*, Great Wrapping

This point represents the wrapping at the level of the Heart. If consolidated it represents the feeling of a big hug. If congested, it can result in full-body pain. This is the accumulation of post-natal karma being processed through the system back to the pre-natal. This affects our diaphragm and the ability of our ribs to function like gills, pumping our breath, while we experience swimming in air, swimming in the Tao Field that is everywhere.

Ren 1   *Hui Yin*, Sea of Yin

Here we have the Sea of Yin, the lowest point on the torso. This is accumulation weighing down the natural upward pumping action of the perineum. As this is lost the structural integrity of the organism collapses, forcing it to crystallize into a holding pattern, with high residual tension and minimal roon for growth, change and adaptability. The organism will be forced to identify with its post-natal configuration as contact with the pre-natal will have been lost.

Yin Wei Vessel- Channel of Our Story

The Story in Our Blood:
Transcription, Stasis, and Transcendence

Other Name - Yin Linking Vessel

The next two channels are paired and are known as the Wei Vessels, or the Linking Vessels. They link together our relationship with time to provide continuity. They are the fabric of our memory, of our experiences, emotions and images that make us the person who we identify with, make up our identity. They are represented by the movement of time over the cycles of 7 & 8, the major events and transitions in our lives. At each of these phases the Yuan Qi is more susceptible to imprinting, which gives us an opportunity to let go and make a change at a fundamental level or to crystallize further into our habituated post-natal processes and limited self-understanding. This is how we age.

The Ren Vessel is the Primal Sea of Yin and the Yin Wei Vessel represents the decline of the body's yin, the entropy of the aging process. This is the way the Ren Vessel is impacted and imprinted by the events of our lives. This is similar to the way a computerized device needs memory to function. We are using up our memory storage through the process of identification with our post-natal existence, through the identification with the experiences of our lives. The Du Vessel is the Primal Sea of Yang and the Yang Wei Vessel represents the same process of memory usage, except more regarding the way the events of our lives impact the Du Vessel. What we are seeing now through modern science is the idea of neural plasticity, and fascial plasticity and the ability to continue learning, to change, to continue evolving the potential of our marrow through an efficient relationship with memory storage.

Record of Images and Feelings

The Yin Wei is the record of the images and feelings attached to our memories. It is our emotional and pictorial record. Memory tends to create constellations of the most disjointed moments of our lives, although on a day-to-day basis our lives tend to be much less disjointed than that. This is the record of our story, of our movie. It is like an autobiography. An autobiography generally consists of the most extreme moments because it makes for better reading. The conundrum here is that the more attached we are to any of the aspects of our story, to any deep nostalgia of the people, places, and events of our past, the less energy that we have available for the present moment. And so it goes, the more attached we are to the past, the more we are consuming our jing.

The Yin Wei Vessel tells the story in our blood and the story in our bones, the story in our yin. If life were a piece of string, the extreme peaks and valleys would consume the string rather quickly. We may have already created those extremes in our life, but we can change our relationship to the memories. We can iron out the peaks and valleys through taking in the essence of those events and how they shaped who we are, and free that energy up for the present. We do not need to live a boring life, but through a certain level of non-attachment, through observer consciousness, we can lead the life we were meant to without unduly impacting the health of our Yuan Qi. This quality of perspective, to be an observer in your own story is beautifully illustrated in the point known as Guest House, Kid 9.

This channel is about continual interaction with the social world, with the "homogenizing principle" of social indoctrination and how much of one's self is actually surviving this process. It is about coming to completion with the elements of our story, the constellations of our trauma, the cementing of our resistance into our Pericardium, the Heart Protector, from fear and survival. We are moving towards completion, through the Completion Gate, the Gate of Hope as represented by Liver 14. We are beginning anew for with every ending comes a new beginning. This is the nature of hope, the possibility of redemption. We are connecting with our Heart and moving into the creativity and authenticity of the throat chakra, as we see on the trajectory of the Yin Wei Vessel.

The Yin Wei is the structure, the yin, it is how the blood and the marrow and the related fascial tension all write one's story through bone remodeling, creating the caverns and crystalline structures. Our only purpose is to be our unique selves, like a snowflake, or a crystal. At the time of our death, or during some Near Death Experiences, the Hun plays us the story of our lives, in our Blood. The Hun plays the movie of the Yin Wei Mai, the Linking Vessel. We are then able to understand the parts of our story that have still been financed by our attachment to the Heart Palaces, until we can learn to be at peace in our Heart, to embody the center of our magic square, so our spirit can return Home.

Yin Wei Meridian Point Energetics

Linking Yin through Time- Weaving the Threads of Our Story

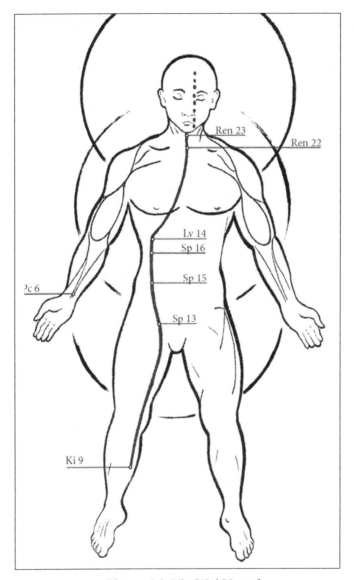

Figure 4.8: Yin Wei Vessel

Opening Point   Pericardium 6   *Nei Guan,* Inner Gate

Yin Wei Vessel Trajectory

Begins at Kidney 9, the Guest House, at the medial aspect of the calves, where it invites the observer consciousness to reflect on the tapestry of the story of our life experiences. From here it ascends through the inguinal region at Sp 13, continuing along the Spleen Channel, representing our post-natal social influences, as it ascends the abdomen to the ribcage to the Completion Gate of Liver 14, to allow the Hun to see the degree to which we have lived our Heavenly Mandate, our Destiny. It continues ascending to the neck and connecting back to the Ren Vessel, from which it originated, at Ren 22 and Ren 23.

Opening Point Pericardium 6 *Nei Guan,* Inner Gate

The holographic emotional record of the images of our story are held in our blood and moved by the pulsation of our Heart. As we hold onto and identify with disjointed images we function less and less from the Heart and more from the Heart Protector, the Heart Constrictor. The Pericardium decides what gets into the inner sanctum of our heart and allows us to experience intimacy and appropriate boundaries. Our ego defines itself in relationship to the Pericardium and our protective mechanism, afraid to lose its self-reference point and accept its place in the single organism of humanity.

Kidney 9 *Zhu Bin,* Guest House

The ability to be the Observer in your own experience, to be detached enough to watch your story with compassion and to trust yourself enough to let go of the over-controlling aspects of the ego.

Spleen 13 *Fu She,* Abode of the Bowels

When we feel at home, our experiences can come and go freely and the bowels move freely. This sense of being at home in society is governed by the Spleen. Encourages letting go of what we don't need and the ability to provide a container for our life.

Spleen 15 *Da Heng,* Great Traverse

This is the post-natal energy of the Spleen/Earth element, as the blood is produced by the Sp/St and the Yin Wei represents how our post-natal experiences imprint us at a level deep enough to resource the yin of the Ren Mai. We are digesting our emotional story in order to extract the essence and free up the yin occupied by memory. We are in the chaos of the winds of change and Spleen 15, due to the fact that it lies on the navel axis, is our ability to trust in our axis, that we have a North Star, a Destiny, and that we will always be able to find our way home.

Spleen 16   *Fu Ai*, Abdomen's Lament

This is the inability to digest our story. The tendency to retreat inward and withdraw love after an incident. Can we digest our story or do we swallow our emotions to the point that we cannot stomach our life?

Liver 14   *Qi Men*, Cycle Gate, Completion Gate, Gate of Hope

The last point in the 12 meridian cycle. With every ending comes the promise of a new beginning, the hope of a fresh start. Here we bring issues that have been stored in our blood to completion, freeing up energy for new growth in the wood element. We are playing parts of the movie of the Hun in order to live and die with no regrets, or at least, less regrets.

Ren 22   *Tian Tu*, Heaven's Chimney

The Yin Wei trajectory returns to the Ren Mai, its source. As we experience completion, the energy of our story is liberated back to the yin. This is the connection to the Upper Dan Tian and Heaven as our story is laid bare before our Heart, the collective and God and is let go up to Heaven.

Ren 23   *Lian Quan*, Angular Ridge Spring

We can speak truth from our Heart and share the wisdom of our journey through our presence and our words if necessary.

Paired Point   Spleen 4   *Gong Sun*, Grandparent/Grandchild

We have less karma in our curriculum, the Chong, as we release and honor our story without regret.

Part 4 Chapter 6

Yang Wei Vessel- Channel of Our Choices
The Brain Marrow Record:
Data Recording for Future Decision-Making

Other Name - Yang Linking Vessel

The Yang Wei Vessel is the complement of the Yin Wei Vessel and they form the warp and woof of our experience. They are the loom that the record of our life, the tapestry of our life is woven onto. The Yang Wei is more about the events, the coordinates, of our memory and Yin Wei is more about what the memories evoke. The Yang Wei can be seen as being more about the actions in our life and the Yin Wei is more about how the actions of others made us feel. The Yang Wei Vessel is also more future-driven. Our energy can be displaced towards the future, generating heat in the body. This often combines with being stuck in the past which relates to holding onto dampness. Together this creates Damp-Heat. This is a very Yang Wei Vessel expression of being. It is also known as a Shaoyang expression which is related to the GB and the San Jiao. It is something that is half this and half that, mediating between internal and external, alternating between latency and expression, something indecisive.

Yang Wei Vessel and the I Ching

The Yang Wei Vessel is very much the brain record of the events of our lives, recording events and their perceived results for future decision-making so that we can make better choices in the future. The ancient oracle and book of wisdom, the *I Ching* or Book of Changes, is often used in a way that benefits the Yang Wei Vessel. The 64 Hexagrams or situations of the *I Ching* are interacted with in a manner that helps us accelerate our understanding of how our choices and the intentions behind them affect our ability to be present with change and the momentum of life. Through reflecting on the archetypal wisdom of the *I Ching*, we can begin to categorize the vibrational configurations of circular time.

As we work with this book of wisdom we begin to see the patterns that continuously roll around and offer us opportunities to refine our character, or perhaps to accept our character and refine our choices. With or without the use of the *I Ching* the idea is that once we have gotten the essence of a lesson we can use our memory storage much more efficiently. Once we understand how the events of our lives relate to a certain type of lesson, we can let go of trying to hold on to the details of so many events, thereby freeing up our essence. We may still remember the details, but they will take up much less energy. We have learned good Feng Shui of the brain marrow, of the 9 Palaces of the Brain. Same lessons, different storage medium.

The Yang Wei Vessel is, like the Belt Channel, a holding ground for accumulation. This is the attempt to process karma in a way that doesn't interfere with our free will in this incarnation. The Yang Wei Vessel has some historical controversy in its trajectory. Some writers believe that it had to return to the Du Vessel as it entered the brain, thereby becoming part of the constitution and the next incarnation. In this scenario, the un-transcended information kept in the memory record will be transmitted for continual learning in the next incarnation.

How Memory affects Our Movement

The Yang Wei Vessel represents how time and memory have affected our movements. How has the post-natal world affected the way we move? Do we move half-hearted? Have we gotten all stiff and rigid in our move-ments because our beliefs have gotten that way? Have we forgotten ways to express the original self? The washing of the marrow record is how one be-comes born again. This is rebirth and the return to innocence. One releases the exterior, the confinement of the connective tissue matrix that has become habituated into a cage. This is the relatively unexplored scientific arena of the relationship between the connective tissue and the brain. Creating neural plasticity as it relates to fascial plasticity is a deprogramming/reprogram-ming of the Yang Wei Vessel and could also be seen as a Divergent Meridian process connecting the Yuan Qi of the brain to the Wei Qi of the fascia.

At this point, similar to the Yin Wei Vessel, we have again learned to stay in the center of our Magic Square. Just as there are the 9 Heart Palac-es, we could look at there being 9 Palaces of the Brain. These are the same palaces, but in the first case the attachment to the palaces is financed by our blood. In the second case, our attachment to the palaces is financed by the Sea of Marrow, the brain. Through the transcendence of the Yang Wei Vessel, we are no longer financing the 9 Palaces with our marrow. We can see through the projections that no longer serve us, we have washed the windows, we have mental flossed. We are able to navigate from our yang energy, able to act in the world according to our purpose, our vision, our positive projection.

The Yang Wei Vessel is about transcending the stasis that we use to protect our self from the movement of life. This is functioning from pre-conceived notions as opposed to existential reality. This is the idea, that maybe if we are not moving, we are safer. This is the safety of the sidelines, of being in the audience, of being the critic, instead of the artist. It is more humble to be the performer, to offer your gifts, to be vulnerable, to play your part. This is how we can be of service. If we can play our part in this big self-organizing pageant of the spirit, there is always a possibility, however, not necessarily a probability. As we have said, in order to be exceptional, we have to be an exception, we have to be the anomaly.

To the degree that we are true to our original nature, to our authenticity, we engage the potential of spirit and the movement towards our Destiny. To the degree that we are unaware of the homogenizing nature of our social and experiential conditioning, our pre-conceived notions, we are on the track of random chance and statistical probability, otherwise known as Fate. Navigating this path is one of the many uses of the *I Ching*, the Book of Change. It allows us to work through our "auto-pilot" settings and be more present, so we can make conscious choices. The stasis in the Yang Wei Vessel could be seen as what we think we should know and the transcendence of the Yang Wei Vessel is the acceptance of our own knowing.

We sit in the center of the Ba Gua. The Ba Gua represents the 8 Directions, the primal forces that become the 10,000 Things, the 64 Hexagrams, the situations of the time-stream that help shape our soul. These situations are a distillation of the vibrations of the universe that we interact with, the constantly changing phenomena. These changes are like the wind, they are like the weather. The un-transcended situations stored as memory keep us from having direct communication with the outside world, the spirit. This is learning as a means of freezing the movement of change, learning as resistance to change, inertia disguised as learning.

As we free up our over-control of the yang energy from the marrow record, as we let go, as we download and upload the applications available from the collective Yuan Qi data-base, we return yang energy to Du Mai. This allows us the strength to express and extend our self into the world to achieve our destiny through the Yang Qiao. The Yang Wei is the mediator of that movement from the core(Du Mai) to the external(Yang Qiao). The resistance to the unimpeded flow of yang energy from the core of our being to direct expression is in the marrow record of the brain, GB, and Yang Wei, based on the karma of our individual and ancestral responses to previous actions in the world.

As the Yin Wei Vessel relates to our Middle Dan Tian and the record of our Heart, the Yang Wei Vessel relates to the Upper Dan Tian and the record of our brain. The washing of the brain marrow allows us to sense the etheric architecture of our aura. We are one with everything and it is important to dissolve in that ocean of unity consciousness. What the Upper Dan Tian allows us to do is to bring differentiation into the infinite.

"Individuality is only possible if it unfolds from wholeness." - David Bohm

Paradoxically, as we are able to enter into a space of profound unity, we become able to truly become an individual. We can learn to play our part and be of service to the whole.

Yang Wei Trajectory and Point Energetics

Linking Yang through Time-
Weaving the Threads of our Story

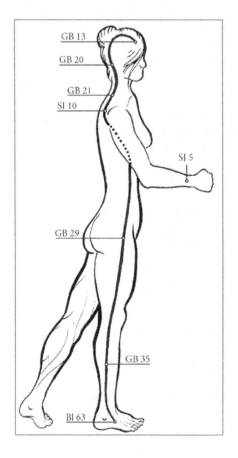

Figure 4.9: Yang Wei Vessel Trajectory[30]

Opening Point **San Jiao 5** *Wai Guan,* Outer Gate

31. *Trajectory from Cecil-Sterman, p.293.*

Yang Wei Vessel Trajectory

Begins at UB 63, the Golden Gate, and ascends up the lateral aspect of the leg crossing with the Yang Qiao at GB 29. From there it goes up to the shoulder and to GB 20. It follows the GB Meridian along the scalp, recording our experiences to be transcended by the brain and ends at GB 13, the Root of the Spirit, anchoring the Shen in the Ling through the liberated brain marrow. Some sources say it enters the brain at Du 15 and Du 16 where it would become part of the constitution, while others say we have the option to keep this from happening through our choices.

Opening Point San Jiao 5, Wai Guan, Outer Gate

The ability to engage the yang qi socially. The ability to express our true self outwardly, to extend our self into the world and the strength of Wei Qi to have appropriate boundaries. Helps clear the fear that blocks self-expression and frees emotions to allow change to occur.

Urinary Bladder 63 Jin Men, The Golden Gate

This is the contact point with the outer world. We begin to be calm about our mission based on witnessing our virtues through our actions. Our Wei Qi can be strong and calm. The Golden Gate is also the Western Gate and the home of *Xi Wang Mu*, the Queen Mother of the West who guards Kunlun Mountain, the gateway between life and death. The lateral malleolus represents Kunlun Mountain and the gate between worlds. This is the ability to wash clean the marrow record in order to return to innocence like a child. This is the transpersonal experience of connection to the Earth energy through our feet. Without dying, we can still connect to the energy and consciousness of the planetary Heart/Mind.

Gall Bladder 35   Yang Jiao, Yang Exchange

Allows the clear yang to move through the dampness of doubt based on previous results to our actions. Removes confusion and provides the strength to make decisions.

Gall Bladder 29 Ju Liao, Inhibited Bone Hole

This is the meeting point of past and present, of Yang Qiao and Yang Wei and how this is reflected in our stance and gait. As a bone hole, it is a key place for storage and loss of latency.

Large Intestine 14 *Bi Nao,* Upper Arm

The ability to handle the new perspective on one's place in the world and the new responsibilities involved.

Small Intestine 10 *Nao Shu,* Upper Arm Hollow

Another meeting point of past and present and how this is reflected in our ability to extend our self out into the world.

Triple Heater 15 *Tian Liao,* Celestial Bone Hole

Diverts heat from entering brain. This can relate to people taking short-cuts on their spiritual path and causing too much kundalini energy to be directed prematurely to the brain.

Gall Bladder 21 *Jian Jing,* Shoulder Well

This opens up all the Jing-Well points of the arms to help us let go. Resuscitates the spirit and opens us up to new possibilities.

Gall Bladder 20 *Feng Shi,* Wind Pool

Allows us to adapt to change and release our habituated responses and armor. Allows us to see with clarity the choices on our path.

Gall Bladder 19 *Nao Kong,* Brain Hollow, Brain Emptiness

Allows the marrow record to be washed anew, so we are not victims of our limited worldview based on our previous actions and choices. Treats brain's holding-patterns of the Sinews. Treats indecision.

Gall Bladder 18 *Cheng Ling,* Spirit Support, Soul Order/Configuration

This is the will to live, supported by our ability to have benevolent projections of our self and our actions into the world. Treats the three ghosts.

Gall Bladder 17 *Zheng Ying,* Upright Construction

Brings fluids to brain. Helps conversion of *Ying,* nutritive qi, into *Zheng,* upright qi and can help with chronic deficiencies.

Gall Bladder 16   *Mu Chang,* Eye Window

The washing of the windows to the soul. The ability to see the past and the present with clarity.

Gall Bladder 15   *Tou Lin Qi,* Head Overlooking Tears

Balances emotions. Helps with tendency to cry over past events.

Gall Bladder 14   *Yang Bai,* Yang Brightness

Treats eye problems and wind conditions. Benefits Lungs.

Gall Bladder 13   *Ben Shen,* Spirit Root

The recording of our actions and life experiences into the brain record. The rooting of the divine into the marrow. A change of mind from a change of heart.

Du 15   *Ya Men,* Gate of Muteness

The ability to articulate our truth, based on the coherence of our heart-mind.

Du 16   *Feng Fu,* Wind Palace

Like the Yin Wei's return to the Ren, we have Yang Wei's return to the Du. The transcendence of our perspective on the actions and choices of our lives allows us to free up the yang energy of the Du and the brain. The inability to transcend will harden and dry up the marrow and the lessons will be recorded for future transcendence.

Part 4 Chapter 7

Yin Qiao Vessel- Channel of Self-Esteem

Inward Journey: Clearing out the Cobwebs/Knowing Thyself

Other Names - Yin Motility Vessel, Yin Heel Vessel

ൟ

The Yin Qiao and Yang Qiao Vessels are about conscious awareness in the present moment. The Qiao represent the Now. They are known as the Heel Vessels or the Motility Vessels and they represent the genetic, constitutional and Yuan Qi level aspects of our stance and posture. As such they are very structural and have a skeletal resonance. This is the availability of Jing Qi, of bone energy in circulation in the moment. If the organization of the charge has been crystallized and financed into the past, there will be no charge available in the present moment. We often learn to adopt a posture that limits the flow of energy through us. This gives us an apparent sense of safety, like driving extra slow, but it keeps us from accessing the power that we need for transformation. Over time this driving extra slow causes wear and tear as if driving with the brakes on.

When engaging in high velocity activities, there is a minimum velocity or speed required to gain the support of gravity, to be centrifugally or centripetally supported. There is a surrender to the flow required with nothing more dangerous than the self-doubt of a hedged bet. At these speeds we tend to gravitate to where our eyes go. We have to learn to focus on where we do want to go and not to focus on where we do not want to go. Life is like this. We are in motion, motility. Interestingly enough, trying to stand in surrender to full alignment with gravity like the static postures of Tai Chi and Qi Gong, follows the exact same principles as high-speed activities. They are all about our relationship to the force of gravity.

Standing Up to Our Self

The Yin Qiao Vessel relates to how we stand up to our self. The Qiao Vessels are related to the eyes and the Yin Qiao represents how we see our self. Our self-esteem, self-worth, self-trust, and self-love are all aspects of the Yin Qiao Vessel. In working with the energy of the Qiao Vessels, we train the structure in conjunction with using the eyes. Using the soft gaze of the eyes in conjunction with movement and awareness of gravity is known as proprioceptive awareness, the awareness of our spatial sense as it relates to our muscle fibers. The Yin Qiao Vessel governs the Yin Sinew Channels, the muscles and fascia of the yin aspects of our body which are related to our posture and our relationship to earth, to our relationship to gravity. The Yang Sinew

Channels are more our big muscle groups associated with movement. Survival issues will reflect in the Qiao Vessels. We break our root to the earth, represented by Kidney 1 on the sole of the foot, in order to accommodate fight or flight which engages the Urinary Bladder Meridian and muscles that break our root such as the gastrocnemius. The suppression of our fight or flight response wreaks havoc in the form of chronic tension in the muscles of our calves, hamstrings, back and neck. Learning to surrender to stillness in relationship to the Earth is how we come back to the present moment.

How We See Our Self

The Yin Qiao Vessel is about looking inward, about having the eyes closed. It is about being receptive and about being seen, being transparent with nothing to hide. It connects our posture, via the genitalia, the Heart and the eyes. This is the present moment reflection of how we see and stand up to our self. The Qiao Vessels are about the potential for self-realization in the moment, the epiphany and connections made in the present moment, the gestalt. Through self-awareness we are able to stay more present, more receptive, without constantly having to put our guard up. Our Wei Qi has been restored to the exterior, giving us lots of room to be our self and to love our self, while still embodying the survival intelligence, awareness and efficiency of the Wei Qi. This is vulnerability not being a sign of weakness. This is trained in the martial art of Tai Chi Chuan for many reasons. We stay more relaxed and clear-headed. We confuse our opponents by not telegraphing the energy of violence. It allows us to lure our opponent into our space to take advantage of the arts of close combat. It also allows us to participate in an outside force, the force of the Earth.

The Yin Qiao Vessel is how we relate to the original imprinting of the Ren Vessel. It is how the social influences have molded the way in which see our self or stand up to our self. This reflects how we relate to yin in the present moment. We can heal the Ren and therefore the Yin Qiao, through being able to mother our self, to provide that nurturing and nourishing container. When we are able to do this for our self, we re-attach our etheric umbilical cord to Mother Earth.

The 3 Worms

As one of the vessels most associated with self-esteem, the Yin Qiao is the Host of the 3 Gui, also known as the 3 Worms or the 3 Ghosts. These are called the Hungry Ghost, the Horny Ghost, and the Wandering Ghost. These represent parasitic influences whether physical or otherwise that can tempt us, create obsession and cause consumption of our Jing-Essence. It is interesting that Charles Darwin, the creator of such a parasitic version of evolution, was suffering from a parasite infection from the tropics that eventually turned him into a recluse and killed him. These are the things that eat away at our self-esteem and slowly consume our resources and finance living out of the moment. These forces try to keep us from accessing our light, the light of the Hun that can illuminate our External Qi Fields. Our lives become darker as these forces continue to eat away at our constitution. Dealing with these sorts of heavy, negative forces has always been a component of shamanism and alchemy. We learn to transform and transmute the dark energies into the light. This cannot be done through resistance, but can only be done through love, acceptance, and neutrality.

The Yin Qiao Vessel is associated with the Kidneys and represents the way that fear can cause us to retreat inward or run away. The degree that fear is always motivating the protective mechanisms of our behavior will always compromise the integrity of the Yin Qiao Vessel. The Yin Qiao Vessel can reflect the energy of being prey. The duality of predator and prey is one of the oldest programs on the planet. The Qiao Vessels began to evolve when we started to walk upright. As we began to walk upright, we were growing out of the limited consciousness of the animal kingdom. Fear can keep us from being able to stand tall, be present, and go after what we want from the world. Fear can also cause us to act out aggressively, which relates more to the unenlightened use of the Yang Qiao Vessel. The Qiao Vessels represent extending our spirituality down through our legs into the Earth, whereby we can finally become Human, Zhen Ren.

The Yin Qiao Vessel reinforces the structure of our axis, our Tai Chi Pole and the Microcosmic Orbit. It gives it shape and context and governs how we relate to the primal energies of the Ren Vessel and the deepest aspects of our blueprint. The Yin Qiao Vessel allows us to physically articulate and embody the energy of our deepest nature.

Yin Qiao Meridian Point Energetics

Standing Up to Your Self

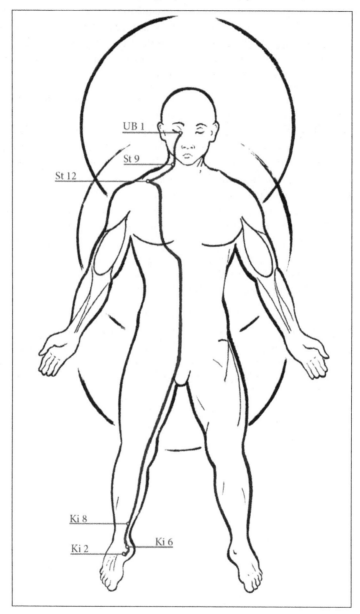

UB 1

St 9

St 12

Ki 8

Ki 2

Ki 6

Figure 4.10: Yin Qiao Vessel[31]

Opening Point   **Kidney 6**   *Zhao Hai*, Shining Sea

31. *Trajectory from Cecil-Sterman, p.301.*

Yin Qiao Vessel Trajectory

Begins at Kidney 6, just below the medial malleolus, acknowledging its role in the way our sinews and bones manage our stance in relationship to the Earth. It then ascends along the Kidney Meridian to the collarbone before going up the SCM muscles and to the eye, representing how we see our self.

❧

Opening Point Kidney 6 *Zhao Hai,* Shining Sea

This is the medial malleolus. The heel vessel. This is how we stand up to our self, how we stand our ground. It is our balance and our relationship to gravity and the Yin Sinews. It is the Shining Sea, the vast untapped potential of the water element on the water planet as we illuminate our understanding of the self.

Kidney 2 *Ran Gu,* Blazing Valley

In order to illuminate the self, we need to direct yang energy into Yin Qiao. We are bringing in the firelight of the divine into the walk through the valley.

Kidney 8 *Jiao Xin,* Trust Exchange/Junction of Faithfulness

The ability to trust in one's self and in one's heart. We must have faith in our self and our beliefs in order to have self-respect and self-esteem. There is a balance between our faith and the fruits of our faith.

Kidney 22 *Bu Lang,* Stepping Gallery, *Water*

We are exploring the mystery, the mystery of one's self. We are looking at our own intrinsic beauty and meaning. We are preparing to view the holographic slideshow of our life that is stored in our blood, in the Yin Wei and read at the time of our death/re-birth.

Kidney 23 *Shen Feng,* Spirit Seal, *Earth*

We are invoking the spirit that resides in the chest. We are making an offering of our post-natal attachment to our ego and showing our integrity in asking for the seal that separates pre-natal from post-natal to be opened so that we may know truth and purpose, and proceed on our quest.

Kidney 24 Ling Xu, Spirit Burial Ground, Wood

We are letting go. Putting our affairs in order. Taking care of regrets and unfinished business and coming to terms with our lives and our self. Letting go of the obstacles, the past, the wishing it were otherwise. Removing the obstacles to acceptance of our lives and self as feeling complete.

Kidney 25 Shen Cang, Spirit Storehouse, Fire

Here we are discovering the essence of our self. The true nature that was buried. The crystal gemstone that has been buried and alchemically transformed through the pressures of the Earth.

Kidney 26 Yu Zhong, Lively Center, Metal

Here we are regaining inspiration. Recovering from the loss of animation of being frozen in post-natal forgetfulness. The Po is regaining sensory awareness with the reverence and wisdom of how to relate to sensation, to fear and desire and sensuality without simply crystallizing into the resistance, the limiting into one perspective.

Kidney 27, Shu Fu, Conveying Palace, Master Point

All the Upper Transport Points unbind the chest and allow the Lungs to be strong enough to cultivate forgiveness, the rectification of the qi and the ability of the Kidneys to grasp that qi and bring it into the world.

Stomach 9 Ren Ying, Man's Welcome, "Welcome Me, Humanity"

The clear articulation and expression of one's self, of one's identity. We are welcomed as we are by society due to our clear understanding of our self. We no longer meet the resistance of the collective because we have transcended the resistance within our self.

Stomach 1 Cheng Qi, Supporting Tears

Allows us to see ourself without judgment. We cleanse the windows of the soul, the doors of perception through a change of perspective. We open the orifice of the eye through the release of a body fluid.

Urinary Bladder 1 *Jing Ming,* Eye's Clarity

Allows us to see our destiny clearly, to see our vision for our life's journey. We can see the world anew because we have changed how we view our self.

Paired Point   ***Lung 7*** *Lie Que,* Broken Sequence, Child Mystery

The strength of the Lungs in releasing judgment and fostering forgiveness. The opening point of the Ren Mai, the mystery of the self that the Yin Qiao stands in relation to.

Part 4 Chapter 8

Yang Qiao Vessel- Channel of Self-Realization

Eyes Wide Open:

Reclaiming Our Birthright/Presence in the World

Other Names - Yang Motility Vessel, Yang Heel Vessel

The Yang Qiao Vessel represents how we stand up to the world and how we see the world. It is how our bones have organized the charge of gravity and modeled around it. How much room for movement in the present moment has been left? Can we carry a high enough charge to participate in the vibration of life? This charge is held in the Bladder as a microcosm of the bladder of our skin that circulates the Wei Qi. The Yang Qiao Vessel has a strong resonance with the Bladder Meridian , the bones and the spine. It is the availability of yang energy in the present moment. It is our interaction point with the world. The Yang Qiao Vessel governs our Yang Sinew Channels, our large muscle groups responsible for movement into the world.

How We Stand Up to the World

As our stance towards the world it is about how we orient our structure towards movement, towards action. How do we stand up to the world? Do we let ourselves get pushed over? Do we brace and resist as much as possible? Do we actively fight to change the world? This is tied in with our perception of the world. How do we see the world? Is it a hostile place? Does it need changing? This at its extreme is the activist that is constantly trying to better the world, to change some wrong that they perceive. As a Chinese Medicine practitioner, the activism is not mine to judge. My job is to convey how this attitude or activity is affecting the person's health and really only if they have asked me to work with them on their health issues on this level.

The healthy Yang Qiao Vessel is represented by the statement that "the world is perfect the way it is. Everything is happening just as it is intended to." The acceptance that everything has happened the way it had to in order to make me the person I am today. This is a tall order of a statement and one that can easily be met with righteous indignation and out-and-out scorn. However, spiritually no other approach truly serves the same function as this highest level of acceptance. Other approaches may certainly feel more appropriate but they will still cause distortion in our view of the world due to being based in resistance. The challenge of the Yang Qiao Vessel is to activate the feedback loop with the universe, to open the windows on the world, to communicate with nature and to have nature

251

communicate with us. To open our eyes and to see and listen with our heart. To see eternity in the present moment.

"To see the world in a grain of sand, and to see heaven in a wild flower, hold infinity in the palm of your hands, and eternity in an hour." -William Blake

Vessel of Self-Realization

The Yang Qiao Vessel is the Vessel of Self-Realization. The healthy Yang Qiao Vessel is an advanced spiritual state. It is the radiance of yang energy coming from the stillness of yin, from the peace within. This is yang energy attracted to the embodiment of yin. Yang energy mobilized through force or sheer will is not the same principle. This is seen in Tai Chi in the surrendering to gravity while maintaining structure, to yield to force while maintaining root, and to activate the natural reflex of the buoyant energy of yang that comes back up from the Earth. The realization of the Yang Qiao Vessel is to surrender to the forces of the world, the winds of change of the 8 directions, while maintaining our center and root, allowing time to flow like a river around us and through us, while we stay present moving forward towards our Destiny the way everything is moving, without resistance and unnecessary tension. We can become the observer, the passenger, once we have established the integrity of our vehicle and learned to trust the driver. The Yang Qiao reinforces the structure of the perimeter of our aura. The Chong is the seed/eggshell form of the bubble, while the definition and integrity of where our boundaries interpenetrate with the world is shaped by the Yang Qiao.

The Yang Qiao Vessel is associated with the energy of the warrior. This energy is also associated with the energy of the predator, something often trained in the martial and magical arts. The predator energy has gifts embedded inside us. One such gift is similar to the energy of the shark, perhaps the world's greatest predator. The shark has the most sensitive vibratory sensors in all of nature along its lateral aspect. We can re-awaken this type of vibratory awareness to all living things through the ears and the lateral aspects of our body. The vibratory conduction of these connective tissue receptors are what allow us to be open to change, to rotate, to change direction at a moment's notice based on communication with nature. The benefit of the energy of predator is that it is often without fear, and therefore can teach humans a lot. These gifts are used in nature to hunt, but we as humans can use them to regain the awareness that everything is one. The predator energy is one of the main energies of the world that is in need of deep healing. Animals are designed to be predators. Humans were never designed to act as predators towards each other. We can learn to use these gifts to play, to pray, to love. We have choice. However, the Yang Qiao Vessel is power and as such one will be tested for their level of responsibility, of response-ability, as they seek to awaken this vessel.

"Between stimulus and response there is a space. In that space is our power to choose our response. In our response lies our growth and our freedom."
- Viktor E. Frankl

Yang Wei is the dormancy of this direct vibratory communication, with too much awareness being in the past or future for direct optimal mediation of vibration. This could also be seen as a Divergent Meridian issue, a loss of instinct over generations. This takes place through our ears and our sense of balance. We have induced latency in these gifts, for so many reasons such as being unable as a species to rectify the potential aggression of great power with the more altruistic virtues of great love and responsibility. Yang Wei is the library of the un-transcended information of these vibrations, vibrations represented by the situations of the *I Ching*.

We screen the information that we do not understand, that we judge. Picking up the raw pheromones of who is stronger and weaker than us, who is available as a sexual mate, whose genetic material is a good match for ours, etc. is a complicated situation for the non-dual spirit. This is the energy of the animal kingdom. It is not intended to merely be acted out upon. That is for the animals to do. That is their nature. In order to drive our further evolution we need to pick up this information without merely attempting domination. We need to learn to let the shen observe, in order for it to show us the appropriate response. We also have to transcend the Yin Qiao Vessel aspects of self-doubt, self-worth and lethargy in order to transcend the dampening of our External Qi fields and return the light to our aura, the San Qing, the Light of the Three Pure Ones. This is the radiance of the awakened Yang Qiao Vessel.

The balanced Yang Qiao Vessel is capable of yielding while pursuing, it is capable of action with receptivity, of strength without resistance. The balancing of the Qiao Vessels holds out a high promise for conflict resolution for the species. Interestingly, the highest realization of the Yang Qiao Vessel is prayer, devotion. The predator is built to pray. To honor creator and creation with eyes, ears, and heart wide open deep in the unity of the present moment is our highest potential. Fearless. Aware. Free of doubt. Alive and in Wu Ji. Wu Ji with Wei Qi. This is the pre-natal nature of ceremonial space, life as living prayer, living devotion, ritual, while paying full attention to our surroundings. When we return to post-natal space, when we leave the temple and return to duality, we integrate the full capacity of the Yang Qiao Vessel over the "compound essence of time." We can integrate the unity space, the coherence of the light patterns of Heaven being integrated into our marrow and bone over seasons.

This present moment awareness calls forth the benevolent energies and forces of the universe, the winds of the directions. This is yang energy attracting light, yang. When we are deep in this yang energy we also attract malevolent energies and forces, the so-called evil winds. The deeper we can be lured into self-doubt into the dark swampy yin of our fears and insecurities, into the jungle of the Yin Qiao Vessel, the deeper these winds can penetrate. It can be a matter of if you soar really high, you may have to go accordingly deep, and there is no perfect way to be prepared. The inward journey is not for the faint of heart.

"When we are no longer able to change a situation - we are challenged to change ourselves."   - Viktor E. Frankl

These are the dark nights of the soul when we may be stuck in an adverse fate, when we cannot change anything in the world, so the only thing we can change is our self. This is water over water in the *I Ching*, when all we can do is wait for the rain to fill the crevice so we can float back on our way. It is often a dangerous situation, one that teaches patience and humility. This is the work that carves the Jing, the uncarved block. When we lose sight of the shore, when we can't see the light from the surface as we sink into the depths, when we feel as though we are drowning, we can learn to swim by becoming still, unlocking the golden flower, the light inside our self, the spirit molecule embedded in matter deep in the cave, deep in the jungle, the iridescence of the deep sea creature, the tree growing out of the high mountain windswept rock.

"What is to give light must endure burning." - Viktor E. Frankl

This is the completion of the Ba Gua Dance. Dancing is the highest use of the warrior energy. It is the highest use of our legs and the Qiao Vessels which began to develop as we started to walk upright. The observer sits in the center and the windows of the directions are open in direct communication with the spirits through the time-stream of the omens. These are the symbols that speak directly to and from the organism of Humanity. As these forms of communication are received in the spirit of gratitude and devotion, our life can become a ceremony of living prayer. This is the purpose of evolution: to evolve an organism that can awaken, so that spirit can learn to get to know itself through us.

Yang Qiao Meridian Point Energetics

Standing Up to the World

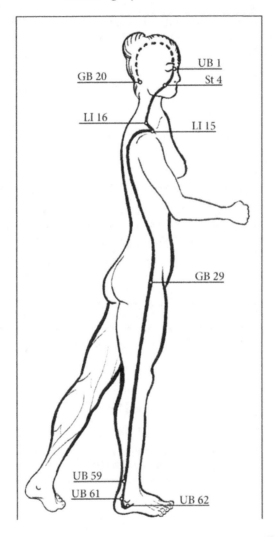

Figure 4.11: Trajectory of Yang Qiao Vessel[32]

Opening Point   Urinary Bladder 62   *Shen Mai*, Extending Vessel

---

32.   *Trajectory from Cecil-Sterman, p.313.*

Yang Qiao Vessel Trajectory

This trajectory begins at UB 62 representing our stance to the world and how we configure our large muscle groups for protection and extension outward. It then travels up the lateral aspect of the leg to the hip where it intersects the Yang Wei Vessel at GB 29. From there it ascends to the shoulder region, to the mouth and to UB 1 at the eyes, representing how we see the world. From here it goes into the brain and to GB 20, the Wind Pool, preparing us to stay present in the now amidst the winds of change. The constancy of self-realization.

Opening Point Urinary Bladder 62 *Shen Mai,* Extending Vessel

This is our stance towards the world, written into our posture and skeletal structure. It is how we see the world. Is it a hostile place? Is it a place that we need to change? Is today a day to enjoy the world or to try to improve upon it? It is the opening point for the Yang Qiao.

Urinary Bladder 61 *Pu Can,* Subservient Visitor, Servant's Partaking

Allows us to serve humanity but not at the expense of our self. Allows us to accept help and receive assistance more gracefully. Helps us be received by humanity.

Gall Bladder 29 *Ju Liao,* Inhibited Bone Hole

This is the meeting point of past and present, of Yang Qiao and Yang Wei and how this is reflected in our stance and gait. The hips allow the articulation of Earth energy in the body and need to be released as if fluid extensions of our torso.

Small Intestine 10 *Nao Shu,* Upper Arm Hollow

Another meeting point of past and present and how this is reflected in our ability to extend our self out into the world.

Large Intestine 15 *Jian Yu,* Shoulder Bone

The ability to reach into the world to connect with our purpose without being held back by doubt. Letting go of previous judgments that held us back from receiving and being received by humanity.

Large Intestine 16   *Ju Gu,* Great Bone

Opens up the shoulders allowing us to handle and embrace life without being held back by the resistances caused by latency.

Stomach 1   *Cheng Qi,* Supporting Tears

Allows us to see others and the world without judgment.

Urinary Bladder 1   *Jing Men,* Eye's Clarity

Allows us to see our destiny clearly, to see our vision for our life's journey with eyes wide open in a world that is always in communication with us.

Paired Point   *Small Intestine 3*   *Hou Xi,* Back Stream

The opening point of Du Mai. Yang Qiao is the ability to extend our Du Meridian into the world in the present moment. This is a strong bone point with just a little padding. This is the point used for the karate chop. The cultivation is that in order to break bricks(move through resistance) our bones need to bend, like a child's. We have learned to extend ourselves into the world with great strength of character and purpose and have learned to have a softer approach that is better received by humanity, based on the adaptability and flexibility of non-attachment. We have learned to be the supple tree that bends in the winds of change and not the rigid tree that breaks.

Integration

The Return from the Journey

After going on the inward alchemical journey to discover the nature of our self, the traveler returns to his or her community to share the gifts that they have uncovered. The Journey into the 8 Extraordinary Vessels is a journey of differentiation of the self. This occurs through discovering the self that is not based in societal influences and conditioning. This is the establishment of the vertical axis between Heaven and Earth. Here we work out the relationship between our morphology and astrology, our ancestry and our destiny.

Once we establish agency in the vertical axis, we have begun to develop our root. In order to develop our root we have had to learn to stand our ground, navigate our boundaries, and embody our truth amidst the pressure from the winds of change of the 8 directions, the horizontal axis. This pressure is the driving force of evolution, the stress fractures in our crystalline matrix that allow us to incarnate, the flaws that allow our hologram to be substantiated. As we are humbled and tumbled, we uncover the ability to shine, to reflect the love of Heaven into the material reality of the Earth. Now we are ready to extend our self back out into the 8 directions, into the sphere of our influence, the mandala of our connections. Now that we have healed our wounds, we can share our creative gifts with Humanity and be received welcomingly by a Humanity that recognizes our gifts. We have come full circle.

Integration is the ability to incorporate the insights we have gained on our journey into our daily lives. This is the infusion of the sacred into the mundane. Though life is filled with constant wonder and mystery, it is the ability to remain grounded within our lives that allows our growth to nourish both our roots and our branches and fruits. One of my favorite aspects of the Chinese Medicine Meridian Matrix and the *I Ching* is that they are fully multi-dimensional. They do this by being a map of the relationships between things. They are descriptions of a ratio between things that holds true at any size or speed. Through doing this they can help us find the constant within constant change and they provide a map for how to take care of our self whether in pre-natal or post-natal space.

Take care of yourself lovingly and may you find peace on your journey.

"Many blessings on your journey of a 1,000 miles through the 10,000 things"

BIBLIOGRAPHY

Abrams, Ralph and Terence McKenna and Rupert Sheldrake, 1992, *Trialogues at the Edge of the West*. Santa Fe, NM: Bear and Company Publishing.

Anthony, Carol, 2007, *A Guide to the I Ching*. Stow, Massachusetts: Anthony Publishing Company.

Birch, Stephen and Kiiko Matsumoto, 1988, *Hara Diagnosis: Reflections on the Sea*. Brookline, Massachusetts: Paradigm Publications.

Bunnell, Lynda and Ra Uru Hu, 2011, *The Definitive Book of Human Design*. Carlsbad, CA: HDC Publishing.

Campbell, Joseph, 1972, *Myths to Live By*. Bantam Books, New York, NY

Cecil-Sterman, Ann, 2012, *Advanced Acupuncture: A Clinical Manual*. New York, NY: Classical Wellness Press.

Chace, Charles and Miki Shima, 2010, *An Exposition on the 8 Extraordinary Vessels*. Seattle, Washington: Eastland Press.

Dechar, Lori, 2005, *Five Spirits*. Lantern Books._

Jacob, Jeffrey, 1996, *The Acupuncturist's Clinical Handbook*. Santa Fe, NM: Aesclipius Press.

Jarrett, Lonny, 1998, *Nourishing Destiny*. Stockbridge, Massachusetts: Spirit Path Press.

Jarrett, Lonny, 2006, *Clinical Practice of Chinese Medicine*. Stockbridge, Massachusetts: Spirit Path Press.

Karcher, Stephen, 2003, *Total I Ching- Myths for Change*. London, England: Sphere.

McKenna, Terence and Dennis McKenna, 1975, *Invisible Landscape- Mind, Hallucinogens, and the I Ching*. San Francisco, California: Harper Collins.

Reich, Wilhelm, 1960, *Selected Works of Wilhelm Reich*. New York, NY: Farrar, Strauss, and Giroux.

Rudd, Richard, 2011, *The Gene Keys*. England, Gene Keys Publishing.

Wilhelm, Richard and Cary F. Baynes, trans., 1967, *The I Ching; or, Book of Changes*. Princeton, New Jersey: Princeton University Press.

Yuen, Dr. Jeffrey, oral transmission. One of the primary sources of oral transmission of Classical Chinese Medicine at an international level is Jeffrey Yuen, the 88th generation of his Daoist Lineage: *Yu Ching Huang Lao Pai*(Jade

Purity School, Yellow Emperor/Lao Tzu sect); 26th generation of *Chuan Chen Lung Men Pai*(Complete Reality School, Dragon Gate Sect).

Yuen, Jeffrey, 2001, "Hun, Po, Ling, Shen: Exploring the Spirits of Chinese Medicine." Transcription of lecture from November 2000.

Glossary

Ba Gua- Literally means "8 sides." This octagon arrangement represents the 8 directions, the 8 trigrams, the 8 primal forces of nature. Essentially an octagon is is a representation of a circle. The foundation for the *I Ching*.

Chong Vessel- One of the 8 Extraordinary Vessels. Also called the Thrusting, Penetrating, or Uterine Vessel. This is our Central Channel, the Channel of our Blueprint and our spiritual curriculum. It is also called the Sea of Blood.

Curious Organs- These organs relate to the Yuan Qi and the 8 Extraordinary Vessels. They are the Uterus, the Bones, the Brain, the Marrow, the Gall Bladder and the Vessels.

Dai Vessel- One of the 8 Extraordinary Vessels. Also called the Belt Channel.

Dao De Jing- The most famous text of Daoism, attributed to Lao-Tze.

De- Translates as virtue, integrity, character, power and original nature.

Divergent Channels- One of the 5 Channel Systems of acupuncture. Connects Yuan Qi to Wei Qi.

Du Vessel- One of the 8 Extraordinary Vessels. The Sea of Yang, the Governing Vessel.

Eight Extraordinary Vessels- One of the 5 Channel Systems of acupuncture. Circulates at the level of the Yuan Qi and connects the Curious Organs. These are the channels most involved in evolution and spiritual growth.

EPF- An acronym for External Pathogenic Factors. Examples are wind, damp, hot, cold, and dry as well as all the metaphoric aspects of these forces.

Gu- Parasite. This is the more substantially based concept of things that literally eat away at us.

Gui- Ghost. This is the more insubstantially based concept of things that eat away at us.

Hun- The Heavenly ethereal soul that is housed by the Liver.

I Ching- The Book of Changes, one of the oldest books of wisdom on the planet. Describes the 64 archetypal situations, represented by hexagrams, that the soul encounters on its journey.

IPF- An acronym for Internal Pathogenic Factors. These are related to emotions, diet, lifestyle and also hereditary influences that may appear over the cycles of 7 & 8.

Jing- One of the Three Treasures. It is our essence, related to our Yuan Qi.

Luo Vessels- One of the 5 Channel Systems of acupuncture. Related to how the body attempts to keep substances and emotions in a state of latency so that they are not in circulation in the blood.

Latency- Anything that is suppressed or repressed. Latency keeps us out of the present moment. Our physical resources get used up financing things in a state of latency. When latency is lost we have the expressions of the disease process.

Ling- The soul. The yin aspect of the spirit housed in the Heart. The soul has Earthly power and influence and has been censored quite often in the transmission of Chinese Medicine as it represents the embodied spiritual power and potential of the individual, of the liberated human being.

Mai- Channel, vessel, or meridian. These words are used interchangeably in this text.

Po- The Earthly corporeal soul. It is related to the Lungs, the lessons of our life and the contract with our ancestry.

Primary Channels- The most commonly understood of the 5 Channel Systems of acupuncture. There are 12 Primary Meridians, named after the Zang-Fu organs that they are associated with.

Qi- Energy, communication, relationship, breath, vitality, life force.

Qi Gong- Any activity related to Qi that requires time and discipline.

Ren Vessel- One of the 8 Extraordinary Vessels. The Sea of Yin, the Conception Vessel.

San Qing- The Three Pure Ones. A concept from religious Daoism related to the Hun. It represents the consciousness associated with the illumination of the ethereal body.

Shen- Spirit, Mind, housed in the Heart.

Sinew Channels- One of the 5 Channel Systems of acupuncture. Circulates the Wei Qi. Represents the material aspect of our self, our form.

Tai Chi- "The supreme ultimate." Represented by the yin/yang symbol. Also a martial art.

Tai Yi- "Supreme one-ness."

Wei Qi- Protective or Defensive Qi.

Wu- One version of this word means shaman. Another version means empty space. Another version is the number 5. All of which are very mystical concepts in the alchemical traditions and a likely source of puns among the alchemically inclined.

Wu Ji- The primordial, eternal "before the beginning."

Wu Wei- Doing/not doing, action/non-action. A zen-like concept representing natural efficiency and right timing. "Without doing, nothing is left undone."

Yang- One of the two principles of polarity. Represented by the sunny side of the mountain.

Yang Qiao Vessel- One of the 8 Extraordinary Vessels.

Yang Wei Vessel- One of the 8 Extraordinary Vessels.

Yi- Intention, focus. An attribute of the Earth element.

Yin- One of the two principles of polarity. Represented by the shaded sound of the mountain.

Yin Qiao Vessel- One of the 8 Extraordinary Vessels.

Yin Wei Vessel- One of the 8 Extraordinary Vessels.

Ying Qi- Nutritive Qi. Includes blood. Associated with the post-natal qi derived from food and air.

Yuan Qi- Source Qi. Primordial energy of nature and the part of ourselves connected to the species' mind and the planetary mind.

Zang Fu- the organ networks of acupuncture. Zang means yin organ and Fu means Yang bowel.

Zhi- One version means Will and one version means Wisdom. Both are attributes of the Kidneys.

Made in United States
North Haven, CT
23 February 2022